HISTORICAL SOUTHERN FAMILIES

VOLUME XI

Harris-Elmore Public Library
300 Toledo Street
Elmore, Ohio 43416

Edited by Mrs. John Bennett Boddie
P.O. Box 2775
Honolulu, Hawaii 96803

Copyright 1967

by

Mrs. John Bennett Boddie

Previous Books

BODDIE & ALLIED FAMILIES

SEVENTEENTH CENTURY ISLE OF WIGHT COUNTY

COLONIAL SURRY

VIRGINIA HISTORICAL GENEALOGIES

SOUTHSIDE VIRGINIA FAMILIES
Volumes I and II

BIRTHS & DEATHS from ALBEMARLE PARISH REGISTER

BRISTOL PARISH REGISTER

HISTORICAL SOUTHERN FAMILIES
Volumes I, II, III, IV, V, VI, VII,
VIII, IX and X.

Publisher and Distributor:
Genealogical Publishing Company
521-523 St. Paul Place
Baltimore, Maryland 21202

TABLE OF CONTENTS

FAMILIES	PAGE

UPSHUR of Virginia, Rose Cottage and
                             Brownsville branches 1
PITT of Virginia and North Carolina 48
BATTS of Surry County, Virginia 57
WILLIAM ROSE of Surry County, Virginia 65
COLLINS of South Carolina, Kentucky and
      Missouri, with related families
      SMITH, ROSS, WYATT, SCOTT,
      FLEETE, HAWTE 76
RAGAN of Georgia, with related families
      SPENCE, TIMMONS, HILLIARD,
      SHEFFIELD, SINGLETON 95
MATHEWS of Virginia and Georgia 105
COX and HUTCHENS of Virginia and North
                            Carolina 109
LAND, ARRINGTON, and BRIDGER of
      Georgia, Virginia, and North Carolina,
      showing DUDLEY descent 119
KNIGHT of Philadelphia, Pennsylvania 127
ALBERTSON of Pennsylvania and New Jersey 140
CHIPLEY of Maryland, Virginia and N. Carolina .. 148
KEMP of England and Virginia 156
McNULTY and KLINE of Pennsylvania and
                            Mississippi 159
WYNN - WYNNS - WYNNE of North Carolina 176
BOAT(W)RIGHT of Virginia 181
BAUGH of Virginia 229
BEESON, GRUBB, BOREN, BOWLES and
      related families of England,
      Pennsylvania, and North Carolina 250
PITCHER and related families of LANCASTER,
      DOUGLAS, GEORGE, JORDAN, BOOTH,
      JACKSON, of Maryland, Virginia, North
      Carolina, Tennessee, and Kentucky...... 259
BREED of South Carolina and Georgia 270

                           ****

EXPLANATION OF ABBREVIATIONS

Cav. and Pioneers	Cavaliers & Pioneers by Nell M. Nugent.
Chn.	Children.
D. Bk.	Deed Book.
d. s. p.	Died single person.
Harl.	Harleian Society Publications.
H. S. F.	Historical Southern Families, by John Bennett Boddie.
Hotten	Original Lists of Immigrants to America, by Hotten.
Ibid.	Reference as above.
O. Bk.	Order Book.
P. Bk.	Patent Book.
P. G.	Prince George County.
R. or Reg.	Parish Register.
17th Cent.	17th Century Isle of Wight County, by Boddie.
S. V. F.	Southside Virginia Families, by Boddie.
V. M.	Virginia Magazine of History.
W. Bk.	Will book.
W. & M. Q.	William and Mary College Quarterly.

****

ERRATUM: H. S. F. Volume X, page 111, line 12:

Troy Woodward Saul, daughter of Luther Kindred Saul and his wife Eula Graham Woodward.

UPSHUR FAMILY in VIRGINIA

ROSE COTTAGE BRANCH

Caleb Upshur
(1744-78)

CALEB UPSHUR, the third and youngest son of Abel I and Rachel (Revell) Upshur, was born in 1744 at "Warwick," - Accomac Co., Virginia. Caleb's mother died when he was five years old and upon the death of his father in 1753 he was left an orphan at the age of nine. Caleb and his brother, John II, were placed under the guardianship of their older brother, Arthur IV. (See H. S. F., Vol. X)

By the will of his father, Caleb was left an 800-acre plantation in Bradford's Neck, near Locustville, Accomack County. The old house on this plantation has been known for generations as "Rose Cottage."

Rose Cottage

By the will of Abel Upshur I, his youngest son, Caleb Upshur, was bequeathed a plantation of about 800 acres in Bradford's Neck, Accomack County. This plantation was about seven miles north of "Warwick," between the towns of Watchapreague and Locustville, just off the seaside road. It was the same plantation that Abel I purchased shortly before his death from William Burton III. On this plantation, facing a small creek, now called Finney Creek, and not far from the Atlantic Ocean. "Rose Cottage" was built nearly 200 years ago.

"Rose Cottage" is characteristic of the type popularly built on the Eastern Shore of Virginia during the period preceding the Revolutionary War, and its construction indicates that it must have grown with the family who lived there. The main house is of brick, laid in Flemish bond with glazed headers, and the top course of the water table has the old beveled-brick treatment. The door and window lintels are of wood. The little house with its high gable roof and small dormer windows has unusually nice lines. A central hall runs through the house from the road side to the creek side, dividing the ground floor into a parlor and dining room. Parlor, cross hall, and dining room all have wainscoting. The mantel in the parlor is exceptionally good; the dining room mantel is plain. Upstairs are two bedrooms, each of which has a fireplace. Additions to the south end of the main section are of a somewhat later date.

"Rose Cottage" has a lovely setting by the water. According to the records the grounds were laid off in symmetrical gardens which sloped down to the creek. However, of the old garden there remains but one box, and no trace of the roses which gave the dwelling its name.

Records fail to show that there were any buildings on the plantation when it was purchased by Abel Upshur I, so it is probable that "Rose Cottage" was built by his son, Caleb, who inherited the plantation in 1753. Caleb married about 1770 and it is reasonable to suppose that he built "Rose Cottage" prior to that date.

The provisions of a deed of sale to "Rose Cottage," recorded January 1, 1842, indicate that members of the Upshur Family were buried here; however, no Upshur tombstones have been found on the property. The deed also indicates that "Rose Cottage" once had a formal garden. A part of the deed is quoted below: (Accomack Deeds, 1842-43, p. 59.)

> "... a certain piece of land in the upper ends of the lower square of the garden, which has been and is now the burying ground of said Upshur's family--Forty-six feet from north to south and thirty feet from east to west which with the right of way to and from the same for purposes of burial--which is not hereby intended to be conveyed but reserved as aforesaid to said Wm

Upshur, his heirs and assigns for the purpose aforesaid."

By reconstructing the gardens from the above record it is possible to locate the Upshur burying grounds. Several marked graves of the Bunting and Finney Families, who later became possessed of the property, are now located in the section which was probably the lower end of the upper square of the garden, on the same side of the middle walk as the unmarked Upshur graves. Caleb's son and heir, John Brown Upshur, inherited "Rose Cottage," and upon his death in 1822, the property descended to his widow and children. The widow and minor children deeded their share to the eldest son, William Stith Upshur, mentioned in the deed quoted previously, and William sold to Edward J. Young. Thus another old Upshur property passed out of the family. (Reference: Whitelaw's "Virginia's Eastern Shore," II, p. 862-65.)

About 1770 Caleb married Anne Brown whose parentage has not been determined, and it was probably about that time that he established his home at "Rose Cottage," about seven miles to the north of "Warwick."

Neither tradition nor the Accomack County records furnish much information about Caleb Upshur. Thomas Teackle Upshur II talked with Caleb's grandchildren who reported their grandfather's reputation as that of a quiet, reserved, and highly respected gentleman whose name was honored by all who knew him. This brief description does not tell much about Caleb, but the fact that his nephew, Littleton Upshur I of "Vaucluse," named his second son in compliment to his uncle indicates that Caleb must have been greatly admired and beloved by that kinsman who was one of the most prominent men of his time on the Eastern Shore.

Caleb Upshur may have been quiet and reserved, but those retiring qualities did not prevent his taking positive action to protect his property when he felt the occasion demanded. An entry dated 1774 in the records of the Virginia House of Burgesses reads: (VIRGINIA JOURNAL OF THE HOUSE OF BURGESSES 1773-1776, p. 129.)

"A Petition of several Persons of the County of Accomack, whose names are thereunto subscribed, was presented to the House, and read; setting forth that the Petitioners and their forefathers, who inhabited the lands lying back from Navigable Water, near Wachapreague Creek, have until very lately, been allowed the privilege of a way over a corner of Land now belonging to Caleb Upshur, to a landing on the said Creek, for taking and bringing away Fish and Oysters, which way being but short along a Bank, and nearly on the line of the said Land, did not interfere with the Owner's enclosures, and was not otherwise considered detrimental to him; but that the said Upshur hath now forbidden the Petitioners from frequenting that Landing, at their Peril, whereby they are in great measure deprived of a comfortable supply of Food; and therefore praying the consideration of the House and such Relief as shall seem Just."

At a meeting of the First Continental Congress in Philadelphia on September 5, 1774, a stringent Continental Association was formed forbidding the colonies to import British goods after December 1, 1774, or to export American goods after September 10, 1775. Congress directed the appointment of Committees of Safety in each town and county with inquisitorial and punitive powers to carry out these provisions. These county committees, consisting for the most part of prominent and trusted patriots, were chosen by the freeholders at the court houses in the same manner that burgesses were elected. Both Caleb Upshur and his eldest brother, Arthur Upshur IV, were chosen members of the Accomack County Committee of Safety of December 23, 1774. (Force, "American Archives", 4th ser., I, 1059.)

Caleb's life was a short one for he died in his thirty-fourth year. He had spent his youth at "Warwick," and there he was buried in the family burying ground with his parents and grandparents. His tombstone may still be seen there bearing the simple epitaph:

In
Memory of
Caleb Upshur
who died October the 17th
1778
In the 34th Year of his
Age

Caleb died intestate. An inventory and appraisement of his estate was taken on December 15, 1778, by order of the Accomack County Court, and his estate was valued in excess of 6780 pounds, a sizeable amount for that period. (For inventory and appraisement of the estate of Caleb Upshur, Accomack Wills, Etc., 1780-84, 495.) Although this was a sizeable estate, it was small in comparison with the estates left by Littleton Upshur I of "Vaucluse" and John Upshur II of "Cedar Grove" (Northampton Wills and Inventories, 1825-29, 137, 168). In this connection it should be mentioned that early Upshur wills and inventories show that considerable property, both real and personal, was passed on to descendants. Little of this property now remains in the Upshur Family, therefore it is urged that heirlooms and memorabilia still possessed by Upshur descendants be cherished and retained, and that family papers or copies thereof be deposited in appropriate libraries for preservation.)

The date and place of burial of Caleb's wife, Anne (Brown) Upshur is unknown. Thomas Teackle Upshur II, genealogist, claimed that Anne married, second, Edmund Read of Drummondtown (now Accomac), born about 1758, died December 25, 1836, and bore Read two daughters, Nancy and Mary. The author has been unable to verify this marriage.

Caleb and Anne (Brown) Upshur had issue: Sally; Leah; Elizabeth Brown; John Brown I.
    I. Sally Upshur. No information has been found concerning this ancestor.
    II. Leah Upshur was born in 1773 at "Rose Cottage," died September 21, 1847, married, January 10, 1793, John Custis Smith of the Eastern Shore of Virginia, born September 16, 1762, died

December 10, 1824. (John Custis Smith
(1762-1824) was son of John Smith (1722-79)
and Susanna (Custis) Smith (1728-85) dau. of
Maj. John Custis (ca. 1701-1732/3) of "Deep
Creek" and Ann (Upshur) Custis. John Smith
(1722-79) was son of John Smith (d. 1745) and
Elizabeth, dau. of Colonel Tully Robinson and
Sarah West. John Smith (d. 1745) was son of
George Smith of London and formerly of
Leicestershire, Eng., who came to the Eastern Shore of Virginia in 1670 and married
Elizabeth, dau. of Colonel William Robinson.)
John and Leah Smith left the Eastern Shore
after the birth of their fourth child, and moved
to Suffolk, Virginia, where they purchased a
large tract of several thousand acres extending
from the present North Carolina highway to
Lake Kilby, known as Smith's Mill Pond when
John Smith owned it. Near the lake John and
Leah built a beautiful home which was burned
in 1860. They were buried in an old family
burying ground nearby where many of their
children and other members of the family were
buried. Issue:

A. Susan Custis Smith, born December 21, 1793, died Feb. 7, 1856, buried at Lake Kilby. Susan never married.
B. John Upshur Smith, born October 13, 1795.
C. Caleb Robinson Smith, born October 19, 1797.
D. Eliza Robinson Smith, born November 20, 1799, died June 12, 1847, buried at Lake Kilby, married K. Hill, and had issue.
E. Anne Upshur Smith, born 1803, died June 2, 1879, married, 1825, Thomas Jefferson Kilby, born April 2, 1803, died June 21, 1881, and had issue. Both were buried at Lake Kilby.
F. John Custis Smith, born 1804, died September 26, 1826, buried at Lake Kilby.
G. Mary Louisa Smith, born October 15, 1808, died May 22, 1837, married Wiley Parker,

Jr., born March 12, 1806, died April 21, 1859, and had issue. Both were buried at Lake Kilby.
H. George Robinson Smith, born September 7, 1815, died July 3, 1872, married Judith Elizabeth Kilby of Suffolk, daughter of Turpin and Martha (Glazebrook) Kilby. This couple had eight children and left many descendants among whom is Telza (Smith) Miller of Suffolk who furnished much of this information about the descendants of Leah Upshur.

III. Elizabeth Brown Upshur was born December 28, 1775, at "Rose Cottage." She married, October 24, 1798, John Upshur of "Brownsville." This couple had four children who are described in the Brownsville branch of this genealogy. Elizabeth died April 21, 1804, and was buried in the family burying ground at "Brownsville."

IV. John Brown Upshur I, only son of Caleb and Anne (Brown) Upshur, was born about 1776 at "Rose Cottage." John's father died intestate in 1778, and Rose Cottage plantation descended to him as son and heir as shown by the following court proceedings:

"John Brown Upshur -- Infant orphan of Caleb Upshur, deceased, by John Upshur, his next friend.
vs. --Ejectment Proceedings.
Wm Stockley.
That the aforesaid Caleb Upshur in his lifetime was seized and in quiet possession of a plantation in Bradford's Neck in the County aforesaid, and died thereof possessed, and the said land descended to the said John Brown Upshur, his son and heir. March 29, 1780." (LAND CAUSES, ACCOMACK COUNTY VIRGINIA, 1727-1826, p. 129; by Nottingham)

Edmund Read of Accomack was appointed guardian to young Upshur so he may have been reared by Read.

As previously mentioned, Thomas Teackle Upshur II wrote that John's mother married, second, Edmund Read but the author has been unable to verify this marriage and is inclined to believe that John's mother died shortly after his birth. Perhaps John and his three young sisters were taken to "Warwick" to be reared by relatives, Abel Upshur II and Elizabeth (Gore) Upshur, who were then living at the old Upshur home plantation.

John Brown Upshur I married (bond dated May 11, 1802) Mary ("Molly") Elizabeth Stith, born September 7, 1786, daughter of William and Sarah (Smith) Stith of Northampton County. John and Mary Elizabeth established their home at "Rose Cottage" where they reared a family of nine children. (See descent later.)

During the War of 1812 John Brown Upshur I served in Captain John Finney's Troop of Cavalry in the Second Regiment of Virginia Militia, Accomack County. (Reference: MUSTER ROLLS OF THE VIRGINIA MILITIA IN THE WAR OF 1812, p. 321.)

John Brown Upshur I died intestate in October 1822, and Rose Cottage plantation was divided among his wife and children. (For letters of administration granted to Severn Eyre Parker on the estate of John Brown Upshur I, Accomack Orders, 1822-24, 85, court of October 28, 1822. For inventory and account of sale of the estate of John Brown Upshur I, Accomack Wills, Etc., 1823-24, 159, 163.) John was probably buried at "Rose Cottage" although his tombstone has not been found there. John's wife survived him by many years. She and her eldest son, William Stith Upshur, joined in selling "Rose Cottage" in 1842, and about that time moved to Northampton County and established their home near Eastville. Mary Elizabeth (Stith) Upshur died in 1851 and was buried at "Vaucluse." (Northampton Wills and Inventories, 1831-1901, p. 87.)

John Brown Upshur I and Mary Elizabeth (Stith) Upshur had issue:
    A. William Stith Upshur was born April 25, 1803, at "Rose Cottage." In 1824 he was licensed to practice law, began his legal profession in Accomack County, and soon acquired the reputation of a very capable lawyer. He marri-

ed, June 6, 1827, Anne Strange Wilson, daughter of Thomas Wilson of Richmond (lineage not traced). This couple settled in Accomack County, and perhaps made their home at "Rose Cottage." Anne Strange (Wilson) Upshur died in the 1830's leaving several small children. In 1842 William Stith Upshur and his mother joined in selling "Rose Cottage" and about that time moved to Northampton County and established their home about three miles from Eastville, just below Shadyside on the western side of the bayside road. Later, William moved to Norfolk where he practiced law until his death in 1868. He was buried in Elmwood Cemetery, Norfolk. William Stith and Anne Strange (Wilson) Upshur had issue:
1. Mary Jane Stith Upshur, born April 7, 1828, at "Rose Cottage," died July 27, 1907, at Monticello, New York. She was a well-known author and wrote for many southern publications under the pen name of "Fanny Fielding." She lived in Norfolk with her father for a number of years, and following his death went to New York. There she met and married, July 2, 1870, Josiah Robert Sturges, born December 4, 1807, died 1876, descendant of the Sturges Family of Fairfield County, Connecticut. Josiah Robert Sturges once owned that tract of land now known as Rock Creek Park, Washington, D. C. Issue:
   a. Mary Upshur Sturges, born July 1, 1871, living 1955, married, 1894, Alois von Isakovics, born July 21, 1870, at Prague, Austria, died June 6, 1917, son of a prominent Austrian family, immigrated to New York in 1886 and founded the Synfleur Scientific Laboratories, Inc., of Monticello where Mary and Alois made their home. Issue:

(1) Marie Aloisia Von Isakovics, b. 1/12/1898, m. 1/21/1921 Luis do Hoyos, b. 7/21/1892 in Spain, immigrated to New York in 1908 and established his home in Monticello, where he was mayor for 16 years. Issue:
(a) Luis Warren de Hoyos, b. 1921, m. 1951 Marian Moore. Child: Debora b. 1953.
(b) Rose de Hoyos, b. 1925.
(2) Paul Von Isakovics, d. in infancy.
(3) Alois von Isakovics Jr., b. 1906, d. 2/24/1947, m. Betty George of Dayton, Ohio. Children: Anne, Alois, and John.
(4) Rosa von Isakovics, m. Martin O' Carroll. Child: Linda.
(5) Johannah von Isakovics, m. Dr. Sidney Austin.

2. Catherine Bullock Upshur, b. at "Rose Cottage", d. aged 18.
3. John Brown Upshur ll, eldest son of William and Anne Upshur, b. 1830 at "Rose Cottage", d. 4/28/1874, m. Anne Andrews, dau. of Dr. Andrews of New Orleans. One son, whose name is not known.
4. Thomas Wilson Upshur, second son of William Stith and Anne Strange (Wilson) Upshur, was born about 1831 at "Rose Cottage." He was listed as a student at the College of William and Mary during 1846-47, although it is possible that the name may refer to his distant cousin, Dr. Thomas Harold Wilson Upshur of the Vaucluse branch who was about the same age. Like his father and elder brother, Thomas studied law which he first practiced in Norfolk. After the Civil War, he moved to Richmond and became a member of the firm of "Wise and Upshur," and other members being the Honorable Henry A. Wise and the Honorable George Douglas Wise of Richmond. Thomas

married, first, Mary Elizabeth Upshur, his first cousin, daughter of John D. and Elizabeth Ann (Faulcon) Upshur. (Elizabeth Ann Faulcon was dau. of John Faulcon of "Melville," Surry County, and Mary Kennon (Cocke) Faulcon (b. 1783), dau. of John Hartwell Cocke (b. 1775) and Elizabeth (Kennon) Cocke. See VA. MAG. OF HIST., 5(1898), p. 76-7. Thomas married, second, Mary Ellen (Dunton) Peed, widow of William J. F. Peed and daughter of George W. and Arnithia Dunton of Church Neck, Nothampton County. Thomas died in Church Neck at the home of his stepchildren. He had no issue by either marriage.

5. Harriet Saltonstal Upshur, born at "Rose Cottage," died in infancy.
6. William Stith Upshur, born at "Rose Cottage," died in infancy.
7. Charles Wingfield Upshur, born at "Rose Cottage," died in infancy.

B. Elizabeth Ann Brown Upshur, eldest daughter of John Brown I and Mary Elizabeth (Stith) Upshur was born April 8, 1805, at "Rose Cottage," died January 17, 1874, married, June 23, 1824, her second cousin, Judge Abel Parker Upshur I, born June 17, 1790, died Feb. 28, 1844, and had issue. (See Vaucluse branch, H.S.F. Vol. X.)

C. Captain Caleb Littleton Upshur I, second son of John Brown I and Mary Elizabeth (Stith) Upshur, was born in June 1807 at "Rose Collage." It may have been this Caleb who, as a boy, carved his name on one of the bricks which was discovered at "Rose Cottage" by the author during his visit there in 1936. When Caleb was fifteen, his father died intestate and Rose Cottage plantation was divided by law among his wife and children. Twelve years later, in 1834, Caleb deeded his part to his elder brother, William Stith Upshur. (Deed to part of Rose Cottage plantation, Caleb Littleton Upshur I to William Stith Upshur, Accomack Deeds, 1834-35, p. 334.) Little is known about Caleb's youth except that he went to sea at an early age, perhaps following his father's death in 1822. He had an adventurous life and in more than fifty years at sea his experiences were many and varied. He was shipwrecked seven times, and on three occasions barely escaped drowning; once he and a seaman were the only survivors, rescued after clinging for many hours to a floating spar. On one voyage Cleb's ship was badly damaged when it struck a great whale, but succeeded in reaching St. Thomas in the Virgin Islands for repairs. He sailed around Cape Horn to the Lobos Islands off the coast of Peru, bringing back guano for his son, Caleb II, pioneer of the fertilizer business in Norfolk. Captain Upshur sailed around the world and during the Civil War ran the blockade in Hampton Roads for the Confederacy.

Captain Upshur often sailed up the Nansemond River, a tributary of Hampton Roads, and frequently stopped at "Pembroke" to dine. "Pembroke," located on the eastern bank of the Nansemond River, was built in the early 1700's. It became the home of James Hunter Goodwin in 1830, and he left it to his daughter, Agnes Goodwin, who married Jeremiah Pinner. Jeremiah's sister, Ann Elizabeth Pinner also lived there. On one of his visits to "Pembroke" Captain Upshur met Ann Elizabeth Pinner, born June 9, 1813, and on April 22, 1835, she became his wife. (Ann Elizabeth Pinner (1813-1854) was dau. of Jeremiah Pinner of Nasemond County and Ann (Stoakley) Goodwin-Pinner (1782-1848). Ann Stoakley may have been a member of the Stockley Family from the Eastern Shore. She was the widow of James Edwin Goodwin when she married Pinner.)

Immediately following their marriage they made their home at "Pembroke," next they moved to Northampton County, but later returned to Nansemond County, establishing their home, so it has been reported, at "Aspen Grove" which the author has been unable to locate. Captain Upshur and his first wife had seven children. Ann Eliza-

beth died December 31, 1854, and was buried at
St. John's Episcopal Church, Chuckatuck, Virginia,
beside her three elder children.

In December 1855, Captain Upshur married,
second, Martha Jane Simmons, born June 7, 1826,
by whom he had three children. (Descent of
Martha Jane Simmons: John Simmons (b. 1751) m.,
1773, Amey Dawley, had Dennis Simmons (1783-
1870) of Knott's Island, N. C., and Norfolk County,
Va., m. Judith Hanes (1787-1865), had Martha
Jane Simmons (1826-99) m. Capt. Caleb Littleton
Upshur I(1807-85).) At the time of her marriage
Martha Jane was living with her parents at their
plantation on Tanner's Creek, a few miles from
Norfolk. Tanner's Creek is now Lafayette River,
and the plantation has become that residential
section of Norfolk known as Algonquin Park. The
old home still stands as a beautiful landmark of
earlier days. Capt. Upshur died Sept. 28, 1885,
at Norfolk, in his seventy-eighth year and was
buried in Elmwood Cemetery beside his son,
Hampden Stith Upshur. No tombstone marks his
grave. Martha Jane d. 2/27/1899 at Norfolk and
buried in Elmwood Cemetery. Capt. Caleb Upshur
and wife Ann (Pinner) had issue:
1. Mary Paulina, b. 5/21/1836, d. 8/19/1850.
2. Ann, b. 1838, d. in childhood.
3. John, b. 1839, d. in childhood.
4. Caleb Littleton Upshur II, b. 9/11/1841 on the
    Eastern Shore, spent his youth mainly in
    Nansemond Co. During the Civil War Caleb II
    served as Captain in the Confederate Army.
    Following the war he married, about 1868,
    Anna Greene Riddick, daughter of Richard
    Riddick, member of the prominent Riddick
    Family on Nansemond County, b. 1842, d.,
    4/1/1914, buried in Elmwood Cemetery.
    Anna inherited a sizeable fortune from her
    father and she and Caleb II bought the old
    Corbell Farm, near Chuckatuck, which they
    developed into a beautiful and productive
    property. They established another residence

in Norfolk where Caleb organized the Upshur Guano Company, and constructed at Bain's Wharf, Portsmouth, the first fertilizer factory in the area. Caleb II became an outstanding citizen of Norfolk, and in addition to civil activities was a Director of the Norfolk College for Young Ladies, founded in 1880. He d. 9/10/1866 and was buried in Elmwood Cemetery. Caleb Upshur II and his wife Anna had issue: (Six chn. d. in infancy.)
- a. Anna, b. 1/24/1869, d. 8/5/1947. She attended Norfolk College for Young Ladies of which her father was a Director. She m. 1/24/1894 Robert Sydney Godwin, b. 5/6/1867, d. 7/1/1915, a member of the Godwin family of Isle of Wight and Nansemond Counties. No issue.
- b. Lucy, b. 7/31/1881, d. s. p. 2/14/1950.
- c. Caleb Littleton III, b. 8/14/1882, engaged in the brokerage business in Norfolk. He m. 6/16/1910 Maude Walker, b. 2/12/1884, dau. of Henry and Florence Walker. Caleb d. 1/28/1919 at Norfolk. Children:
  - (1) Caleb Littleton Upshur IV, b. 5/14, 1911, m. 10/19/1936 Nancy Davis, dau. of Cornelius and Sallie Davis. One child: Nancy, b. 1938, m. 1957 Robert Charles McAllister.
  - (2) Henry Walker Upshur, b. 11/6/1913, m. 1939 Frances Dawson, dau. of Cary and Elizabeth Dawson. Children: Cary and Henry Upshur Jr.
- d. Littleton, d. in infancy.
5. Elizabeth Upshur, b. 8/11/1843, d. 3/2/1888, m. 10/26/1876 John P. Keeling (1842-1917). No issue.
6. Nancy Upshur, b. 5/6/1845, m. 12/17/1868 John Richard Whitaker, b. 5/1/1842. Lived in Enfield, N. C. Issue:
  - a. John Richard Jr., b. 4/30/1874, m. 7/29/1901 Grace Jennys, b. 5/3/1883. Issue:
    - (1) Fenton J. Whitaker, b. 1/3/1906.

(2) John Richard Whitaker III, b. 11/29/1907.
b. Elizabeth, b. 12/30/1876, m. 6/29/1904 Walter Clement, b. 11/3/1866. Issue: Walter Jr. and Nancy Clement.
7. Hampden Stith Upshur, b. 5/1/1850, d. s. p. 1881.

Capt. Caleb Littleton Upshur I and Martha Jane (Simmons) Upshur his second wife had issue:
8. Judith Upshur, b. 1856, d. in infancy.
9. Sallie Hanes Upshur, b. 8/3/1859 at Norfolk. She m. 7/28/1876 John R. Young, b. 3/14/1849, d. 11/30/1937. Sallie d. 4/10/1913. Issue:
   a. Royden Young, b. 1877, d. in infancy.
   b. Murray Young, b. 1878, d. in infancy.
   c. John Young Jr., b. 1881, d. 1902.
   d. Emma Gertrude Young, b. 7/22/1883, d. 11/21/1950, m. 11/4/1905 Donald Cheatham, b. 12/10/1880, d. 6/3/1931, son of the Rev. Henry Cheatham and his wife Emma. Issue:
      (1) Richard Young Cheatham, b. 12/30/1907, m. 7/27/1940 Jean Hudgins. One child: Laurel Cheatham, b. 1944.
      (2) Helen Littleton Cheatham, b. 10/27/1919.
   e. Helen Upshur Young, b. 8/5/1885, m. 1920 Col. Elmore Beach Gray, U.S. Army. No issue.
   f. Raymond Giraud Young, b. 11/5/1887, d. 2/22/1953, m. 1913 Naomi Phillips, b. 3/15/1893. Issue:
      (1) Sallie Young, b. 8/18/1914, m. 1941 Cleland Leaman. One child, Bruce Leaman, b. 1946.
      (2) Margaret Young, b. 1/10/1918, m. 1948 Harry Hunter Roper.
   g. Marie Louise Young, b. 2/13/1892, d. 2/13/1904.
10. Robert Lee Upshur, youngest child of Capt. Caleb Littleton and Martha Jane (Simmons)

Upshur, was born Dec. 7, 1862, at Norfolk. At that time his father was running the blockade in Hampton Roads on the side of the Confederacy, so Robert's mother took her infant son and young daughter, Sallie, to her father's plantation on Tanner's Creek. Robert grew up on the big farm with its orchards, cattle, and magnificent waterfront. During this time he attended a private school conducted by a Mr. Jones about two miles from the plantation.

Following the death of his grandfather, Dennis Simmons, the plantation was divided among his four daughters, and Robert's mother inherited the large tract about one mile from the old homeplace. On this tract, also beautifully situated on Tanner's Creek, she tried to farm with an incompetent overseer but the results were unsatisfactory. Robert was sent to Norfolk to live with his older half-brother, Caleb Littleton Upshur II, and there attended Gatewood Military Academy. At sixteen Robert was taken into the office of his half-brother to learn the fertilizer business and he continued in that type of work until a few years before his death.

Robert married, Jan. 17, 1888, Julia Estelle ("Stella") Andrews, born November 23, 1866, at Benevolence, Georgia. (Descent of Julia Estelle Andrews: Isham Andrews left Virginia for Georgia about 1769, had Micajah Andrews m. a Miss Quarterman, had Edward Quarterman Andrews (1800-78), Methodist Minister, m. Elizabeth Beasley, had Christopher Columbus Andrews (1829-76), Methodist Minister, m. Mary Stedman Raboteau (1834-1918), had Julia Estelle Andrews (b. 1866) m. Robert Lee Upshur (1862-1935). (Andrews Family genealogical tree in possession of the author.) Mary Stedman Raboteau, supra, was dau. of John Samuel Raboteau II (1805-81) of Fayetteville, N.C., m. Esther Barclay. John and Esther also had a dau.,

Catherine, m. Allison Francis Page of Cary,
N. C., had Walter Hines Page, Ambassador
to Great Britain during World War I. John
Samuel Raboteau II was son of John Samuel
Raboteau I (1766-1838), born in Philadelphia,
m. Susannah Graeff of Germantown, Pa.,and
said John Raboteau I was son of Charles Cornelius Raboteau of New Providence, Penn.,
m. Elizabeth Klein.) When she was a young
girl her widowed mother moved the family to
Norfolk where "Stella" attended Norfolk College for Young Ladies. A brief paragraph is
inadequate to describe "Stella" who, in later
years, became the matriarch of her family.
Author and advisor to family and friends, she
wrote for the Norfolk newspapers at the age
of eighty-nine, and her mind was as bright
and keen as it was when she was eighteen.
She was loved by all who knew her and her
powerful influence for good has been felt by
many. She died Dec. 23, 1956 and was buried
in Forest Lawn Cemetery, Norfolk, beside
her husband, who d. 3/7/1935. Issue:
a. Mary Lee Upshur, b. 12/27/1888 at Norfolk, m. 6/14/1915 Roy Elliott, b. 11/1/1884, son of Samuel and Martha Elliott
of Ohio. Issue:
(1) David Upshur Elliott, b. 7/6/1917,
m. 1945 Ethel Bauer, dau. of George
and Louise Bauer of Louisville, Ky.
Their chn: David, b. 1947, and
Anne, b. 1950.
(2) Margaret Lee Elliott, b. 8/16/1919,
m. 1944 Robert Knox Jr., who d.
1960. No issue.
(3) Mary Upshur Elliott, b. 4/17/1928,
m. 1950 William Ross. She m. (2)
Thomas Downing. They have Lelia
and Robert Downing.
b. Robert Littleton Upshur, b. 4/13/1891,
m. 5/13/1917 Penelope Jackson, dau. of
William and Sallie Jackson of Princess

Anne Co., Va. Issue:
- (1) Jane Upshur, b. 2/5/1919, m. 1941 Alfred Woodward, b. Illinois 12/15/1913. She m. (2) Thomas L. Barnes. Issue: Robert, Anne, and David Woodward.
- (2) Martha Lee Upshur, b. 7/31/1920, m. 1942 Charles Pritchard, b. 8/3/1912. Issue: Penelope, Charles, and Littleton Pritchard.
- (3) Stella Andrews Upshur, b. 5/18/1926, m. 1948 William W. Thompson, Jr., b. 3/6/1925. Issue: Elizabeth, William, Robert and Thomas Thompson.
- c. Gladys Estelle Upshur, b. 5/30/1895, d. 6/11/1920, m. 1918 Barney L. Jones of Fuquay Springs, N.C. (1891-1925). Issue:
  - (1) Rev. Barney L. Jones Jr., b. 1920, m. Marjorie Curts, of Middletown, Conn. Issue: Roy, Stella, Walter, and Christopher Jones.
- d. John Andrews Upshur, (author of this genealogy), b. 1/9/1899 at Norfolk. He graduated from the U.S. Naval Academy in 1921. During WWI, while a Midshipman, he performed active service aboard the U.S.S. MAINE. Later, as an officer, he served for several years aboard the U.S.S. OKLAHOMA in the Pacific, spent four years on destroyers in the Atlantic, completed a tour of duty as Instructor at the Naval Academy, and served for three years on destroyers on the Asiatic Station. After leaving active service in the Navy in 1933, he made his home in Smithfield, Virginia, for a few years. In 1937, he joined the staff of Colonial Williamsburg as Director of their Merchandising Division. Following the outbreak of World War II he took leave of absence to return to active duty in the Navy, serving most of his duty at the Naval Operating Base,

Norfolk, as Executive Officer to the Commander Inshore Patrol, and Administrative Officer for District Operations. Following the surrender of Japan he resumed his former position with Colonial Williamsburg, to retire eventually to the Eastern Shore of Virginia, and make his home at Drummonds Mill Farm, near Accomac.

He married, 7/14/1928, Eleanor Eve Walton of Augusta, Georgia, born 11/27/1905, graduate of Smith College, and a descendant of that prominent Walton Family of Virginia and Georgia of which George Walton, Signer of the Declaration of Independence, was a distinguished member. (Descent of Eleanor Eve Walton: Robert Walton (d. 1734) of New Kent County, Va., m. Frances, had George Walton (1724/5-1797) of Prince Edward County m. Martha Hughes (b. 1734), had Robert Walton (1754-1800) immigrated to Richmond Co., Ga., prior to the Revolution m. Blanche Glasscock (b. 1757), had Robert Walton (1791-1870) of Augusta m. Evelina Sarah Watkins (1796-1868), had Robert Walton (1826-1908) of Augusta m. Virginia Meals Combs (1833-1918), had Robert Walton (1867-1939) of Augusta m. Lucy Eleanor Wilson (b. 1870) of Barnwell County, S.C., had Eleanor Eve Walton (b. 1905). Robert Walton Robertson, "Walton Genealogy," HISTORICAL COLLECTION, GEORGIA CHAPTER, D.A.R., II, p. 329-40). Issue:

(1) Eleanor Walton Upshur, b. 12/9/1931, graduated with honors from Mary Washington College, m. 6/5/1965 John Melville Whittock Jr., b. 5/26/1916, son of John and Gertrude (Baker) Whittock.

(2) John Andrews Upshur Jr., b. 7/26/

1933 at Annapolis, Md., graduated
from Yale University 1956, later
attended the University of Michigan
where he received graduate degrees.
 e. Margaret Esther Upshur, b. 12/19/1902,
m. 1928 William Bowen Ault of Enterprise,
Oregon, b. 10/6/1898, graduated from U.
S. Naval Academy 1922. Killed in action
1942. She m. (2) William S. Meacham, b.
1/15/1900. Issue:
- (1) William Upshur Ault, b. 12/8/1932, m. 1957 Beverly Owens. Issue: William, James, and Margaret Ault.
- (2) Robert Bowen Ault, b. 4/23/1937, m. Virginia Kelly. They have Robert Ault Jr., b. 1963.

D. John D. Upshur, born in 1809 at "Rose Cottage", married, 1836, Elizabeth Ann Faulcon of Surry County. John died July 26, 1838, perhaps at "Cedar Cottage," his home on Warehouse Creek, Northampton County. John and Elizabeth Ann (Faulcon) Upshur had issue:
 1. Mary Elizabeth Upshur, b. about 1837, m. her first cousin, Thomas Wilson Upshur. No issue.

E. Mary Jane Upshur was b. at "Rose Cottage" but the dates of her birth and death have not been determined. Although Thomas Teackle Upshur II wrote that she never married, the author believes that she may have been the Mary Upshur of Norfolk who married Major William Goode, b. Jan. 7, 1791.

F. Robert Stith Upshur, b. in 1815 at "Rose Cottage," died Dec. 6, 1883. In 1842 he went to New Orleans where he entered the U.S. Customs Service, and after the Civil War became Collector of Accounts in that city. On April 6, 1847, he married Angelina Lafferranderie, b. 7/1/1826, d. 5/4/1895. Issue:
 1. Robert Brown Upshur, b. 5/17/1851. He m. 10/29/1878 Adele Nores, a native of France, who d. 3/11/1919. Robert was living in 1937. Issue:
  a. Robert Ashton Upshur, b. 3/13/1880, d.

          in infancy.
- b. Albert Sidney Upshur, b. 3/13/1882, d. in infancy.
- c. Lilia (twin) b. 3/13/1882, m. 1910 Theodore du Fossat Soniat. Issue:
  - (1) Theodore Soniat, b. 10/4/1811, m. 1936 Mary Thomas of New Orleans. They have Robert and Thomas Soniat.
  - (2) Edwin Soniat, b. 12/26/1915.
  - (3) Joel Soniat, b. 4/12/1918.
  - (4) Yvonne Soniat, b. 10/8/1920.
 2. Estelle Upshur, b. 11/17/1854, d. 6/9/1867.
G. Sallie Stith Upshur, b. 12/26/1815 at "Rose Cottage", d. s. p. 12/25/1871.
H. Abel Brown Upshur, b. 10/25/1821 at "Rose Cottage". During the Civil War served in the Office of Ordnance and Hydrography of the Confederate Navy in Richmond. He m. Columbia Wingfield Williams, b. 7/11/1828 at "Tudor Place", Georgetown, D.C. She d. 4/18/1886, and was a great gr. daughter of Martha (Dandridge) Custis-Washington, wife of George Washington. Abel d. 2/6/1895. No issue.
I. Hampden Stith Upshur was b. at "Rose Cottage" but the date is not known. d. s. p.

BROWNSVILLE BRANCH

Thomas Upshur I
(ca. 1713-1751)

    Thomas Upshur I, youngest son of Authur II and Sarah (Browne) Upshur, was born about 1713 at "Warwick." The exact date of his birth has not been determined and his tombstone has not been found, but he died in 1750/1 for his will was dated and proved in court during that year.
    In 1734 Thomas I entered into a covenant deed with his parents for the plantation which for generations has been known as "Brownsville." (Deed of Gift to Thomas Upshur I for "Brownsville," Northampton Deeds, 1733-50, p. 30.) He agreed to surrender the plantation to his parents whenever they should call upon him to do so, thus his

parents retained a life interest in the property. Thomas I is the first Upshur who is definitely known to have lived at "Brownsville," although his father, Arthur Upshur II, may have lived there for a short time following his marriage to Sarah Browne.

About 1738 Thomas Upshur I married Sarah Bell who bore him two sons, Thomas Upshur II and Brown Upshur. (Descent of Sarah Bell: Thomas Bell I (ca. 1618-78) of Northampton County, E.S. Va. immigrant, had Robert Bell (d. 1724) m. Mary Cutting, sister of William Cutting (d. 1704), had Thomas Bell (d. ca. 1768) m. Mary Watson, dau. of Robert Watson (d. 1708/9), had Sarah Bell m. Thomas Upshur I(ca. 1713-51). All the above lived on the E.S. Va. For Bell Family of E.S. Va., Northampton and Accomack County records, PASSIM; Whitelaw, VIRGINIA'S EASTERN SHORE, PASSIM; Nottingham, WILLS AND ADMINISTRATIONS, ACCOMACK COUNTY, VIRGINIA, 1663-1800, PASSIM; Johnston, SOCIETY OF COLONIAL WARS IN THE STATE OF MARYLAND, plate II, p. 22) After the death of Thomas I his widow(bond dated April 14, 1752) Henry Gascoigne, and bore him a daughter, Sarah, and probably other children. (Will of Thomas Upshur I, Northampton Wills, Invs., Divs., Etc., 1750-54, p. 28-9; IBID., 73-5, for inventory of his estate.)

Thomas I and Sarah (Bell) Upshur had issue:
I. Thomas Upshur II was born July 2, 1739, at "Brownsville." He inherited this plantation upon the death of his father, and in 1785 added to his real estate by the purchase of an adjoining farm to the north called "Upshurshire." (Thomas Upshur II left this farm to his son, Thomas Stockley Upshur (ca. 1768-ca. 1796). Upon the latter's death the title went to his sister, Anne Stockley Upshur (b. ca. 1765), who married John Teackle II(1762-1811) of "Craddock." In his will of 1811, Teackle called the farm "Upshurshire." His son, Dr. John Upshur Teackle (1803-50) of Baltimore, sold the farm in 1833, and the deed called it "Uppershire," the spelling generally used by Upshur decendants.)

   Like his father, Thomas II was a planter, and records indicate that he was very successful.

He was frequently referred to in old family records as Captain Thomas Upshur, and Thomas Teackle Upshur II claimed that he served as an officer in a company of Minute Men during the Revolutionary War. (There are several Revolutionary War records of a Thomas Upshur of Virginia, but the author believes each refers to Thomas Upshaw of the Upshaw branch from Essex and Caroline Counties. However, the names of many officers and men who served as Minute Men during the Revolutionary War were never entered in the official records, and the omission of the name of Thomas Upshur II is a case in point for family records and tradition indicate that he served as a Minute Man.)

On Feb. 1, 1761, Thomas II married Anne Stockley, (see later), born 1739, died Oct. 22, 1817, by whom he had six children who lived to be grown. Thomas II died Dec. 19, 1792, at "Brownsville," and both he and his wife are buried there in the family burying ground with many of their descendants. (Will of Thomas Upshur II dated June 10, 1789, Northampton Wills, Etc., 1792-95, p. 100.) Issue:

A. John Upshur was b. 12/29/1761, at "Brownsville." He was a prominent, wealthy, and highly respected citizen of the Eastern Shore. He was a successful planter and merchant, and for a time was High Sheriff of Northampton County. Among his various enterprises was the operation of a castor oil mill. He was a large shipper of corn to New England ports, using chartered vessels which loaded at his wharf on Brownsville Creek. By the will of his father John Upshur, he inherited the northern half of "Brownsville" contaning 631 acres, and in 1806 built the present home now occupied by his descendants. In 1823 he purchased the southern half of the tract, thus reuniting the entire tract first patented by his ancestor, John Browne. He added further to his real estate through the purchase of a 470-acre tract, later known as "Merton," on the bayside and "Essex" in Upshur's Neck.

John Upshur, usually referred to in the family as John Upshur of "Brownsville," married three times. He m. (1) 5/14/1792 Elizabeth Gore, widow of his second cousin Abel Upshur 11. Elizabeth bore John no children and d. 1/16/1794. John Upshur m. (2) 10/24/1798 his second cousin Elizabeth Brown Upshur, dau. of Caleb and Anne (Brown) Upshur of Rose Cottage, b. 12/28/1804. She bore John four children, and after her death John Upshur m. (3) 6/9/1808 Elizabeth Upshur (Teackle) Yerby, b. 3/17/1776, d. 2/8/1837, buried at "Brownsville." Elizabeth Upshur Teackle was dau. of Col. Thomas Teackle III (ca. 1734-84) and Elizabeth (Upshur) Teackle (ca. 1740-82) of "Craddock.") She was the widow of Dr. George Yerby of Lancaster County when she married John. By her first husband she had one child, Dr. George Teackle Yerby of Northampton County, able physician and Delegate to the Virginia legislature for sixteen years. Elizabeth bore John four children. John Upshur d. 9/29/1842, at "Brownsville" and was buried in the family burying ground with his last two wives.

John Upshur and Elizabeth Brown (Upshur) Upshur, his second wife, had issue:
1. Thomas Brown Upshur, b. 7/17/1799, d. in infancy.
2. William Brown Upshur I, b. 11/5/1801, d. 8/23/1884, m. 11/3/1851 Catherine Teackle Neale who d. 2/26/1911. (Catherine was dau. of William Neale and Elizabeth Teackle (Smith) Neale (1798-1857), dau. of Charles and Catherine (Teackle) Smith (b. 1768) of "Moratico Hall", Richmond Co. This couple had no issue and were buried at "Brownsville".
3. Anne Upshur, b. 10/26/1802, d. in infancy.
4. John Caleb Upshur, b. 3/24/1804, d. in

infancy.

John Upshur and Elizabeth Upshur (Teackle) Yerby Upshur, his third wife, had issue:
5. Anne Elizabeth Upshur, b. 9/1/1809, d. s. p. 1885 in Maryland.
6. Sallie Teackle Brown Upshur, b. 8/21/1811, d. 5/30/1892, m. 10/7/1834 William W. Handy of Princess Anne, b. 2/21/1802, d. 7/31/1857. Sallie was his second wife. Issue:
   a. The Rev. William Collins Handy.
   b. Sallie Brown Upshur Handy.
7. A son, b. 5/28/1816, d. in infancy.
8. Thomas Teackle Upshur I, b. 9/4/1817 at "Brownsville", d. 7/1/1889. Studied medicine at the University of Va. He m. 4/12/1842 Elizabeth Teackle Smith, b. 6/15/1822, d. 2/7/1886. (Elizabeth was the dau. of Isaac Smith III (1768-1846) of "Sea View", near Eastville; son of Isaac Smith II (1734-1813) of "Selma", Eastville. The mother of Elizabeth was Anne Stockley (Teackle) Smith (1788-1862), dau. of John Teackle II, (1762-1811), son of Col. Thomas Teackle III (ca. 1734-1784). Anne was the second wife of Isaac Smith III, his first wife having been Maria, dau. of Judge Francis Hopkinson of Philadelphia, Signer of the Declaration of Independence.) Elizabeth and Thomas were natives of Northampton Co., but spent the latter part of their lives in Princess Anne, where they died. Both are buried in the Manokin Presbyterian Church of that town. Issue:
   a. John Upshur, b. 9/1/1843, d. 6/21/1887 at Princess Anne.
   b. Thomas Teackle Upshur II, b. 12/22/1844 at "Upshurshire". He entered Va. Military Institute in 1859 and continued his studies there until the Civil War began. On 6/8/1861 he

enlisted in the Confederate Army and served bravely throughout the war. Following the war, he went to Sumter, S.C., where he m. 9/5/1871 Caroline DeSaussure Blanding, b. 6/14/1852, d. 3/26/1940. (Caroline was dau. of Col. James Douglas Blanding (1831-86), dau. of Capt. James Dickey and Frances Adelaide (Spiers) McFaddin, all of Sumter, S.C.) After working for several years in Sumter, and a few years in Texas trying his fortune at sheep raising, Thomas II and his family moved to Virginia in 1884, and established their home at "Brownsville." Here he began his historical and genealogical work in which he was steadfastly engaged for more than twenty-five years. He spent many years in restoring and transcribing the early court records of Northampton and Accomack Counties, thus helping to preserve the oldest continuous court records in America. He was recognized as an authority on the Eastern Shore, and was an outstanding genealogist of the period. His manuscripts include the history of every important family then living on the Eastern Shore of Virginia. Thomas II died Jan. 14, 1910, at "Brownsville" where both he and his wife were buried.

Except for one or two pamphlets and a number of articles in historical magazines, he died before his great store of knowledge could put into print for permanent record.

Thomas Teackle Upshur II and Caroline DeSaussure (Blanding) Upshur had issue:

(1) Elizabeth Upshur, b. 11/24/1872, d. 8/25/1887.
(2) James Blanding Upshur, b. 8/21/1874, d. 10/2/1889.
(3) Lenora McFaddin Upshur, b. 12/11/1876, m. 8/9/1899 Thomas Percival Robinson, b. 5/7/1856, d. 1/5/1916. They made their home in Germantown, Pa. Issue:
   (a) Lenora Blanding Robinson, b. 5/11/1900, m. 1921 Reginald Evans Graeff. They have James and Elizabeth Graeff.
   (b) Anna Barney Robinson, b. 2/10/1908, m. 1943 Joshua B. Westcott.
(4) William Brown Upshur III, b. 11/28/1878, d. 6/29/1929, m. 6/4/1903 Caroline Payne Martin, b. 10/24/1881, dau. of Col James and Florence (Watkins) Martin of Winston, N.C. They lived in Sumter, S.C. Issue:
   (a) James Blanding Upshur, b. 4/6/1904, m. 1929 Martha Poag; they have William, Rebecca, and Martha Poag.
   (b) John Dupuy Upshur, b. 1906, d. in infancy.
   (c) William Brown Upshur, b. 6/11/1909, d. young.
   (d) Dorothy DeSaussure Upshur, b. 1/20/1911, m. 1937 Henry Glenn Oetgen, (1913-1953).
   (e) Donald Martin Upshur, b. 7/17/1912, d. 9/14/1950, m. 1942 Claire Powell, dau. of Clayton Powell, dau. of Clayton L. Powell of Riverside, Ill. They had John and Gertrude Upshur.

- (f) Dr. Thomas Teackle Upshur IV, b. 2/22/1915, m. 1942 Betsy Cox of Mobile, Ala. They have Diana, Elizabeth, Fontain, Carol and Thomas Upshur.
- (g) Robert Irving Upshur, b. 5/30/1918, m. 1950 Helen Nash, b. 10/21/1922, dau. of John and Jessie Nash. They have David and John Upshur.

(5) Florence Irving Upshur, b. 9/13/1880, m. 12/27/1917 John Ashby Dick, b. 9/29/1868, d. 2/2/1943. Issue:
- (a) Anne Floyd Dick, b. 7/13/1919, m. 1946 William H. Cockerill. They have Anne, William, Charles and Thomas Cockerill.
- (b) Esther Macdonald Dick, b. 12/29/1921, m. 1940 Woodrow W. Bralley, b. 10/2/1912. They have David, Stephen, and Richard Bralley.

(6) Anne Floyd Upshur, b. 10/25/1882, who has lived at "Brownsville" since early childhood. She collaborated with Ralph T. Whitelaw in writing "Virginia's Eastern Shore", and perhaps knows more about the history of the Eastern Shore and the Upshur family than anyone now living. She has been of great help to the author of this lineage.

(7) Caroline DeSaussure Upshur, b. 1/30/1886, d 9/18/1848, m. 9/10/1910 Henry Ball Baker, b. 6/18/1882. They made their home in West Chester, Pa. Issue:
- (a) Henry Ball Baker Jr., b.

1/4/1912, m. 1941 Betty
Worrel, b. 9/15/1914. They
have David, Henry, Benja-
min, and Rob Baker.
  (b) Caroline Upshur Baker, b.
5/23/1913, m. 1934 Clarence
W. Woodcock, b. 5/23/1910.
They have Carolyn, Claire,
and Clarence Woodcock.
  (c) Elizabeth Fontain Baker, b.
1/31/1915, m. 1936 Raymond
E. Olmstead, b. 1/10/1914.
They have Sarita and Fontain
Olmstead.
  (d) Thomas Upshur Baker, b. 1/
5/1925.
(8) Thomas Teackle Upshur III, b.
8/17/1888, d. 5/31/1915.
(9) Henry DeSaussure Blanding Upshur, b. 11/4/1890, d. 2/25/1956,
m. 12/28/1920 Eleanor L. Lambert, b. 8/30/1890. Issue:
  (a) Eleanor Lambert Upshur,
b. 1/16/1923, m. 1942
George W. Poythress. They
have one dau. Virginia.
  (b) Hamilton Brown Upshur, b.
8/3/1924, m. 1949 Martha
Ellis.
(10) Sarita Reed Upshur, b. 4/28/1895,
d. 9/18/1934, m. 4/2/1921 Curry
Thomas (1888-1936). No issue.
c. Florence Upshur, b. 3/7/1847, d. 8/
18/1900, m. 11/15/1865 Judge Levin
Thomas Handy Irving, b. 4/8/1828
near Salisbury, Md. , d. 8/23/1892.
Judge Irving was an able lawyer and
statesman, and was Judge of the
Court of Appeals in Maryland for
many years. He was the son of Dr.
Thomas Handy Irving and Margaret
(Ker) of the Eastern Shore of Mary-

land. Judge Irving and his wife are buried in the Manokin Church Cemetery. Issue: one daughter, who died at birth.
- d. Alice Brown Upshur, b. 6/9/1849, d. in infancy.
- e. William Brown Upshur, b. 11/13/1854, d. in infancy.
- f. Anne Elizabeth Upshur, b. 10/19/1857, d. s. p. before 1926.
- g. Sallie Brown Upshur, b. 7/3/1859, d. 12/19/1886, m. 3/19/1884 William Handy Dashiell. No issue.
- h. Mary Graham Upshur, b. 2/5/1861, d. at birth.

B. Anne Stockley Upshur, eldest dau. of Thomas II and Anne (Stockley) Upshur, b. at "Brownsville" ca. 1765, m. 12/18/1783 Col. John Teackle II of "Craddock", b. 1/12/1762, d. 2/18/1811, son of Col. Thomas Teackle III and Elizabeth (Upshur) Teackle. Issue:
1. Elizabeth Upshur Teackle, b. 9/26/1784, d. 4/6/1806, m. Harrison Ball of Richmond Co. and had issue. (Ref: Hayden's Va. Genealogies, p. 104).
2. Thomas Upshur Teackle, b. 3/29/1786, d. in infancy.
3. Anne Stockley Teackle, b. 3/17/1788, d. 12/11/1862, m. 4/6/1814 Isaac Smith III of "Sea View", b. 11/8/1768, d. 11/27/1846. Anne was his second wife and bore him several children, one of whom was Elizabeth Teackle Smith who m. Thomas Teackle Upshur III.
4. Mary Upshur Teackle, b. 4/29/1790, d. 1846, m. John Rutter of Baltimore and had issue.
5. Lavinia Upshur Teackle, b. 10/11/1792, d. 3/25/1853, m. Capt. William Graham of Newry, Ireland, b. 7/4/1787, d. 11/30/1864 in Baltimore. Issue:
6. Sarah Upshur Teackle, b. 5/7/1795, d. 10/30/1867, m. William S. Pawson of Baltimore, b. 8/24/1798, d. 5/30/1884. Issue:

7. Thomas Upshur Teackle, b. 11/2/1797, d. 9/ 13/1863, m. 4/23/1839 Emma Wilson (d. 12/19/ 1861), dau. of Thomas Wilson of Baltimore. Issue.
8. Susanna Brown Upshur Teackle, b. 4/26/1800, d. 6/11/1881 at "Avon" near Baltimore, m. 9/5/1820 Francis Hopkinson Smith I, b. 3/14/ 1797 at "Ingleside" near Eastville, d. 2/14/1872. (Francis Hopkinson Smith I (1797-1872) was son of Isaac Smith III (1768-1846) and his first wife Maria (Hopkinson) Smith (1773-1806). This couple had nine children among whom was Francis Hopkinson Smith II, b. 10/23/1838, d. 4/8/1915, distinguished author who m. Josephine, dau. of William Vandeventer of Astoria, Long Island, and had issue.
9. Dr. John Upshur Teackle, b. 10/15/1803, d. s. p. 6/9/1851, in Baltimore.
10. St. George Williamson Teackle, b. 1/26/1806, d. 3/26/1874, was a prominent Baltimore lawyer. He m. 10/27/1836 Catherine Hays of Baltimore, b. 9/2/1815, d. 4/17/1896. Issue.

C. Sarah Brown Upshur, third child of Thomas II and Anne (Stockley) Upshur, was b. 4/14/1767 at "Brownsville', d. 1/23/1819, m. 10/23/1786 Col. Peter Hack of "Fairview", on Nadua Creek near Craddockville, Accomac Co., b. 4/11/1754, d. 10/18/1844. He was brother of Ann Hack (b. 1750) who m. Abel Upshur II (1756-1790). Sarah was his second wife. Issue:
1. Dr. Peter Thomas Upshur Hack, b. 1/15/1793, d. 7/31/1838, m. (1) Sallie Selby and (2) Harriet Fleming Selby. Issue by both wives.
2. Sallie Brown Upshur Hack, d. 1874, m. Col. Thomas Hatton Kellam of "Evergreen", Accomac Co. No issue.
3. John William Hack, m. Sabra, dau. of Thomas Cropper of Accomac Co. Issue.
4. Melinda Upshur Hack, d. s. p. ca. 1862.
5. Ann Hack, d. s. p. 1827.
6. Cave Jones Hack, m. Charlotte Dennis.

D. Thomas Stockley Upshur, second son of Thomas

II and Anne (Stockley), b. ca. 1768 at "Brownsville", d. ca. 1796 d. s. p. He studied law and practiced in Richmond. He inherited "Upshurshire", which after his death, passed to his sister Anne Stockley (Upshur) Teackle and then to her son Dr. John Upshur Teackle of Baltimore.
E. William Bell Eyre Upshur, d. aged 18.
F. Mary Upshur (twin of William), m. (bond dated 1/14/1794) the Rev. Cave Jones, an early Rector of St. George's Church, Accomac Co. They removed to New York where he became assistant Rector of Trinity Church. Issue:
1. Lydia Jones, d. s. p. at an advanced age.
2. Anne Jones, d. s. p. ca. 1895. She bequeathed her property to the Va. Theological Seminary in Alexandria and to the Washington and Lee University in Lexington.
G. Other children (names unknown) d. in infancy.
II. Brown Upshur, second son of Thomas I and Sarah (Bell) Upshur, was b. ca. 1740. Died young.

****

ANCESTRY OF MARY ELIZABETH STITH

Mary ("Molly") Elizabeth Stith, born September 7, 1786, died July 2, 1851, married (bond dated May 11, 1802) (Stratton Nottingham, THE MARRIAGE LICENSE BONDS OF NORTHAMPTON COUNTY, VIRGINIA, from 1706-1754 (Onancock, Va., 1929), p. 100). John Brown Upshur I of "Rose Cottage," born about 1776, died October 1822. As of interest to numerous descendants of this couple, several ancestral lines of Mary Elizabeth Stith follow:

Descent from Major John Stith (For Stith lineage, WM. AND MARY QUAR., 1st ser., 21 (1912-13), 181-93, 269-78; ibid., 1st ser., 22 (1914), 44-51; Upshur, SIR GEORGE YARDLEY, 29-30.)
1. Major John Stith immigrated to Virginia before 1656, settled in Charles City County.
2. Lt.-Col. Durry Stith (d. 1741) m. Susanna, dau. of

Lancelot Bathurst of New Kent County, son of Sir
Edward Bathurst of Gloucester County, Eng. Drury
Stith had a brother, Capt. John Stith, m. Mary, dau.
of William and Mary (Isham) Randolph of Turkey
Island, Va., parents of the Rev. William Stith, historian and early President of the College of William
and Mary.
3. Lt.-Col. Drury Stith (ca. 1695-1740) m. Elizabeth,
dau. of Maj. William Buckner (d. 1716) of Yorktown.
4. Griffin Stith (1720-84) m. Mary (b. 1726/7), dau. of
William Blaikley (d. 1736) and Catherine (Kaidyee)
Blaikley (1698-1771) of James City County. Griffin
Stith was Clerk of the Northampton County Court
1743-83.
5. William Stith (d. 1794), Clerk of the Northampton
County Court, m. Sarah, dau. of Isaac Smith II
(1734-1813) and Elizabeth Custis (Teackle) Smith
(1742-1822).
6. Mary Elizabeth Stith (1786-1851) m. John Brown
Upshur I (ca. 1776-1822) of "Rose Cottage."

Descent from Isaac Smith I: (For Smith lineage,
Upshur, SIR GEORGE YARDLEY, ch. 4; VA. MAG.
OF HIST., 58 (1950), 396-403; Whitelaw, VA's
EASTERN SHORE, PASSIM; Smith, "Smith, Teackle,
Upshur Families"; Upshur, MSS.
1. Isaac Smith I (d. 1760) of E. S. Va., m. Sarah,
youngest dau. of Maj. John West (the Younger) and
Frances (Yardley) West, dau. of Capt. Argoll Yardley II and Sarah (Michael) Yardley.
2. Isaac Smith II (1734-1813) of Northampton County m.
Elizabeth Custis Teackle (1742-1822), dau. of Thomas
Teackle II (1711-69) and Elizabeth (Custis) Teackle
(b. 1718), dau. of Thomas Custis (ca. 1685-1721) of
"Deep Creek" and Anne (Kendall) Custis, dau. of
Capt. William Kendall II (1659-96) and Ann (Mason)
Kendall. Isaac II and Elizabeth first lived in Accomack County, then at "Moratico Hall" on the Rappahannock River, and then at "Selma," near Eastville.
3. Sarah Smith m. William Stith (d. 1794).
4. Mary Elizabeth Stith (1786-1851) m. John Brown Upshur I (ca. 1776-1822) of "Rose Cottage."

Descent from the Reverend Thomas Teackle

1. Rev. Thomas Teackle (1624-1695/6), born in Gloucester County, Eng., settled on the E.S. Va. prior to 1653. He m. 2d, Margaret, dau. of Robert Nelson of "Gray's Inn," London, and Mary (Temple) Nelson, dau. of Sir John Temple and Dorothy (Lee) Temple, dau. of Edmund Lee.
2. Maj. John Teackle (1693-1721) of "Craddock," Accomack County, m. Susanna (b. ca. 1693), dau. of Arthur Upshur II (ca. 1654-1738) and Sarah (Browne) Upshur.
3. Thomas Teackle II (1711-69) of "Craddock" m. Elizabeth Custis (b. 1718).
4. Elizabeth Custis Teackle (1742-1822) m. Isaac Smith II (1734-1813).
5. Sarah Smith m. William Stith (1786-1851) m. John Brown Upshur I (ca. 1776-1822) of "Rose Cottage."

Descent from John Custis I
(For Custis, Scarburgh, Whittington, and Smart lineages, Harrison, HARRISON, WAPLES AND ALLIED FAMILIES: Whitelaw, VA's EASTERN SHORE, PASSIM.)

1. John Custis I (b. ca. 1599), Englishman, is believed to have immigrated to the E. S. Va. about 1650, m. Joane Powell.
2. Thomas Custis (b. ca. 1628) of Baltimore, Ireland, brother of Maj.-Gen. John Custis II (ca. 1630-1695/6) of "Arlington," Northampton County, E. S. Va. immigrant.
3. Edmund Custis (ca. 1650-1701) of "Deep Creek," Accomack County, was brought to the E. S. Va. by his uncle, Maj.-Gen. John Custis II. Edmund m. Tabitha Scarburgh Whittington, dau. of Col. William and Tabitha Scarburgh (Smart) Whittington.
4. Thomas Custis (ca. 1685-1721) of "Deep Creek" m. 2d, Anne, dau. of Capt. William Kendall II (1659-96) and Ann (Mason) Kendall.
5. Elizabeth Custis (b. 1718) m. Thomas Teackle II (1711-69) of "Craddock."
6. Elizabeth Custis Teackle (1742-1822) m. Isaac Smith II (1734-1813).
7. Sarah Smith m. William Stith (d. 1794).
8. Mary Elizabeth Stith (1786-1851) m. John Brown

Upshur I (ca. 1776-1822) of "Rose Cottage."
<u>Descent from Sir George Yardley</u> (For Yardley
lineage, SIR GEORGE YARDLEY: Captain J. H. R.
Yardley, BEFORE THE MAYFLOWER (New York,
1931). For Michael, Thorogood, West, Offley, and
Osborne lineages, Harrison, HARRISON, WAPLES
AND ALLIED FAMILIES; VA. MAG. OF HIST., 58
(1950), 396-403; Upshur, MSS; Whitelaw, VA's
EASTERN SHORE, PASSIM; Smith, "Smith, Teackle,
Upshur Families."
1. Sir George Yardley (1588-1627), Knt., Gov., and Capt. Gen. of Virginia, was born in Southwark, Eng. He left England for Virginia in 1609 on the SEA ADVENTURE, was shipwrecked off Bermuda, but finally arrived at Jamestown on the DELIVERANCE in 1610. In 1619, during his term as Governor, he summoned the First Legislative Assembly in America at Jamestown. He died there in 1627, and it is believed that he was buried in the so-called Knight's Tomb in the old Jamestown Church. Sir George m. Temperance Flowerdew who descended from an ancient and distinguished family. She came to Jamestown on the FALCON in 1609. She survived Sir George and m. 2d, Capt. Francis West, brother of Lord De la Warr. She had no issue by her second husband.
2. Col. Argoll Yardley I (1621-55) was born at Jamestown, m. 2d, Ann, dau. of John Custis I (b. ca. 1599), and settled on the E. S. Va. His son is believed to be a child by his first wife (name unknown).
3. Capt. Argoll Yardley II (d. 1682) of Northampton County, m. Sarah, dau. of Capt. John Michael (ca. 1625-78) and Elizabeth (Thorogood) Michael, dau. of Capt. Adam Thorogood (1603-40) of Norfolk County, Eng., and Sarah (Offley) Thorogood (bap. 1609).
4. Frances Yardley m. Maj. John West (the younger) (d. 1718/19) son of Lt.-Col. John West (1638/9-1703) and Matilda (Scarburgh) West, dau. of Col. Edmund Scarburgh II (1617-71). Lt.-Col. John West was son of Anthony West (ca. 1600-52) who immigrated to Jamestown in 1622 on the JAMES.
5. Sarah West m. Isaac Smith I (d. 1760).

6. Isaac Smith II (1734-1813) m. Elizabeth Custis Teackle (1742-1822).
7. Sarah Smith m. William Stith (d. 1794).
8. Mary Elizabeth Stith (1786-1851) m. John Brown Upshur I (ca. 1776-1822) of "Rose Cottage."

Descent from Captain Edmund Scarburgh I (For Scarburgh, Smart, Whittington, and Custis lineages, Harrison, HARRISON, WAPLES AND ALLIED FAMILIES: Whitelaw, Va's EASTERN SHORE, PASSIM.

1. Capt. Edmund Scarburgh I (ca. 1584-ca. 1635) emigrated from England to the E. S. Va. before 1629. He served in the Virginia House of Burgesses for several years, and was one of the first Commissioners for the Plantacon of Acchawmacke in 1632. He m. Hannah, dau. of Robert Butler.
2. Col. Edmund Scarburgh II (1617-71) was bap. at St. Martin-in-the-Fields, London. It is believed that he was left in England for his education and that he immigrated to the E. S. Va. when he learned of his father's death. He became one of the most important men in the Colony of Virginia and held many offices including those of Surveyor Gen. of Virginia, Speaker of the House of Burgesses, and Commander-in-Chief of all the Inhabitants of the E. S. Va. His wife's name was Mary but her parentage has never been definitely determined.
3. Tabitha Scarburgh (b. 1640) m. 1st, John Smart, born in Bristol, Eng., 2d, Devereaux Browne, 3d. Maj.-Gen. John Custis II, 4th, Col. Edward Hill of "Shirley," Charles City County.
4. Tabitha Scarburgh Smart m. Col. William Whittington (ca. 1653-1719/20), son of Capt. William and Elizabeth (Weston) Whittington of Northampton County. Col. Whittington was a member of the Virginia House of Burgesses for several years.
5. Tabitha Scarburgh Whittington m. Edmund Custis (ca. 1650-1701) of "Deep Creek."
6. Thomas Custis (ca. 1685-1721) of "Deep Creek" m. 2d, Anne, dau. of Capt. William Kendall II (1659-96) and Ann (Mason) Kendall.
7. Elizabeth Custis (b. 1718) m. Thomas Teackle II

(1711-69) of "Craddock."
8. Elizabeth Custis Teackle (1742-1822) m. Isaac Smith II (1734-1813).
9. Sarah Smith m. William Stith (d. 1794).
10. Mary Elizabeth Stith (1786-1851) m. John Brown Upshur I (ca. 1776-1822) of "Rose Cottage."

Descent from Captain Adam Thorogood (For Thorogood, Michael, Offley, and Osborne lineages, Harrison, HARRISON, WAPLES AND ALLIED FAMILIES; Whitelaw, VA's EASTERN SHORE, PASSIM; Upshur, SIR GEORGE YARDLEY.

1. Capt. Adam Thorogood (1603-40) immigrated to Virginia on the CHARLES in 1621. He m. Sarah Offley (bap. 1609) dau. of Robert Offley and Anne (Osborne) Offley, dau. of Sir Edward Osborne, Knt., and Lord Mayor of London in 1582. Capt. Thorogood was one of the principal figures in the history of Virginia during the seventeenth century, and he named Norfolk, Va., after Norfolk, England.
2. Elizabeth Thorogood, m. Capt. John Michael (ca. 1625-78). Capt. Michael immigrated to Virginia and settled on the E. S. Va. He was a prominent colonist and a man of wealth. He served as a Commissioner for Northampton County, and a Justice of the Peace in 1665 and subsequent years.
3. Sarah Michael m. Capt. Argoll Yardley II (d. 1682).
4. Frances Yardley m. Maj. John West (the Younger) (d. 1718/19).
5. Sarah West m. Isaac Smith I (d. 1760).
6. Isaac Smith II (1734-1813) m. Elizabeth Custis Teackle (1742-1822).
7. Sarah Smith m. William Stith (d. 1794).
8. Mary Elizabeth Stith (1786-1851) m. John Brown Upshur I (ca. 1776-1822) of "Rose Cottage."

xxxxxxxxxx

ANCESTRY OF ANNE STOCKLEY

Anne Stockley, born 1739, died October 22, 1817, married (bond dated January 29, 1761) (Nottingham, THE MARRIAGE LICENSE BONDS OF NORTHAMPTON

COUNTY, VIRGINIA, from 1706-1754, p. 100). Thomas Upshur II of "Brownsville," born July 2, 1739, died December 19, 1792. As of interest to numerous descendants of this couple, several ancestral lines of Anne Stockley follow:

Descent from John Stockley
1. John Stockley (d. ca. 1673) of Accomack County, son or brother of Francis Stockley I (d. 1656) of Northampton County, m. Elizabeth whose parentage has not been determined.
2. Francis Stockley II (d. 1698), wife Sarah.
3. Francis Stockley III (d. 1741) m. Elizabeth Eyre, dau. of John (d. 1719) and Elizabeth (Tilney) Eyre.
4. Eyre Stockley (d. 1740) m. Mary Bell (d. 1784), dau. of Nathaniel Bell (1689-1745/6) and Mary Scarburgh (West) Bell (b. 1691).
5. Anne Stockley (1739-1817) m. Thomas Upshur II (1739-92) of "Brownsville."

Descent from Anthony West (For West lineage, Harrison, HARRISON, WAPLES AND ALLIED FAMILIES; Whitelaw, VA's EASTERN SHORE, PASSIM: VA: MAG. OF HIST., 58 (1950), 396-403; Johnston, SOCIETY OF COLONIAL WARS IN THE STATE OF MARYLAND, plate II, 22; Upshur, MSS; Smith, "Smith, Teackle, Upshur Families.")
1. Anthony West (ca. 1600-52), wife Anne, immigrated to Virginia on the JAMES in 1622. Genealogists believe that he was the same.Anthony West who was on the E.S. Va. as early as 1649, and who died there in 1652.
2. Lt.-Col. John West (ca. 1638-1703) of Accomack County m. Matilda Scarburgh, dau. of Col. Edmund Scarburgh II (1617-71).
3. Anthony West (d. ca. 1717) m. Elizabeth Rowles.
4. Mary Scarburgh West (b. 1691) m. Nathaniel Bell (1689-1745/6).
5. Mary Bell (d. 1784) m. Eyre Stockley (d. 1740).
6. Anne Stockley (1739-1817) m. Thomas Upshur II (1739-92) of "Brownsville."

Descent from Thomas Bell I (For Bell lineage,Nottingham, WILLS AND ADMINISTRATIONS, ACCOMACK COUNTY, VIRGINIA, 1663-1800; Whitelaw, VA's EAST-

ERN SHORE, PASSIM; Johnston, SOCIETY OF COLONIAL WARS IN THE STATE OF MARYLAND, plate II, p. 22.)
1. Thomas Bell I (ca. 1618-1678) emigrated from Gravesend, Eng., to Virginia on the THOMAS and JOHN in 1635 at the age of seventeen and settled on the E. S. Va. (According to Thomas Teackle Upshur II).
2. Robert Bell (d. 1724) m. Mary Cutting, sister of William Cutting (d. 1704).
3. Nathaniel Bell (1689-1745/6), brother of Thomas Bell (d. ca. 1768), m. Mary Scarburgh West (b. 1691), dau. of Anthony (d. ca. 1717) and Elizabeth (Rowles) West.
4. Mary Bell (d. 1784) m. (1) Eyre Stockley (d. 1740), m. (2) Nathaniel Beavens.
5. Anne Stockley (1739-1817) m. Thomas Upshur II (1739-92) of "Brownsville."

Descent from Thomas Eyre I (Eyre lineage, Whitelaw, VA's EASTERN SHORE, PASSIM; Johnston, SOCIETY OF COLONIAL WARS IN THE STATE OF MARYLAND, plate II, 22; Upshur, MSS; Smith, "Smith, Teackle, Upshur Families."
1. Thomas Eyre I (d. 1657), E. S. Va. immigrant, m. (1) Susannah Baker.
2. John Eyre (d. 1719), brother of Thomas Eyre II (d. 1715), m. Elizabeth Tilney, dau. of Lt.-Col. John Tilney and Ann (Hinman) Tilney, dau. of Richard Hinman. (According to Thomas Teackle Upshur II).
3. Elizabeth Eyre m. Francis Stockley III (d. 1741).
4. Eyre Stockley (d. 1740) m. Mary Bell (d. 1784).
5. Anne Stockley (1739-1817) m. Thomas Upshur II (1739-92) of "Brownsville."

xxxxxxxx

UPCHER FAMILY IN ENGLAND

Arthur Upcher (Arthur Upshur I), Eastern Shore of Virginia immigrant, was born in Essex County, England, about 1624. His parentage has not been determined. It has been mentioned that his parents might have been Thomas Upcher of Colchester, Essex County, and Anne (Ayre)

Upcher of London, who were granted a marriage bond by the Bishop of London in 1621. The date of the marriage bond, 1621, and the date of Arthur's birth, 1624, make this parentage a reasonable possiblity. However, at the beginning of the seventeenth century there were in Essex County numerous Upchers from whom Arthur might have descended.

Although the author has accumulated many early records of the English Upchers, they are inconclusive as to Arthur's parentage. He hopes to continue the search of the English records, particularly those of Essex County where the Upcher name has been in evidence for many centuries. Parish registers in the possession of the Society of Genealogists, Chaucer House, London, court rolls, chancery bills, and subsidy rolls should also be explored. Full transcriptions of Virginia's historical records are being made in England and in the future should be available at the Virginia State Library; these records, too, should be studied. When a careful investigation of these additional sources can be made it is believed that Arthur's parentage will be revealed.

The origin of the Upcher name is a matter of speculation. It is possible that it was derived by the first bearer from his residence at Upsall in Yorkshire, or at Upshire, a hamlet in Waltham Hundred, Essex County. Among the earliest records of the name are those of Geoffrey de Upsal and Richard de Upsale of Yorkshire in the year 1273.

In ancient English and early American records the name appears variously as Upchar, Upcher, Upchur, Upchurch, Upcott, Upsal, Upshall, Upshaw, Upshear, Upsher, Upshire, Upshor, Upshott, Upshur, and others. Of these the name UPCHER in England, and UPSHUR and UPSHAW in America have been most generally in evidence during the past three hundred years.

During the past one hundred and fifty years, "Sheringham Hall" has been the principal seat of the Upcher Family in England. (For Upcher lineage, BURKE'S LANDED GENTRY (London, 1937), p. 2311-12.) In 1812 Abbot Upcher bought Sheringham estate on the North Sea, near Cromer, Norfolk County, England, and the next year laid the first stone for "Sheringham Hall." Abbot died in 1819 before the Hall was completed, but his son,

Henry Ramey Upcher, finished the construction in 1838 at the time of his marriage. The furniture came by sea from London; the ship was beached at high tide and the furniture was loaded into wagons and drawn to the Hall.

Six generations of the Upcher Family have already lived at "Sheringham Hall." During the past eighty-five years an intermittent correspondence has been carried on between the Upshurs in Virginia and the Upchers at "Sheringham Hall." A letter dated February 24, 1937, from the late Miss Caroline Edith Sparke Upcher extends a cordial invitation to the author to visit "Sheringham Hall" which she describes"... this beloved and beautiful home, both inside and out ... many large and spacious rooms ... wonderful setting with park and woods and sea ... mile drive of lovely rhododendrons and cedars ..." It is hoped that members of the Upshur Family who visit England will call at "Sheringham Hall" and meet their English Cousins.

xxxxxxxx

REAR-ADMIRAL JOHN HENRY UPSHUR
(1823-1917)

John Henry Upshur, son of John E. Nottingham and Elizabeth Parker (Upshur) Nottingham, was born December 5, 1823, in Northampton County, perhaps at "Selma," near Eastville. Following the death of his father, his mother had John Henry's surname and that of his brother, George, changed in 1841 from Nottingham to Upshur by act of the Virginia Assembly. (THE NATIONAL CYCLOPEDIA OF AMERICAN BIOGRAPHY (New York, 1893), IV, p. 316; APPLETON'S CYCLOPEDIA OF AMERICAN BIOGRAPHY, VI, p. 214; DICTIONARY OF AMERICAN BIOGRAPHY, XIX, p. 128; Upshur, AS I RECALL THEM, PASSIM; "Arlington and Mount Vernon, 1856," VA. MAG. OF HIST., 57 (1949), p. 140-75).

Upshur was a student at the College of William and Mary during 1837-40, and in 1841 entered the U. S. Navy as Midshipman. During 1843-46 he cruised in the U.S.S. ST. MARY'S in which he joined the Atlantic Squadron in the Gulf of Mexico at the time of the Mexican War. He served in the naval battery at the bombardment of Vera

Cruz in March 1847. After the fall of that city he returned to the United States to enter the Naval School, later to become the U.S. Naval Academy, where he was a member of the class of 1847. His uncle, Commander George Parker Upshur, was Superintendent of the Naval Academy at that time.

John Henry Upshur was promoted to Master in July 1855, and served aboard the U.S.S. CUMBERLAND off the coast of Africa to suppress the slave trade during 1858-59. Later he became an Instructor at the Naval Academy. When the Civil War began he was assigned to the North Atlantic Blockading Squadron, and participated in the capture of the forts at Hatteras Inlet and in the sounds of North Carolina during 1861. Although a native Virginian, Upshur strongly and sincerely believed that his first duty was to the Union.

He was Executive Officer of the U.S.S. WABASH at the capture of Port Royal, and commanded four boats in Commander Rodger's expedition in the inland waters in the vicinity of Port Royal and Beaufort, South Carolina. He commanded the U.S.S. FLAMBEAU of the South Atlantic Blockading Squadron during 1862-63 in operations off the coast of South Carolina.

In July 1862 he was promoted to Lieutenant Commander, and during 1863-64 served aboard the U.S.S. MINNESOTA of the North Atlantic Blockading Squadron. He commanded the U.S.S. FROLIC during 1864-65, taking part in both engagements at Fort Fisher. He served in the Mediterranean during 1865-67, was promoted to Commander in July 1866, to Captain in January 1872, and served as member of the Naval Board of Inspection during 1877-80. Following this tour of duty he took a leave of absence and visited England and Europe. Upon his return he became a member of the Naval Board of Examiners.

He served as Commandant of the Brooklyn Navy Yard during 1882-84. He was promoted to Rear Admiral in 1884 and appointed Commander-in-Chief of the Pacific Station. In June 1885 he was voluntarily placed on the retired list.

Rear-Admiral Upshur died May 30, 1917, and was buried in Arlington National Cemetery. At the time of his death he was the senior Rear Admiral of the Navy, and the last surviving officer of Commodore Perry's historic expedition to Japan in 1853. Admiral Upshur's record as a sailorman placed him among the most valued of his profession, and his loyalty to the flag endeared him to his country. He died at the age of ninety-four in full possession of his faculties. He was an earnest Christian, a noble gentleman, and loved and respected by all who knew him.

xxxxxxx

UPCHER COAT OF ARMS*

Arms Argent, on a chevron azure, between three foxes' heads erased, gules, and many pears slipped Or.

Crest On a wreath Argent and gules a plume of five ostrich feathers alternately Argent and Or, before them a Unicorn's head couped azure, gorged with a ducal coronet Or.

Motto: Praestat Opes Sapientia.

---

*Howard and Crisp, VISITATIONS OF ENGLAND AND WALES, III, p. 25; BURKE'S LANDED GENTRY (London, 1937 issue), p. 2311-12.

The arms and crest were assigned by patent dated February 18, 1777, to Peter Upcher of Sudbury, Suffolk County, England, only surviving child and heir of Abbot Upcher, Clerk in Holy Orders, Rector of St. Gregory's and St. Peter's in that town, by Mary, his wife, daughter and co-heir of John Foxwell, Clerk, Rector of Rattlesden, Suffolk County, by Bridget, his wife, daughter and co-heir of John Brownrigg of Willisham in the said county. Abbot Upcher was the eldest son and heir of Peter Upcher of Sudbury, a Justice of the Peace for Suffolk, by Susan, his wife, daughter and heir of Charles Abbot of Sudbury, and grandson of Robert Upcher, sometime of Colchester and afterwards of Wormingford, Essex County.

The arms and crest were to be used by the aforesaid Peter Upcher and by the descendants of his grandfather, Peter Upcher. The motto was not assigned but was probably adopted by the Peter Upcher to whom the arms and crest were granted.

In order that a right to this coat of arms may be recognized by the College of Arms, London, it is necessary to enter in the books at the Herald's Office a pedigree showing descent from one of the ancestors specified in the patent. Thus, if the laws of heraldry were strictly complied with, descendants of Arthur Upcher, the immigrant, would not use this coat of arms because this ancestor was born at least two generations before the earliest Upcher mentioned in the grant of arms. However, since both the English and Virginia branches of the family presumably had a common ancestor as late as 1600, and as the most useful prupose of heraldry today is the identification of family and alliances, the use of these arms by the Upshur Family in Virginia should be encouraged.

A letter dated May 1936 from Miss Caroline Edith Sparke Upcher of "Sheringham Hall" to the author explains that the foxes' heads used in the arms came from Mary Foxwell, Peter Upcher's mother. It is not known why the other charges and heraldic devices were assigned but their description and meaning as generally used follows:

UNICORN   The heraldic unicorn has the body of a horse, the legs of a stag, the tail of a lion, a fine mane, a single horn springing from its forehead, and often tufts of hair under its chin. The horn was regarded as a sovereign cure for many dire diseases, and a grand antidote against all poisons. The unicorn was first used in England by James I, and is used as a charge, a crest, and a supporter. It is almost invariably white or silver, and is usually armed and unguled of gold.

OSTRICH FEATHERS   The use of the ostrich and ostrich feathers can be traced back to the time of the Crusades when returning crusaders brought this symbol from the East. The ostrich was a symbol of endurance and martial ardor. The middle feather is usually shown curling forward while the others are shorter and curve forward and outward.

DUCAL CORONET   The ducal coronet is a charge very commonly used in heraldry upon the necks of birds and animals. Such

birds and animals are said to be ducally gorged. The
coronet also forms part of many crests, the heads of
birds and animals issuing from it. The heraldic ducal
coronet has no reference to ducal or any other rank, and
is usually represented as a chased circle heightened by
four strawberry leaves, three of which are shown.

PEARS   Pears are often emblazoned on English
and French coats of arms. Fruit when
slipped is represented as having a stalk.

FOXES   Foxes are commonly used as charges.
The fox is an emblem of cunning, deceit,
and rapacity.

In the Parish of Ormesby St. Michael, and in Sheringham Parish, both of Norfolk County, England, are tablets on the walls of the chancels showing a quartering of the Upcher arms with those of the Abbot Family of Colchester, Essex County. (Edmund Farrer, THE CHURCH HERALDRY OF NORFOLK (Norwich, 1887-93), I, p. 340, II, p. 440-41.)

In 1867 Rear-Admiral John Henry Upshur went to England in command of the U.S.S. CANANDAIGO. According to his son, the late George Lyttleton Upshur, the Admiral visited the Upchers of "Sheringham Hall" and determined a common ancestor. Later, the Admiral designed a somewhat new coat of arms by changing the colors in the Upcher arms, then quartered with the Abbot Family, and registered the revised arms in his name at the Herald's Office. The author has been unable to verify this registration. At any rate, the Admiral and several members of the Upshur Family in Virginia have used the new arms which are emblazoned:

> Arms Quarterly; first and fourth Argent, on a chevron
> azure between three foxes' heads erased gules
> as many pears slipped Or; second and third gules
> a chevron Or between three pears of the second.
>
> Crest: On a wreath Argent and azure a plume of five
> ostrich feathers alternately azure and Or before
> them a unicorn's head couped Argent gorged with
> a ducal coronet gules.
>
> Motto: Praestat Opes Sapientia.

According to Admiral Upshur the charges in the revised arms symbolize incidents associated with the Upshur Family in Virginia. The pears represent "Pear Plain," the home of Littleton Upshur II in Northampton County. The foxes' heads symbolize the noble sacrifice of Rachel (Revell) Upshur who was bitten by a mad fox at "Warwick" and later died of hydrophobia.

The original Upcher coat of arms has been used for several generations by various members of the Upshur Family in Virginia, and the author recommends its continued use in preference to the revised arms designed by the Admiral.

xxxxxxxx

WARWICK

By patent dated September 28, 1664, Arthur Upshur I was granted 2000 acres of land in Matchipungo Neck on the seaside of Accomack County between Matchipungo River on the west and Upshur's Bay on the east. Soon this tract became known as Upshur's Neck and it is so called today. About 1674 Arthur I completed the manor house for this plantation which became known as "Warwick" after Warwick County, England, the original home of his last wife, Mary (Clarke) Hamond-Jacob-Upshur.

Five generations of the Upshur Family had lived at "Warwick" before it was burned by the British during the Revolutionary War. Arthur Upshur IV, then owner of "Warwick," was an officer in a company of Minute Men on a mission with his command watching for the enemy to land from Chincoteague Bay, farther up the coast. When information was received that the British had put into Upshur's Bay and had taken possession of "Warwick," Arthur IV and his men hastened south to attack. Upon reaching "Warwick" they opened fire upon the British who were reembarking in their barges. Arthur's wife then informed him that nothing had been harmed, and that the British only wished to fill their water casks and buy some meat. Suspecting that the British would return for vengeance, Arthur IV removed all his valuables during the remainder of the day and night. Early the next morning the British returned in force, burned the house and outbuildings, and carried away everything of value that remained.

The present house is part brick and part frame; in the former part, the bricks are laid in Flemish bond with glazed headers, and the top course of the water table is of the early beveled-brick type. It is undoubtedly very old as indicated by its seventeenth-century architectural characteristics which support the tradition that Arthur Upshur IV rebuilt "Warwick" at the close of the Revolutionary War, and incorporated into his new house that part of the older dwelling which survived the fire. Moreover, when "Warwick" was restored in 1927 by the late Ralph T. Whitelaw, it was necessary to remove the original shell lime plaster from the walls of one room on the first floor of the old brick section. Charred door lintels were discovered at that time in the center on the front and back walls, thus furnishing mute evidence of the traditional fire, and showing that originally this part had entrances at the front and rear. The frame part of the present house was probably added after the fire, and the interior woodwork both there and in the brick part are correct for that period. (Whitelaw, VA's EASTERN SHORE, I, p. 581-7).

Arthur Upshur I, his last wife, and many descendants were buried at "Warwick." All the tombstone inscriptions are still legible.

Every member of the Upshur Family owes a debt of gratitude to the late Ralph T. Whitelaw for his careful restoration of "Warwick," thus preserving the oldest known home of the Upshur Family in America. The Upshur Family is also indebted to the present owners, Mr. and Mrs. Richard Hollerith, for maintaining "Warwick" in a high state of preservation, and for the interest they have shown and the care they have given to the house and grounds.

xxxxxxx

See H. S. F., VOL. X for other branches of the Upshur family in Virginia.

xxxxxxx

Contributed by: John Andrews Upshur, Drummonds Mill Farm, Accomac, Virginia.

PITT OF VIRGINIA AND NORTH CAROLINA

ROBERT PITT was born in Virginia ca 1738 and d. ca 1806. He was not mentioned in the will of his father, Henry Pitt Sr. Neither was his brother Joseph. The will of Henry Pitt Jr., recorded in Isle of Wight Co., Va., 1775 names wife Julia, son Edmund, daughters Salley and Esther. Executors: wife and brother Joseph Pitt. Will probated by Julia Pitt and Samuel Bridger, her bondsman. (W. Bk. 8, p. 357).

ROBERT PITT is believed to be the son of Henry Pitt the elder for the following reason: Robert married ca. 1758 Mary Bridger, b. in Va. ca 1742, d. 12/18/1812, daughter of Joseph Bridger of Isle of Wight Co. Robert and Mary Pitt named their first son Joseph, after Mary's father; they named their second son Henry, after Robert's father.

Robert Pitt's marriage to Mary Bridger is recorded in Isle of Wight Order Bk., 1759-63, pp. 177-207. The Pitts and Bridgers were related through several intermarriages. Col. Joseph Bridger, 1627-1686, who had a distinguished record in Isle of Wight Co., m. Hester, daughter of Col. Robert Pitt, brother of Henry Pitt, ancester of this line of Pitts. (Ref: 17th Century Isle of Wight Co., by Boddie; also LAND lineage, this volume.)

Mary Bridger was the daughter of Joseph Bridger 3rd and his wife Sarah Davis. Joseph 3rd. was the son of Joseph Bridger 2nd and his wife Elizabeth Norsworthy.

Robert Pitt moved to Edgecombe County, N.C., before the Revolution. He served in the war and received fifteen pounds in pay vouchers. (N.C. Rev. Army Accounts, Vol. S, p. 17 Folio 4.) Joseph Pitt, son of Robert and Mary Pitt, received a pension for his services in the army. Son Henry also served. (Army Accounts, V., p. 78. Folio 2.)

Robert and Mary Pitt had issue:
1. HENRY PITT, of whom later.
2. Joseph Pitt, b. 1762.
3. Thomas Pitt, b. 1767.
4. James Pitt, b. 8/21/1769, d. 1830. Married Leah Phillips ca 1796. Lived in Edgecombe Co. Will filed

there 6/21/1830. Leah Phillips, b. 11/10/1777, d. 1824, was the dau of David and Sarah Phillips. Children:
i. Joab Phillips Pitt, b. 12/22/1798, d. 8/22/1854, m. Elizabeth Hopkins ca 1820. Will filed Edgecombe Co., August Court of 1854. (W. Bk. G, 80). Elizabeth was b. 1/5/1806, d. 10/7/1847 (tombstone records). Joab m. (2) Winnifred Warren, no issue in 1849. (See later.)
ii - viii Other children of James and Leah Phillips Pitt were: Ralph, Dawson, John, Rebecca, Pernetta, Jedidah, and Bennett Pitt, of whom we have incomplete records.
5. Arthur Pitt, b. 1771.
6. Keziah Pitt, b. 1775, m. Jesse Johnston.
7. Davis Pitt, b. 1777.
8. Bridgers Pitt, b. 1779.
9. Esther Pitt, b. ? m. Edward Bayhine.
10. Sally Pitt, b. ? m. _____ Stringer.
11. Ralph Pitt, b. ?

HENRY PITT, son of Robert and Mary Pitt, was b. 1759, removed in 1796 to Sumner Co., Tenn., where he d. 2/13/1845. He m. Zilpha (?) who was an early member of Lower Town Creek Baptist Church. Henry Pitt applied for a Federal Pension on 8/20/1832 for his war services. (Claim S-3689). Henry and Zilpha Pitt had issue (four sons and 2 daughters shown in 1790 census, D. Bk. 6, p. 82):
1. John Pitt, b. 1780. m. Susannah Strother 3/12/1808 in Sumner Co., Tenn.
2. Elizabeth Pitt, b. 1782, m. _____ Harder of Tenn.
3. William Pitt, b. 1784, m. Jane Robertson (b. 1794) of Sumner Co. 1/9/1813; two daus. under 10 years shown in 1830 census, p. 207.
4. Stephen Pitt, b. 1786. m. Nancy Gamblin 1/11/1809.
5. Catherine Pitt, b. 1788, m. James Jobe of Sumner Co., 9/10/1808. (Bonded by Robert Pitt.)
6. Robert Pitt, b. 1790.
7. Susannah Pitt, b. 4/23/1791.
8. Joseph Pitt, b. 1793.
9. James Pitt, b. 1795. Unmarried in the census of 1820, Sumner Co.
10. Polly Pitt, b. 1797, m. Britton Rogers 4/17/1819,

who was bequeathed 80 acres in the will of his father, Abraham Rogers (wife Tabitha) of Sumner Co., on 3/17/1807. (W. Bk. 1, p. 113).

Children of Joab and Elizabeth (Hopkins) Pitt: (Son of James and Leah (Phillips) Pitt)
1. Henry Bridger Shirley Pitt, b. 4/5/1821, d. 11/14/1894 (tombstone records, Hickory, N.C.) m. Susan Routh Bennett, b. 9/14/1830, d. 3/13/1871 (or 1877). (See later.)
2. Robert Shirley Pitt, b. 12/2/1824, d. 4/24/1884, m. on 1/5/1849 Penninah Porter, who was b. 5/28/1830, d. 8/5/1870. Lived in Edgecombe Co. Issue: William, Bennett, Penninah, John, Anna, Robert, Gatsey, Rebecca and Edward Pitt.

Lineage of Henry Bridger Shirley Pitt:
Joab Phillips Pitt made two deeds to his son Henry Shirley Pitt, one on 8/14/1847 in Edgecombe Co. (D. Bk. 24, p. 373) and the other in which he refers to him as "my son". (D.Bk. 26, p. 310). Joab also bought nine $100.00 shares of stock in the first Railroad Company in N.C. These matured one hundred years later and were inherited by his few remaining grandchildren and by his great-grandchildren. Joab lived at "Pine Tops", Edgecombe Co., N.C. Materials for his home were shipped from his native England. Joab's will was filed in Edgecombe Co. 6/21/1830, probated February Court, 1831. He did not mention his son Henry Bridger Shirley Pitt in his will, and it is believed that Henry received his share of the estate before his father's death, as shown in the deeds previously mentioned.

Henry m. Susan Routh Bennett, dau of Mark H. Bennett and Elizabeth Kettlewell Routh Bridger, widow of John L. Bridger Sr. Issue of Henry and Susan Pitt:
1. Elizabeth Pitt, b. 1848, d. in infancy.
2. Lulu Bridger Pitt, b. 8/19/1850, d. 4/8/1883, m. Lynn Adams 1870. (See later.)
3. Ada Elinor Pitt, b. 8/18/1852, d.s.p. 4/15/1932.
4. Elizabeth Routh Pitt, b. 1854, d. 12/30/1894, m. Robert Liggett 1870. (See later.)
5. Gattie Ainsworth Pitt, 1855-1926, m. Thomas H. Bailey, b. 1855. (See later.)
6. Margaret Bennett Pitt, b. 4/13/1856, d. 3/14/1950.

m. _____ Dean, no issue.
7. Mark Bennett Pitt, of whom later.
8. Anna Lewis Pitt, b. 11/11/1861, d. 4/9/1938. m. Frank Thomas 12/20/1883. (See later.)
9. Henry Franklin Pitt, b. 10/28/1864, d. 3/8/1910 in Calif., of whom later.
MARK BENNETT PITT, b. 9/9/1859 in Rocky Mount, N.C., d. 11/9/1934 in St. Tammany Parish, Slidell, La. He m. (1) Cora Moon. Issue:
1. Hugh Bennett Pitt, b. 11/26/1887, d. 7/2/1952, m. (1) Elizabeth Sales of Washington, Ga., (2) Ruth L. Sales. No issue.
2. Thad J. Pitt, b. 1889, d. ca. 1942, m. Jo Hayes. One daughter, Thadyne Pitt, b. 1929. Living 1952 in Brunswick, Ga.
Mark Bennett m. (2) Hannah Mary Wood, b. 2/22/1892 Carbon Hill, Ala., d. 3/8/1930 in Selma, Calif. Children of this union:
3. Whitney Bennett Pitt, b. 8/11/1908, m. Mattie L. Clark of Miss. 9/21/1929. Reside (1966) in Houston, Texas. Children:
   i. Patricia Yvonne Pitt (surviving twin) b. 9/30/1930, m. 11/18/1955 in Houston to Harry Lee Ashcroft.
   ii. Nelda Lee Pitt, b. 9/18/1933, m. Lt. Joe Turner 8/20/1955 in Houston.
4. Fred Horne Pitt, b. 3/17/1910, m. Bernadine Hope of San Antonio 7/9/1936, who was b. 10/19/1918, dau of Henry Elmer Hope and wife Elizabeth. Issue:
   i. Frederick Henry Pitt, b. 4/11/1937, m. (1) Doris Marie Wilder, b. 2/9/1942 in New Mexico; marriage dissolved 1965. Children: Fred Henry Pitt, b. 1/2/1959 in San Antonio, Texas; and Eddie Joe Pitt, b. 1/3/1960 in Hurst, Texas. He m. (2) Geraldine Monroe Roberts, b. 3/10/1938 in Dadeville, Ala.
   ii. Douglas Ray Pitt, b. 5/24/1939, m. Marlene Jackson Dyrkinson, b. 11/23/1939, in Hurst, Texas, 5/16/1964. Son: Michael Ray Pitt, b. 7/22/65.
   iii. Robert Ernest Pitt, b. 2/14/1948 San Antonio, Texas.
   iv. John Michael Pitt, b. 2/19/1951, d. in infancy.

v. Annie Elizabeth Pitt, b. 7/18/1953 San Antonio.
5. Dudley Roy Pitt Sr., b. 12/15/1911, m. in San Diego, Calif., Elvira M. Stoltz 2/8/1933, who was b. 9/5/1912 in New Orleans, La., dau of Follene Albert Stoltz and Annie E. (Koenig) Stoltz. He was educated in Carriere, Miss., and served in the U.S. Navy, 1931-33. Issue:
i. Dudley Roy Pitt Jr., b. 8/1/1934 in New Orleans, La. Graduated from La. State University and now on the staff of N.W. La. State College in Natchitoches. m. Tinnetto Talley, dau of Vernon A Talley 8/26/1956. Issue: Melanie Diane Pitt, b. 1/24/1958; Dudley Roy Pitt 3rd, b. 9/1/1961.

HENRY FRANKLIN PITT, son of Henry and Susan (Bennett) Pitt, m. (1) Mary Jane Daws, dau of Henrietta and Miles Daws of Edgecombe Co., N.C., who d. 1890. Child:
1. Mary Maude Pitt, b. 10/19/1889 in Hickory, N.C. m. Howard Warren Hooper, son of Charlie Tipton Hooper and Laura Louise Wyatt, in Doyle, Tenn., 3/31/1912. He d. 1/23/1966 in Orlando, Fla., and his wife d. 4/7/1956 in Nashville, Tenn. Both buried there. Issue:
i. James Warren Hooper, b. 10/25/1913 in Nashville, Tenn., m. Ophelia Ann Patton, widow of _____ Evans, b. 8/14/1907 in Nashville. Issue:
   a. Judy Elise Hooper, b. 8/10/1942 in Nashville, m. Aaron E. Pirtle, b. 2/27/1942 in Nashville, son of Sam Davis Pirtle and wife Mary Carney. m. 12/16/1960 in Nashville. Son: Eddie Warren Pirtle, b. 8/11/1962.
   b. Betty Louise Hooper, b. 12/18/1950.
ii. Mary Louise Hooper, b. 4/18/1916, m. 5/20/1935 in Franklin, Ky., Urby Moss Davidson, son of Archie Pilcher and Amelia Moss Davidson of Primm Springs, Tenn., b. 3/24/1910. Issue:
   a. Randall Lee Davidson, b. 3/29/1938 in Nashville, m. Carol Ann Swan, b. 12/19/1938 in Gainesboro, Tenn., m. 7/2/1957, dau of Charlie and Ina Swan. Children: Randall Jr., b. 1959, Gregory Pitt, b. 1962, and Carol Davidson, b. 1964.
   b. Kenneth Warren Davidson (twin), b. 3/12/1940

in Nashville, m. Billye Bader, dau of William Bader of Fayetteville, Tenn., b. 1/12/ 1940, m. 6/13/1961 in Nashville. Child: William Warren Davidson, b. 11/25/1965 in Nashville.
    c. Wayne Moss Davidson (twin), b. 3/12/1940, m. Joyce Marie Chunn, dau of James and Mabel Chunn of Franklin, Tenn., b. 10/18/ 1937, m. 10/9/1964 in Nashville.
    d. Walter Hooper Davidson, b. 8/10/1948 in Nashville.
  iii. Thelma Elise Hooper, b. 4/17/1920, m. John Blake Eastham Jr., b. 5/11/1919, son of John and Anna Eastham, in Nashville, m. 12/24/1942. Issue:
    a. Daniel Harman Eastham, b. 4/14/1948.
    b. John Howard Eastham, b. 2/11/1950.

HENRY FRANKLIN PITT m. (2) in 1892, Margaret Burris of Greenburg, N.C., b. 7/21/1876, living (1966) in San Diego, Calif. Issue:

2. Herman Franklin Pitt, b. 8/17/1894 in LaGrange, N. C., d. 3/2/1942 in San Diego, Calif., m. Lena Inez Cash 11/10/1897. Issue:
  i. Mary Lucille Pitt, b. 3/25/1918 in Los Angeles, Calif., m. Robert A. Bradley, b. 9/27/1911, d. 10/22/1964, m. 12/25/1938. Issue:
    a. Garvin Blaine Bradley, b. 10/16/1947 Santa Ana, Calif.
    b. Janice Elaine Bradley, b. 12/28/1948.
  ii. Ethel Louise Pitt, b. 10/25/1920 in San Diego, m. Joseph T. Haley, b. 7/17/1916, m. 4/8/1939. Issue:
    a. Patricia Louise Haley, b. 1/6/1943 in Los Angeles, m. Richard Wellington Evans, b. 10/1/1937, m. 7/1/1961. They have Richard Jr., b. 1962, and David Evans, b. 1965.
    b. Virginia Aileen Haley, b. 2/27/1953 Inglewood, Calif.
    c. Bette Jean Haley, b. 2/25/1955 Inglewood.
  iii. Pearl Elizabeth Pitt, b. 10/5/1922 in San Diego, m. Charles Grace Nixon, b. 7/17/1917, m. 3/27/ 1942 San Diego. Child:

  a. Barbara Ann Nixon, b. 10/26/1943, accidentally killed 1/6/1948 in San Diego.
3. Paul Noble Pitt, b. 3/27/1898 in Chattanooga, Tenn., m. Theodora Johnson, b. 12/7/1900, d. 11/25/1937, m. 6/30/1919. Paul Pitt d. 8/3/1936. Issue:
 i. Helen Elizabeth Pitt, b. 8/4/1920 in San Francisco, Calif., m. (1) Buehl E. Gray, b. 11/21/1915, m. 6/5/1942. Issue:
  a. Guy E. Gray, b. 11/29/1943, m. Linda Baker 11/21/1965.
 Helen E. Gray m. (2) Robert Milner, b. 3/13/1920, m. 11/29/1948. Child:
  b. Debra Milner, b. 8/11/1954.
4. Margaret Bell Pitt, b. 8/2/1900 in Chattanooga, Tenn., d. 11/5/1905.

    ****

Issue of Gattie Anisworth Pitt and Thomas Henry Bailey (b. 1855, d. 3/5/1906):
1. Ida (Cecelia) Bailey, b. 2/4/1891, m. Emmett Richardson; reside Greensboro, N.C. Issue:
 i. Wesley Richardson, b. 5/20/1923, m. Stella Arguello 5/9/1955 in Las Vegas, Arizona, reside Riverside, Calif. They have two daus.
 ii. Jack H. Richardson, b. 3/18/1920, m. Margaret Smith in Miss. 9/21/1954. Two daus. Reside New Orleans.
2. Warner Lee Bailey, b. 1888, da. 2/11/1908, accidentally killed.
3. James Bertrand Bailey, b. 1889, d. ca. 1918. m. Annie Scott. Their son: Clyde Bailey, b. 3/22/1911.
4. Elinor Ada Bailey, b. 1894, d. 9/28/1932. m. Clyde Bergman. Issue:
 i. Clyde Bergman Jr., b. 1915.
 ii. Ida Lee Bergman, b. 1917.
 iii. Elinor Bergman, b. 1922.
 iv. Margaret Bergman, b. 1927.
5. Troy Homer Bailey, b. 9/22/1899, m. (1) Blanche Fowler. m. (2) Hazel Dawkins. Issue:
 i. Millard Wilson Bailey, b. 1935, m. Joyce _____.
 ii. Troy Henry Bailey, b. 1937, m. Barbara Pulley.
 iii. Daniel James Bailey, b. 1940, m. Carolyn Carter.

iv. Helen Ann Bailey, b. 1942.
v. Gattie Ida Bailey, b. 1941.

Issue of Elizabeth Routh Pitt and Robert Liggett (b. ? - d. 1926) m. ca. 1888 in Pitt County, N.C.:
1. Maude Liggett, b. 1890. m., no issue.
2. Irene Liggett, b. 1892, d. 1940. m. J.H. Heath. Issue: 10 children.

Issue of Anna Lewis Pitt and Frank A. Thomas, m. 12/20/1883:
1. Charles Routh Thomas, b. 1886, m. Annie Gentz 1917. Issue:
   i. Iona Thomas, no record.
   ii. Ruth Thomas, m. a Mr. Jordan; their daughter, Adrienna Jordan.
2. Ivy Thomas, b. 8/7/1889, lives in Winston Salem, N.C. (1966).
3. Allison Thomas, b. 1891, d. 10/21/1962, m. Bessie Ball 1917. Issue:
   i. Ivy Pauline Thomas, b. 1919, m. 1938 in Rahway, N.J., _____ Suiter; they have Patricia and Eileen Suiter.
   ii. Willie Frank Thomas, b. 1917 in Winston Salem, d. 1962. m. in North Brunswick, N.J. Ruth ____. Issue: Willie, Susan, Jack (m. Kathyrn Scalf), Billy (m. Euretha Wilson), Charles, and Robert Thomas.
4. Ada Thomas, twin to Allison, d. in infancy.
5. Henry Thomas, b. 1884, d. in infancy.

Issue of Lulu Bridgers Pitt and Lynn Adams, (b. 1/8/1818 in Wake Co., N.C.) m. 1870 in Hickory, N.C.:
1. Florence Sue Adams, b. 2/18/1878, d. ca. 1956, m. S.A. Jenkins (b. 1872, d. 1942) 3/24/1897. Resided in Ayden, N.C. Issue:
   i. John Lynn Jenkins, b. 1898, d. 1951. m. in N.C. 1928. One son.
   ii. Lulu Mae Jenkins, 1900-1945.
   iii. Routh Thomas Jenkins, b. 1902, d. in infancy.
   iv. Bruce Adams Jenkins, b. 1904, d.s.p. 1918.
   v. Alta Lee Jenkins, b. 1906, m. Clifton Worthing-

       ton, resides Winterville, N. C.
- vi. Walter Ivey Jenkins, b. 9/17/1908, m. in Florida and d. before 1954.
- vii. Remo Adams Jenkins, b. 1910, m. Robert Hawkins. Lived in Raleigh, N. C., one son, Robert Hawkins Jr.
2. Lynn Adams, b. 1879, d. 9/30/1934, m. in Ga., no issue.
3. Walter Henry Adams, b. 12/15/1881, d. s. p. 1964 in Dunn, N. C.
4. Routh Bennett Adams, b. ?, m. and had issue:
  - i. Margaret Adams, m. Dr. L. W. Jackson and lived in Ohio.
  - ii. Bennett Routh Adams, lived in Atlanta, Ga.

              Data supplied by: Mrs. Dudley R. Pitt Sr.,
                              Talisheek, La.

BATTS OF SURRY COUNTY, VIRGINIA

William Batts, 1691-1742, of Surry Co., Va., m. (1) Sarah Thorpe, daughter of Thomas Thorpe and his wife Martha Jennings of Isle of Wight Co., Va., and widow of William George. Martha Jennings Thorpe was a daughter of John Jennings and his wife Martha Harris (dau. of Robert Harris, son of Thomas Harris). William Batts and Sarah (Thorpe) Batts had five children named in his will: William, John (of whom later), Mary, Martha, and Elizabeth Batts.

Ref: W.Bk.Surry Co., 1738-1754, p. 419.

"In the name of God Amen. I, William Batts of Southwark Parish in the County of Surry have thought fit to make this my last Will and Testament absolutely revoking all other wills heretofore made by me and as for temporall estate it hath pleased God to bless me with I give in manner and form following:

Viz: *Item*: I give and bequeath to my dear and loving wife the use of my plantation whereon I now live during her natural life and after her decease I give the sd. plantation to my son John and to his heirs forever. I likewise give to my wife the labour of my negro man Jemmy during her life and after her decease I give sd. negro man Jemmy to my daughter Martha and her heirs forever. I likewise give to my wife the feather bed and furniture I commonly ly on and one trunk and one chest and four pewter dishes and six plates and one large iron pott and two cows and calves and provision to support the family the first year after my death and likewise five ews and my gray mare and side saddle and four chairs and new spinning wheele and cards and one brass kittle.

I give and bequeath to my son William the Plantation I bought of Hen. Taylor to him and his heirs forever and my negro man called Sam and one feather bed and furniture and my horse colt called York and three pewter dishes and six plates and three chairs and one iron pott and one pan and six head of cattle and five sheep and all my troopers armes and one new saddle and one chest and one small trunk. I give and bequeath to my son John one negro girl called Hannah after my wifes decease. I likewise give my son John ten pounds cash. I give and bequeath to my daughter Mary one negro woman called Phyllis to her and her heirs forever and one feather bed and furniture.

Item: I give and bequeath to my daughter Elizabeth one negro girl call'd Judy to her and her heirs forever and one feather bed and furniture. I give and bequeath to my daughter Martha one large Bible and one brass skillet. I give and bequeath to my grandson William Batts one feather bed and furniture and ten pounds cash when he comes to the age of twenty one years.

I give and bequeath to my grandson William Lain one violen and forty shillings to be laid out in his schooling and all the rest of my estate of what nature or quality soever I desire may be equally divided between my loving wife and my five children and I do nominate and appoint my wife and my son William whole and sole extor's of this my last will and testament. In witness whereof I've hereunto set my hand and fixt my seal this 31st day of December 1741.

                      William W. Batts (LS)
                          signum

Sign'd sealed and published in
presence of us
Charls. Binns, Henry Holt, David Drew.

At a Court held for Surry County the 17 day of November, 1742.

"The within Last Will and Testament of William Batts was presented in Court by the Executors therein named who made oath thereunto according to law and the same being proved by the oaths of Charles Binns and Henry Holt witnesses thereto who also made oath that they saw David Drew the other witness subscribe his name thereto as such it is thereupon ordered to be recorded.

                    Teste: Aug. Claiborne, Clk.
                    Teste: V. E. Savedge, Clerk."

John Batts, 1717-1785, m. (1) Lucy Hart. They had a
son, William Batts. John Batts m. (2) Mary Warren, dau.
of Thomas and Lucy Warren. (See will of Thomas Warren,
Surry Co., Va., H.S.F., Vol. IX, Boddie.) Their children: Frederick, Henry, Patty, Sally, John, Bejamin (of
whom later), and Betsy Batts.
Ref: W. Bk., Surry Co., 1783-1792, p. 70.
"In the name of God Amen. I, John Batts of the County
of Surry & Parish of Southwark being weak of body but of
sound mind and disposing memory, thanks be to God for
the same, Therefore do make and ordain this to by my
last Will and Testament, in manner and form following:
Viz; Imprimus: I give to my beloved wife Mary Batts the
use of all my land and plantation, likewise two negros
namely Philip & Cate, one Sorrel horse, one side saddle,
two feather beds and furniture, one chest of drawers, all
my pewter, one copper coffee pot, one loom and harness,
one spinning wheel, one pair cotton cards, one pair wool
ditto, six chairs, one cart and wheels, and all my stock
of cattle & hogs, likewise two pots & one frying pan
dureing her natural life, but if my said wife Mary Batts
should die before my son Benjamin Batts arrives to the
age of twelve years old, then my will and desire is that
the two negros above mentioned, to wit: Philip & Cate,
should be hired out till my son Benjamin Batts arrives
to the age of twelve years old and the money arising from
said hire to be laid out for the support and schooling my
three youngest children viz: Betsy, John, and Benjamin
Batts, and at the end of the said twelve years or the death
of my wife, the two said negroes Philip & Cate to be sold
and the money arising from the sale thereof to be equally
divided among all my children then living to them and
their heirs forever. My will and desire is that at the death
of my wife, my land & plantation & all the personal Estate above mentioned should be sold, and the money arising from the sale thereof to be equally divided among all
my children before mentioned, to them and their heirs
forever.
Item: I give and bequeath to my son Frederick Batts one
horse named Ball, and he the said Frederick Batts to pay
to my daughter Patty Batts the sum of four pounds specie,
and to my daughter Sally Batts, the sum of two pounds

five shillings specie, to them and their heirs forever and the said Frederick to have the said horse for him and his heirs forever.

Item: I give and bequeath to my son Henry Batts all my wearing clothes, to him and his heirs forever.

Item: I give and bequeath to my wife above mentioned all my provision both corn & bacon for the use of the family.

Item: My will and desire is that the remainder of my estate of all kinds whatsoever should be sold and the money arising from the sale thereof after all my just debts are paid to be equally divided among all my children before mentioned to them and their heirs forever, but if either of my children should die before they arrive to the age of twenty one years old, then his or her part of my estate to be equally divided among the surviving ones, to them & their heirs forever. Lastly I do nominate and appoint my wife Mary Batts Executrix and Jesse Cocks & Richard Rowell Sen. Exors. to this my last Will and Testament, revoking & making null and void all other wills formerly by me made & do pronounce this to be my last. In Witness whereof I have hereunto set my hand and affixed my seal this fourteenth day of March Anno one thousand seven hundred & eighty-five.

       John Batts (L.S.)

Signed & seal'd in presence of
  her
Elizabeth   X   Savidge
  mark
Joel Savidge
Robt. Rowell

 At a Court held in Surry County April 26, 1785:

 The afore written last Will and Testament of the within named John Batts deceased was presented in Court by Jesse Cocks one of the Exors. therein named who made oath thereto according to law, the same was proved by the oaths of Elizabeth Savidge and Joel Savidge two of the witnesses thereto and ordered to be recorded. And on the motion of the said Jesse Cocks who entered into bond certificate is granted him for obtaining a probate thereof in due form and liberty reserved the other Executors to join therein when they shall think fit.

Examined:
Copy

Teste: Jacob Faulcon, Cl. Ct.

Teste: V.E. Savidge, Clerk

Benjamin Batts, b. 1780, d. in Sussex Co., Va., 1834, served in the War of 1812. He m. Sarah Hicks Rainey, dau of Daniel Rainey, in 1804 in Sussex or Surry Co., 25 miles from Petersburg. They had eleven children who grew to maturity.
1. William Evans Batts, b. 1806 in Essex or Dinwiddie Co., Va., d. 1860 in La. Married and had issue.
2. Wilkins Warren Batts. (See lineage in H.S.F., Vol. 2, p. 69.)
3. John Batts, lived and died in North Alabama. m. and had issue.
4. Robert Hicks Batts, d.s.p. 1852.
5. George Washington Batts, lived and died in N. Ala. Had issue.
6. Henry Batts, d. 1852 in Ascension Parish, La. No issue.
7. Andrew Jackson Batts, of whom later.
8. Mary Batts, d. in Ala. m. _____ Gresham. (?)
9. Martha Batts. m. _____ Morris.
10. Sarah Batts, m. _____ Morris, Louisville, Ky.
11. Rebecca Batts, m. _____ Connolly, had issue.

ANDREW JACKSON BATTS, b. 4/19/1831, d. 8/3/1901, son of Benjamin Batts and wife Sarah. At the age of five he was sent to live with his uncle John Rainey in Limestone Co., Ala. In 1860 he m. Julia Rice, b. 6/18/1844, d. 7/21/1926, m. at Bastrop, Texas. Children:
1. Charlie A. Batts, b. 8/10/1861, d. 4/22/1879.
2. Benjamin Batts, d. young.
3. Julie Batts, b. 5/19/1868, d. 7/7/1925. No issue.
4. Ella Batts, b. 5/30/1866, d. 10/27/1944, m. Henry Newton Bell, who was b. 8/27/1856 in Jackson Co., Ark., d. 11/15/1934 in Bastrop, Texas. Their son:
   i. Henry Newton Bell Jr., b. 1/11/1902, m. Mildred Smith, b. 3/7/1903, d. 9/7/1963. Their son, Henry Newton Bell 3rd., b. 3/5/1941 Temple,

Texas, m. Pamela Roberts 1964 at San Antonio, Texas.
5. Robert Lynn Batts, b. 11/1/1864, d. 3/4/1937, m. Harriet Fiquet Boak, b. 11/10/1867, d. 3/4/1937. Both are buried in Oakwood Cemetery, Austin, Texas. After his marriage, Robert L. Batts practiced law for a short time in Bastrop then was appointed Professor of Law at the University of Texas, 1893 - 1900. He was later in private practice; in 1917 he was appointed to the U.S. Fifth Circuit Court of Appeals. In 1919 he resigned to become General Counsel for Gulf Oil Co. In 1927 he was appointed to the Board of Regents, University of Texas. Children:
   i. Robert Edward Lee Batts, b. 11/25/1890 at Bastrop. m. (1) Mynette Long, b. 9/7/1889, d. 11/30/1944. Children:
      a. Margaret Douglas Batts, b. 8/20/1917, m. Donald Cameron Duncan 2/14/1942. They have Margaret Batts Duncan, who m. John Tinkle: (Child: Margaret Tinkle.) Caroline Bowie Duncan, and Donald Cameron Duncan Jr.
      b. Robert Edward Lee Batts Jr., b. 9/14/1930, m. Minerva Hobart 12/20/1952, dau of Frederick and Minerva (Jones) Hobart. Children: Stewart, Robert and Mary Batts.
   ii. Mary Ella Batts, b. 2/28/1892 at Bastrop, Texas, m. Sawnie Robertson Aldredge, b. 11/13/1890, d. 5/13/1949, son of George Nathan Aldredge and Betty Warren Hearne Aldredge. Sawnie R. Aldredge was native of Dallas and Mayor 1921-23. Chn:
      a. Sawnie Robertson Aldredge Jr., m. (1) Carol Rogers; m. (2) Mildred Payne 11/20/1954 at Dallas. They have Sawnie Robertson Aldredge 3rd and Amy Payne Aldredge.
      b. Mary Lynn Aldredge, m. John Barto McEntire Jr. 4/19/1947. They have Lynn, John, Sawnie, and Mary McEntire.
   iii. Margaret Lynn Batts, b. 7/28/1898 in Austin, Texas, m. Edgar Gardner Tobin, b. 9/4/1896, d. 1/10/1954. Margaret Batts Tobin lives in San

Antonio (1966) and is active in civic life. Child: Robert Lynn Batts Tobin.
6. Laura Vivian Batts, b. 7/1/1875, d. 10/6/1943, m. 12/31/1895 Michael Augustus Wallace, b. 10/4/1874 in Travis Co., Texas, d. 1950, eldest son of W.D. Wallace and his wife Caledonia (Fowler) Wallace. Children:
   i. Ada Lynn Wallace, b. 10/26/1906, m. 4/19/1931 Hubert Harden. No issue.
   ii. Priscilla Wallace, b. 1/4/1908, m. 12/9/1924 Sherman Ellsworth Matthews, b. 12/11/1902 in Kansas. Chn: Betty, Billy, Sherman, and Priscilla Matthews.
7. Edward Lee Batts, b. 1/18/1872 at Bastrop, d. 11/1/1933 at San Angelo, Texas, m. Bonnie Green b. 1/19/1899, d. 1/23/1955, m. 7/20/1921. Children:
   i. Jane Batts, b. 5/10/1922, d. 12/28/1940.
   ii. Edward Lee Batts Jr., b. 2/17/1925, m. Jean Hines.
   iii. Mary Batts, b. 9/10/1928, m. Richard Floyd, (b. 6/6/1928, a surgeon) m. 3/31/1951. They live in Lexington, Ky., and have Richard, Bonnie, Mary, and Margaret Floyd.

****

Lineage of Mary Sue Driver:

Thomas Warren of Smiths Fort, Surry Co., Va., m. (3) Jane, widow of John King. Their son
Thomas Warren Jr., b. 1659, will proved 1721 in Surry Co., m. Elizabeth _____, will dated 1724 Surry Co., probated 1730. Their son
John Warren, inventory 1731, Surry Co., m. Sarah Deberry of Isle of Wight Co., 1712, dau of Peter Deberry who mentions his daughter Sarah as wife of John Warren, and leaves her 100 acres of land in Pigeon Swamp. Their son
Thomas Warren, will dated 1759 in Surry Co., m. Lucy _____, (her will dated 1783, Surry Co.) Their daughter
Mary Warren, named in her mother's will as Mary Batts,

m. John Batts, will dated 1785, Surry Co. Their son
Benjamin Batt(s), will dated 1830 Sussex Co., m. Sally
Hicks Rainey. Their son
Wilkins Warren Batt, m. Amanda Robinson. Their dau.
Rosa Ann Batt m. William Roger Poyner. Their dau.
Susan Amanda Poyner m. Dr. John Davis Driver, parents of
Mary Sue Driver

****

Data contributed by: Mary Sue Driver
Dallas, Texas.

and Mary Batts Aldredge
Dallas, Texas

WILLIAM ROSE[1] OF SURRY COUNTY, VIRGINIA

In order that we may understand the conditions existing in Virginia at the time when William Rose arrived, it is necessary to look back a few years earlier into the history of the colony. Virginia was the first permanent English settlement in America. In 1606 an expedition was sent by the London Company - a little over one hundred men sailed in three ships and landed at Jamestown in May 1607. However, the site they had chosen for their settlement was not climatically suitable, the colonists were inexperienced and unsuited to pioneer life, and the Indians were hostile. By the end of 1607 only thirty eight men still survived.

During the next two years additional colonists arrived, and for a time under the leadership of Captain John Smith conditions improved. In 1609 Captain Smith had to return to England, and without strong leadership the colony once again suffered. Strife, disease and starvation soon set in. The Indians, who were thoroughly hostile by now, killed anyone who ventured into the forests to hunt for food. When Sir Thomas Gates arrived in 1610 he found that half the people were dead and the rest weak and in despair. His supplies were limited, and the decision was made to leave the colony. They boarded the boats, and as they neared the mouth of the river they met the new governor, Lord De la Warr, who was bringing other colonists and plentiful supplies. Their hopes now restored, they were persuaded to return.

During the next few years new colonists constantly arrived, and many "indentured" servants, who agreed to work for a period of time in exchange for passage, usually seven years, were imported as laborers. Tobacco culture became the prime vocation.

In 1619 the first representative assembly in North America, the Virginia House of Burgesses, was organized. This same year saw the first negroes brought into the colony, and also in 1619 one hundred women arrived to marry colonists.

In 1622 the Indians attacked and killed 350 persons. (A Thomas Rose or Rosse who was living in Charles

City Corp. in 1621 was reported killed there in the Indian attack of 1622). Sickness and famine once again descended upon the colony and the population was reduced by nearly one-half; however, they recovered from this severe setback. The tobacco industry grew in importance and the settlers built their homes farther inland.

A second Indian attack, in 1644, which resulted in the death of several hundred settlers, scarcely retarded the rapid growth of the colony. The population by 1648 was 15,000.

Into this early settlement came William Rose, born about 1622, probably a native of England or of Scotland. He arrived during a time of English settlement of the Jamestown area and did not use the traditional Scottish names in his family, yet the Scottish Roses were sending many of their younger men into Virginia. Perhaps further research will disclose the name of the port from whence he sailed and his family's origin.

William was in the Colony by 1650, though there is a possibility he was here even earlier, or that he made the trip to Virginia more than once. If he did indeed arrive earlier, the records would not be in Surry County, for it was formed in 1652 from James City County. The latter records unfortunately were destroyed in the Richmond fire during the Civil War (where they had been sent for safekeeping!)

William Rose married, probably around 1650, to Anne, whose maiden name in unknown. She also was born in distant lands, and came with her husband to Virginia. She outlived him - William Rose died in 1671 or 1672 at the age of forty nine, which left her to raise their children, some of whom were still very young. Anne probably remarried very soon - there was a shortage of women in the colony and widows often re-married several times. Her deed of gift recorded in 1672 in which she is called widow might have been made in preparation of a second marriage, for it was common for a widow to make a gift of her deceased father's property before entering a second marriage. However, if she did re-marry the facts are not known to us, and her date of death is also unknown.

William Rose made his first and only purchase of land in Virginia in 1652, and sold it in 1654. Later Francis

Sowerby acquired this land in two parcels of 105 1/2 acres each, and many years later William Rose's son Richard would marry Francis Sowerby's daughter Elizabeth. That William continued to reside near his old neighbors is indicated by various records showing his name among theirs. George Rose comments, "Since the Roses continued to reside in the same area it is concluded that the description of the 211 acres on the fork of Gray's Creek (see record later) indicates fairly accurately where William Rose was seated. He was therefore within two or three miles of the John Rolfe house and perhaps four miles in direct line south and west of Swann Point. These landmarks are well indentified even now. This is a pleasant land of fertile soil and splendid trees. The feel of the area is definitely rural to this day."

It is a matter of interest that William Rose could write and sign his name, and that at lease one document is known to exist entirely in his own hand. George H. Rose, who has made two trips to Virginia in search of details on the early Roses says: "The glimpses I get of William Rose of Surry remind me of a colonial merchant I once researched. William bought at a sale, bought a servant maid, had an indentured man servant, collected on a debt, paid his obligations to an estate, was handy when court was in session, appeared as a claimant against an estate, sent Joseph Sulway a letter asking him to appear in court for him, and then appears in an enigmatic pledge of certain goods in 1671. He showed no disposition to hold and cultivate land though he did acquire and hold 211 acres for about two years and surely could have acquired additional land if he could afford a man servant or a maid or farm animals. His son, William, was adjudged a man of sufficient resources to be in the mounted militia, which designation fell upon one in a rather well composed letter suggests that he came from a background of some attainment. I suspect that he was either a merchant or a tradesman who also cultivated a small amount of land and whose original holding of 211 acres probably earned him the designation - planter."

Children of William Rose and his wife Anne:
1. Jane born ante 1655, probably ca 1651 (called eldest in 1677); m. 1st Richard Avery; m. 2nd Edward Booky.

2. Anne born ante 1655, probably ca 1653 (of age in 1677, but probably older than her brother William who had just recently attained his majority then); m. Thomas Flood, Jr.
3. William born ca 1655 (he declares in 1689 that he is age 34); m. Lucy (Corker) Jordan.
4. Mary born 1656-1666 (still a minor in 1677 for she had a guardian, but named in a 1666 document); further on she is unknown, perhaps died before marrying.
5. Richard born ca 1669 (not named in a 1666 document of his parents, but born by 1669 for he purchased land in 1690 and had to be of age. He had a guardian as late as 1686. (There are several records proving he was a son of William and Anne Rose, most notably a gift recorded in 1672 by his mother, in which he is named); m. Elizabeth Sowerby.

Following is a chronological list of all known records naming William Rose[1]. In some instances the quotes indicate wording in the original document, in other instances quotes are used to show wording in a copied record, such as a published book. See reference at end of each item to ascertain if record is original or copied. Comments are indented at end of each item. See last page of Chapter for bibliography.

SOURCE RECORDS:

<u>1650</u>   On 3 Feb. 1645 John Cawsey of James City
<u>1652</u>   sold to David Hamey a servant maid named
Frances Jones for the term of five years three quarters, at which time she was to be free. On 26 Mar. 1649 Edw. Hamey assigned the maid to Thos. Crafton. On the reverse is another assignment dated 3 Feb. 1650 in which Mary Crafton, relict of Thomas Crafton, deceased, assigns her rights in the servant to John Cooper - witnessed by Geo. Jordan and <u>Wm. Rose</u>. This matter came to court in Surry in 1652 and at this time "Wm. Rose, aged 30 years or thereabouts" testified that Jno. Cooper bought the maid. Signed: William Rose. (Surry Book I p. 15) (Davis abstracts p. 3)

Two important points are established - that William Rose was in the colony by 1650 and that he was born ca 1622.

<u>1652</u>   25th of Feb., 1652. John Jennings "doe give Mr. Jno. Orchard full power for me in my place and action in behalf of the whole right of a patent for land belonging unto me containing 211 acres as by the patent appeared unto Wm. Rose." Assigns to Wm. Rose all rights in 211 acres of land, in the patent, bounding upon the land of Thomas Woodhouse, 4 Jan. 1652. (Surry Book I p. 23) (Davis abstracts p. 6)

>This is the only known land purchase of William Rose. In 1666 when Francis Sowerby renewed this patent the boundaries were described as "Upon the heads of the two northernmost branches of Greyes Cr., N.E. & S.E. upon land of Thomas Woodhouse, N.E. & S.E. upon Jno. Watkins & S.E. upon James Mason." (Cav. and Pion. p. 562-63)

<u>1653</u>   "...7 Mar. 1653. Deposition of Thos. Gray, Sr., aged 60 years or thereabouts that Daniel Hutton did bequeath his whole estate to Rebeckah his wife. Wm. Rose, aged 30, testified to the same. 27 Mar. 1653." (Surry Book I p. 41) (Davis abstracts p. 11)

>Again William's age is established as circa 1622.

<u>1653</u>   "William Knott, 200 acs. in Surry Co., on S. Side of James Riv., about 1 1/2 mi. from same. Last of Mar. 1653, p. 256 (Patent Book III). S.W. by S. into the woods, cross the reedy Swamp runn. on the N.W. by W. Side of Mr. Benjamin Harrysons devdt., by the round island, and N.W. by W. Towards upper Chip Oaks Cr. Trans of 4 pers: William Rose, & his wife, Anto. Wightman, Dorothy Woofe..." (Cav. and Pion. p. 287)

>This patent shows that the wife of William Rose also was an immigrant. In early Virginia, a person responsible for bringing others over received 50 acres per person, regardless of how many times the person entered the colony, and these persons were referred to

as "headrights". There are records in this same source of other early arrivals by the same name; (1) Capt. Thomas Paulett gr. 2000 ac. in "Chas. Citty Co." on 15 Jan. 1637, his list incl. Wm. Rose, (2) Nicholas Merywether gr. 3000 ac. in Westmoreland Co. 1 June 1654, his list incl. William Rose, (3) Thomas Rowe gr. 500 ac. upon "Potomeck in the freshes" on 15 July 1657, his list incl. Wm. Rose. Any of these records could apply to William Rose of Surry County, though it was usual for the patentee to apply for land in the same vicinity where his headrights settled.

1654 "...30 March 1654. Wm. Rose, for himself and his heirs etc. to Mathew Battell and Richard Tias 211 acres of land." (Surry Book I p. 39) (Davis abstracts p. 11)
This is a disposition of the land that he obtained in 1652 - later purchased by Francis Sowerby.

1655 In the year 1655 William Rose acquired for 800 pounds of tobacco a maid who was to be "delivered to my (new? now?) dwelling house in Southwark Parish." (Surry Book I p. 80) (GHR Notes)

1656 The name of Wm. Rose appears in a list of accounts for goods sold by Wm. Thomas for the accounts of Henry and John Richards, the year was 1656. (Surry Book I p. 54) (Davis abstracts p. 21)

1656 4 Oct. 1656 - James Mason, Overseer of the Estate of John Spilltimber, dec. to acquit and discharge Wm. Rose and Robert Stanborn of a bill of 360 pounds of tobacco which was due the estate of said dec'd. Signed: James Mason.
Reference unclear - perhaps Surry Book I p. 79 or 89. This suggests a possible partnership: Rose-Stanborn.

1657   "Mr. Joseph Sulway---Whereas you are baile for me to the sheriff to attend to a suit of Colonel Swann for the court at Surry, I therefore hereby authorize you to appear for me at said Colonel Swann's suit & to counsel duly for me and this shall be your warrant issued by my hand this 19 of February, I sign 1657. Wm. Rose"
   This letter, which was found by George H. Rose as a loose paper among Surry records, is unusual in that it appears to be entirely written by William Rose.

1658   "...James Hugate, examined, said that Roger Potter persuaded him to run away secretly to a remote part of the bay..." - involved in this matter was "Wm. Rose his boy" which apparently refers to his servant. Date inferred as 10 ber 24, 1658 or December 24, 1658 old style. (Surry Book I p. 123) (Davis abstracts p. 39 & 40)

1659   "...17 Oct. 1659. The body of Wm. Hawkes was viewed, he being the servant of Coll. Thos. Swann. He fell from an ox cart, the wheels of which passed over him. Robert Stanton, Wm. Rose, Thos. Andrews, Wm. Browne, Wm. Fisher, Thos. Wise, Fra. Sowerby, Hen. Browne, Arth. Owen, Rich. Case." (Surry Book I p. 150) (Davis abstracts p. 46)
   William Rose served on coroner's juries several times.

1660   Robert Storey, servant of William Rose, planter, hanged himself in the woods. 1660. (Surry Book I p. 150)
   Davis abstracts show this name as Rose_r_. Note the designation, planter. Robert Storey was no doubt an indentured servant.

1662   "...Capt. Thos. Swann obtained judgment against the Est. of Richard Stanton in the Quarter Court, upon an attachment formerly served upon sd Richard Stanton, his estate, in the Hands of Robert Stanton, and the latter to give an account of the est. of

Richard Stanton, satisfying judgment etc..." A long list of names follows, which included that of Wm. Rose. Dated 13 July 1662, wit: Thomas Flood and Joseph Trafton. (Surry Book I p. 212) (Davis abstracts p. 62)

1666   In two transactions dated July 3, 1666, Barth: Owen transfers to Wm. Rose & Anne Rose his wife a gray mare four years old called Liddey for the use and benefit of Jane, Wm., Anne & Mary Rose, the son and daughters of Wm. Rose and Anne his wife. Purchase is made by some cattle belonging to the children "given to them by some (?) friends." Signed: Barth: Owen. Wit: Luke (his mark) Mizell and John Morecocke. In the next record Wm. Rose & Anne Rose his wife "bargained & Sold & enchanged for & in behalfe of Jane Wm Anne & Mary Rose three Cowe & three Calves & two Steares with Mr. Barth: Owen for a gray Mare of fower yeares ould Called Liddey..." - this stock belonged to the children and consisted of a black cow called Coale, a red cow called Cherry, a black cow called (Lagg?) and their increase, and two steers. Signed: William Rose and Anne (her mark) Rose. Wit: Luke (his mark) Mizell and John Morecocke. (Surry Book I p. 271-272) (STR photocopies)

> This is not a gift of stock from parents to children - the children had received the stock as a gift and the parents are now making an exchange for their benefit. George Rose says "This strongly indicates that either William Rose or his wife or both had relatives in the area. Livestock was very hard to come by, for animals were brought over by boat and losses were heavy. Though either Barth: Owen or the clerk uses the words "friends", a gift of livestock was an almost sure sign of propinquity!"

1667   "...6 March 1667. Thos. Cruse and Rich. Case declared that the body of Baton Brown found at Coll Swann's landing came to his death by drowning. Samuel Goose, Samuel Magott, Wm. Rose." (Surry Book I p. 300) (Davis abstracts p. 85)

1668   William Rose was on a list of tithables in 1668, with some of his neighbors: Thomas Gray, Francis Gray, Capt. Wm. Brown, Francis Sowerby, Thomas Sowerby (brother), Sam Maggett, Luke Mizell, Capt. Corker. (Wm. and Mary Mag. Series I pp. 163-4) (GHR Notes)

1668   "...Feb. 20, 1668. Thos. Flood, Coroner, for the time being, two men drowned watering a horse. Jury - Wm. Rose, Fra. Hogwood, Robt. Warren, John Bird, Fra. Gray, John Meare, Rob. Lee." (Surry Book I p. 323) (Davis abstracts p. 88)

1668   "October 15th Anno. 1668. Certaine goods Carpenters tooles & other Chattells sold att an (auction?) by the widow Creed being Lawfully Cryed by the Shirrife & sold for tobb. payable the 10th of Novem 1669 & bought in these severall parcels by these severall persons as followeth. Imp:^{r} A Chest of Carpenters tools Contining 5 Augers inserts 4 good chessells 2 chessells more 2 large plaines 6 hand plaines for Joyners worke 1 large peircer a handsaw, broad Az; new ____? hamer & 1 file to whet Saws 2 plaines & Irons More?, Cauckin Iron 1 good peircer & stock & rest for a Saw & the chest & all wth one pare of Compasses sold to Wm Rose for 305 lb tobb & Caske bill taken & Capt Browne security..." (Surry Book I p. 317) (STR photocopies)

    This purchase seems to favor the idea that William Rose might have been a merchant or tradesman. Some clothing was sold at the same sale.

1671   "...3 Jan. 1671. Wm. Rose makes a pledge of certain goods of John Salway, live stock, negroe woman etc. for the security of a debt of tobacco owed to John Salway, 12 Oct. 1671. Wit. John Carr, Robert Palmer." (Surry Book I p. 402) (Davis abstracts p. 104)

    This is the latest record known of William Rose. We infer from the style used in Davis abstracts that this record was dated 12 Oct. 1671 and recorded 3 Jan. 1671/2. William

Rose died between the date of the above and 1672, when his wife is called widow.

1672 Anne Rose, widow , petitions for the recordation of a gift to her children as follows: "I give to my sonn Wm Rose one Cow & two 2 yere old heifers with all theire female increase one fetherbed with a boulster & Rugg to be delivered him at ye age of 21 yrs halfe a mare & halfe a filly aboute 5 months old with theire increase male & female I give to my Daughter Anne Rose one quarter prte of ye above sd Mare & filly I give to my Daughter Mary Rose ye other (prte? qrte?) of ye sd Mare & filly with theire increase two Cows & one Calfe with theire female increase I give to my sonn Rich: Rose one Cow & one two yeare old heifer." Signed: Anne A Rose (or, Anne, her A mark, Rose). Test: Geo. Watkin (Surry Guardian's Accounts 1672-1750 p. 4) (STR photocopies)

 This record establishes that William Rose was deceased and that they had a son Richard not named in the 1666 document. The recordation date does not appear, but its order in the book indicates it was recorded 1672.

1677 "Surry County ye 8th of December 1677. William Rose Senio[r] did in his lifetime Record a Mare w:[th] her whole Increase for the use & benefit of 4 of his children viz[t] Jane, William Ann and Mary, which Mare & her Increase was to remain in a Joynt Stock untill the said Children came to Lawfull Age or were married, and then was to receive an Equall Share out of them, Jane the Eldest Married & her husband sould her share to W[m] Rose, now W[m] Rose being at age Desires to have the Stock Divided & to be possest with his prte being the halfe. The whole Stock being as followeth. one Mare aboute 8 yr old valued 1300 lb tobo one horse aboute 4 yr old valued at 0800 lb tobo one horse aboute 2 yr 8 months old valued at 0600 lb tobo one Colt about 8 month old still to run in a Joynte Stock untill a better Conveniency presents to divide it W[m] Rose his lott was to have the two horses at 1400 & is thereby indebted to his two sisters fifty pounds of tobo & the mare to be wholly theirs viz[t] Ann Rose & Mary Rose unto which division each party herein con-

cerned have with the advise of theire friends Consented
as witness their hands this day and yeare above written."
Signed W^m (perhaps his W sign) Rose, Ann (x), Richard
Avery Guardian of Mary Rose. Wit: Willm Browne, John
Moring, contents read in court Jan. 1, 1677, recorded
Jan. 18, 1677 (old style date). (Surry Book II p.162)
(STR photocopies).

The probable order in which the children
were born is established - Jane is eldest
and married; Ann at least 21 for she signs;
William newly 21 (in 1689 he declares he is
34); Mary is still a minor needing a guardian.
The total value of the stock to be divided is
2700 lbs of tobacco - William Jr.'s two
horses valued at 1400 is 50 lbs more than
his half, and he is thus indebted to his two
sisters 50 lbs. of tobacco or 25 lbs. each.

This ends the known records naming William Rose[1].

BIBLIOGRAPHY:

1) **Surry County Records, Surry County, Virginia 1652-1684**, Books I and II abstracted by Elizabeth T. Davis, abbreviated as Davis abstracts.
2) **Cavaliers and Pioneers, Abstracts of Virginia Land Patents and Grants 1623-1666** by Nell Marion Nugent, 1934, abbreviated as "Cav. and Pion."
3) Research records of **George H. Rose,** made largely during two trips to Virginia, abbreviated as "GHR notes."
4) Research records of **Seymour T. Rose** consisting of photocopies of early Rose documents, abbreviated as STR photocopies.
5) **Rose Notes** by Augusta B. Fothergill, deposited in Virginia State Library.
6) Research notes of **Wickliffe Rose** (now deceased), made in 1930-31, in possession of his son H. Wickliffe Rose.

****

Contributed by: Seymour & Christine Rose
3676 Manda Drive,
San Jose, California

COLLINS OF SOUTH CAROLINA, KENTUCKY, MISSOURI,
with related lineages, Smith, Ross, Wyatt, Scott, Fleete, Hawte.

William Collins, of York, England, m. Mary Campbell, descendant of Robert the Bruce. They had Thomas Collins.

THOMAS COLLINS, b. 1729 in York, England; d. Spartanburg, S.C. 9/11/1796; m. in York, Rosanna Dodds, b. 1729 in York, d. Spartanburg, S.C. 1796. Their gravestones are still legible and can be seen in Old Nazareth Church Graveyard. Thomas and Rosanna emigrated to Pennsylvania, where their first child, John Collins, was b. in 1754. Their second child William was b. there in 1755. In 1760 the family was living in Rockingham, Va., but in 1761 Thomas and Rosanna with their children had taken up a large survey on the Tyger River, Spartanburg District, S.C. (Ref: Howe's "History of the Presbyterian Church", Vol. 1, p. 544).

Children:
1. John Collins, b. Pa. 1754, d. 4/4/1841. m. Elizabeth Brown of Newberry Dist., S.C.
2. WILLIAM COLLINS, b. 1755. (see later)
3. Richard Collins. (see later)
4. Frances Collins, (Fanny), m. _____ Allen.
5. Joseph Alexander Collins, b. 2/10/1763, d. 8/24/1847. m. Elizabeth Fleming.
6. Jane Collins, (Jennie), b. 6/23/1764, d. 11/9/1849. m. Col. William Austin.
7. Nancy Collins, b. 1768, d. 1859.
8. Alexander Collins. Named in his father's will.
9. Mary Collins. m. _____ White. Named in her father's will.

REVN. WAR RECORD OF THESE CHILDREN:
Capt. John Collins, S.C. Militia. (Record in Washington, D.C.)
Richard Collins, of Roebuck's Company. (Marker in Old Nazareth Churchyard).
Joseph Collins served as a scout. (S.C. Indents).
Jane Collins served by carrying important despatches

in her saddlebag, at night and alone; swimming two
rivers to N.C. (Ref: Austin and Allied Families, p. 35).
Capt. William Collins served under Lt. Col. Marion.
(Refs: Marker in Old Nazareth Churchyard; Pettis' "Johnson Co., Mo., Biographical History", under John A.
Collins; History of Lafayette Co., Mo., pp. 406-407-522;
S.A.R. Year Bk., 1896, p. 83.)

The will of Thomas Collins, dated Aug. 22, 1796, may
be found in Box 7, pkg. 27, at Spartanburg. Rosanna d.
10/1/1796. (Gravestone ref.)

After the War, William and his brother Richard went
to Kentucky. They settled in Warren Co., but Richard
returned later to S.C., as there is a record showing
that he served as "Citizen Attorney" in a land matter,
and his WILL is there. He was on the Tax List of Warren
Co., Ky., in 1800 and 1801. Both Capt. William Collins
and his brother Richard were Bounty Recipients.

Kentucky was then a frontier, over-run with Indians
and with wild beasts. There is an interesting story in
records of Western Ky. University concerning Richard.
One night, he was sleeping under a tree with four or
five companions, when Indians surprised and killed them
all except Richard, who escaped to a Dutch settlement
clad only in his shirt. An old Dutchman kindly took him
in, and clothed him in his own blue britches and yellow
jacket, and as Richard was tall and thin, and the old
Dutchman was short and fat, Richard's appearance was
a source of great merriment to the young daughters of
the family. The women of the house soon wove and made
a new suit for Richard.

Richard died in Spartanburg, and his WILL leaves his
personal effects to his brother Joseph Collins, who cared
for him in his last illness.

Capt. William Collins was about 20 at the outbreak of
the War. He fought in almost every battle in the area -
at King's Mountain, at the Battle of Cowpens, and was
among those who chased Tarleton out of the South. He
was twice wounded. His sister Jennie, alone at night,
carried important despatches.

William took up a large survey in Warren Co., Ky.,
near Bowling Green (as it is today). There he m. a Miss
Wright, b. in Va., (probably a dau. of John Wright,) m.

ca. 1796. Children: Sarah, b. 1798; Richard, b. 1800; William, b. ca. 1802; Thomas, b. ca. 1805; Christine, Rosey and Joseph, dates unknown.

William Collins m. (2) Nancy Moore Dyer, widow of Abner Dyer. (Ref: Warren Co., Ky., Marriages, 1707-1857, p. 16.) They were m. 3/8/1818.

Marriage Register records:
William Collins mar. Nancy Dyer 3/28/1818,
Richard Collins mar. Caty Ennis (Innes) 4/16/1818. (p. 16)
Christine Collins mar. LeRoy Barton, 8/2/1827. (p. 8)
Sarah Collins mar. Elijah Key 9/24/1799. (p. 58)
William Collins mar. Susannah Bowmer 7/18/1818. (p. 15)

****

(From "Graves Inscriptions of Warren Co., Ky.," by Hardcastle, p. 44):
Rachael, wife of John Ennis, b. 9/6/1797; d. Sept. 1820.
Mary Ann Ennis, b. Mar. 1740; d. 1827.
(From Wills and Inventories, 1823-1827):
John Ennis, Inv. Jan. 15, 1824; Sale List; no WILL.

****

By his second marriage, Capt. William Collins had a daughter Harriet Adaline Columbia Ann (called by a shortened form of Columbia), b. 1/27/1818, m. Ira Anderson; and another child d. in infancy.

William Collins was an important land owner of Warren Co. He was Deputy Sheriff; Tax Collector; was chosen "Defender of Orphans", bondsman, etc; appointed "Chairman of Riders" (to ride and guard against unlawful assembly of slaves); road surveyor. He was a man of affluence and renown, respected by all; known as "Handsome Big Bill". (Ref: Records in Western Ky. University Library; Warren Co. Minute Bks., and Court Records, Bowling Green, Ky.)

In 1825 we find him with his family, sons-in-law, and friends, settling in Davis Township, Lafayette Co., Mo., lush, rich land surrounding what is today the town of

Lexington. He d. there in April, 1835. His son RICHARD, who had settled on a farm about two miles south-west of what is today Higginsville, Mo., administered William's estate, will filed 11/12/1835, probated 1836, Lafayette Co., Mo. The slaves were disposed of 7/25/1836; the farmland was later bought by a Mr. Aull, from whom the town of Aullville gets its name. (Ref: Pettis' History, p. 522; History of Lafayette Co. (pub. 1888) pp 406-407; "Revolutionary Sketches", pub. in the Carolina Spartan, Spartanburg, S.C., 1/23/1898; and data at Cowpens Nat'l. Monument, S.C. State Hwy. #11.)

HEIRS OF WILLIAM COLLINS: William Collins; Richard Collins; Larkin Graham for wife Sarah, nee Collins; Wheeler O. Harris for wife Rosey, nee Collins; Thomas Collins; Leroy Barton for wife Christine, nee Collins; Harriet A.C.A. Collins; and wife Nancy Collins. Son Joseph Collins is not mentioned in this list of heirs, but he had been sent back to Warren Co., Ky., to dispose of some property for his father, and on his return to Mo., d. in St. Louis, Mo., 1856. Perhaps he was to receive the proceeds from the sale of the Ky. property.

RICHARD COLLINS, son of Capt. William Collins, was b. ca. 1800 at Bowling Green, Warren Co., Ky., where he m. Catherine Innes (Ennis) 4/16/1818. He was a commissioned officer in the Cornstalk Militia. With his father and their friends and other relatives, he removed in 1825 to a farm where Higginsville, Mo., is today located, in Lafayette Co. His first child, named Lafayette, was the first white child to be born in that area, and the town of Fayetteville took his name. Lafayette Collins became a merchant and shortly before the Civil War removed to Texas, where he prospered, and his family became well-known.

Children of RICHARD AND "CATY" COLLINS:
1. Lafayette Collins, b. 1827, m. Elizabeth Davis, dau. of General Davis of Johnson Co., Mo.
2. Mary Ann Collins, eldest dau. b. ca. 1828, m. William Young; d. before her father.
3. Sarah Collins, second dau. b. ca. 1829, m. Solomon Clay.
4. William George Collins, b. ca. 1830, m. Ann Mariah, dau. of John Davis Smith. (see Smith lineage later).

5. Rachael Collins, b. ? m. James Clay.
6. Nancy Collins, b. 1835, m. 1855 her cousin William Collins, son of Thomas Collins.

Richard Collins left no WILL, but his estate was filed 6/30/1851, and Lafayette Collins names the heirs of Richard as:- William I. Young who resides in Andrew Co., Mo.; Sarah Clay who resides in Johnson Co., Mo; Lafayette Collins; Nancy J. Collins; and William George Collins who resides in Johnson Co., Mo. Sworn and subscribed to June 1851; signed Lafayette Collins; filed 6/30/1851.

"To the Honorable Court of Johnson Co., Mo., the undersigned petitioners Lafayette Collins, William George Collins, Catherine Collins, Wm. M. Collins and Nancy Collins his wife, - all of Johnson Co., Mo., - and James Clay and Rachael Clay his wife, both of the Co. of Lafayette, Mo., respectfully beg leave to state to your Honors that Richard Collins, late of said Johnson Co., Mo., departed this life on or about 22nd. of May in 1851 without leaving a WILL, and leaving the following named heirs:- Catherine Collins his widow; Lafayette Collins and William George Collins his sons; Rachael Clay (nee Collins); Nancy Collins who intermarried with Wm. M. Collins; Sarah Clay, late Sarah Collins, who intermarried with Solomon Clay, his daughters; and also Georgianna Young, Richard Young. Sarah K. Young, Thomas Young, and Mary A. Young, who are the children and heirs of Mary A. Young, the late Mary A. Collins, who intermarried with Wm. I. Young and departed this life before the death of her said father Richard Collins."

The said petitioners state that the said Georgianna Young, Sarah K. Young, Richard Young, Thomas S. Young and Mary A. Young are infants of tender age (to wit, within the age of 21) and that they, together with their father, reside in Andrew Co., Mo., and that the said Solomon Clay resides in the State of California. Then follows a statement of the slaves owned by Richard, and that the estate was not involved in any debt. Filled 11/11/1851. Cost of Tombstone - $30.00. Warrensburg, Mo.

WILLIAM GEORGE COLLINS, son of Richard and

Caty Collins, was b. in Lafayette Co., Mo., 1830. He
m. 10/17/1858 in Johnson Co., Mo., Ann Mariah Smith,
eldest dau. of John Davis Smith and his wife Susan Oldham
Geiger, (see Smith lineage later). William and his wife
owned and operated the Mansion House Hotel, in Warrensburg, Mo., (inherited from John Davis Smith,) the largest
and finest hotel in that part of the country. Ann's sister
Mary had married William's cousin, John A. Collins,
son of Thomas Collins, and they ran the livery stable
in connection with the hotel. These were large proper-
ties, enclosing two entire blocks of the town. Warrensburg was an "entry" to the West, and times were prosperous until the outbreak of the Civil War. The Smiths
and the Collinses were Southerners; some of their
neighbours were also, but not all; and across the State
Line lay Kansas; murders, lynchings, fires abounded.
Both the "North" and the "South" commandeered the hotel
in turn, ate what they wanted, burned and looted. John
Collins joined the Confederate Army and was captured;
William had suffered injury to his eye by a burning, so
was unable to go to war, but after his cousin was released from prisoner-of-war camp, both families decided to leave Warrensburg. They removed to Washington,
Mo., where once again William and John entered the
hotel and livery business. William Collins operated
three hotels there, the Elm Street Hotel, at Main and
Lafayette, "Gregory House", and "Washington House"
at Main and Jefferson Streets.

    Mary (Smith) Collins, wife of John A. Collins, d.
12/20/1879, and is buried in the cemetery at Washington, Mo. (Ref: Washington Historical Society records.)
John re-married, and removed to Sedalia, Mo., where
he entered politics and eventually became Mayor of that
city.

    Early in 1883, William Collins left Washington and
went to St. Louis, Mo., to seek better medical help for
his eyes. In 1893 he purchased land at "Eden", near
Sparta, Randolph Co., Ill., where he d. 7/17/1899. His
wife Ann (Smith) Collins d. there 6/22/1903. Both are
buried in Old Warrensburg Cemetery, Mo. (Ref: Land
purchase at "Eden" recorded 10/17/1893, D.B. 42, p.
233.)

Children of William George Collins and his wife Ann:
1. John L. Collins, b. 1860, Warrensburg, Mo.
2. Catherine Emma (Kate) Collins, b. 6/13/1861. (see later)
3. Henry Collins, b. 1867.
4. Thomas Collins, b. 1869.
5. Abington Collins.
6. Mattie Drucilla Collins.

KATE EMMA COLLINS, b. 6/13/1861 at Warrensburg, Mo., m. at Washington, Mo., 8/30/1876, Samuel Robinson Avery, son of Edward Morehouse Avery and his wife Sarah Robinson Avery, of Webster Groves, Mo. (Note: Samuel Avery's lineage may be found in "The Groton Avery Clan", Vols. 1 and 2, by E.M. Avery, pub. 1912.) This is a distinguished lineage, originating in this country in 1630 in Mass. and Connecticut. Thus, for the first time in the history of either family, northern and southern families are joined in marriage. It seems fitting that this occurred in Missouri, the "Compromise State".

Samuel R. Avery d. at Union, Mo., 6/2/1930, and is buried in Mt. Hope Cemetery, Union. Kate (Collins) Avery died at the home of her son Harry Avery, a lawyer, of St. Louis, Mo., 7/12/1943. She is buried at Union also.

Children of Kate Emma (Collins) Avery and Samuel Avery:
1. Mary Collins Avery. (see later)
2. Grace Robison Avery, b. 2/19/1881 at Richmond, Mo.; m. Robert F. Thias.
3. Edward Mark Avery, b. 6/2/1882, at St. Joseph, Mo. Accidentally killed in Vancouver during a storm.
4. Carlyn Tilden Avery, b. 9/5/1888 at St. Charles, Mo., m. Walter Mateer, d. Houston, Texas. No children.
5. Samuel Richard Avery, b. 10/17/1895 at St. Louis, Mo., d. in California ca. 1959. His son, Stephen Avery, a Methodist minister in Texas.
6. Henry Christopher Avery (Harry), b. 4/21/1902 at St. Louis, Mo., m. Adele Saxenmeyer.

MARY COLLINS AVERY, b. 5/14/1878 at Washington, Mo.; attended Avery Grade School, Webster Groves, Mo.,

(named for her grandfather Edward Morehouse Avery), and old Central High and Normal Schools in St. Louis. She eloped with Charles Henry Mason Jr., and they married 6/1/1901. He was b. in St. Louis, Mo., 8/28/ 1877, the only son of Charles Henry and Hannah (Dunham) Mason, who had m. in Holywell Church, Huntingdon, England, 1/15/1873, and emigrated to America and settled at Ellardville, then a suburb of St. Louis, Mo. Charles H. Mason Jr. d. 12/5/1943, buried in Fairview Cemetery, Staten Island, N.Y. Mary Collins (Avery) Mason d. 1/4/1956, buried in the Mason plot, Valhalla Cemetery, St. Louis, Mo. Children of Mary Avery Mason and Charles H. Mason:
1. Esther Marye Mason, b. 4/12/1903, m. 6/30/1926, St. Louis, Mo., to Kenneth Heggs. (see later)
2. Charles Avery Mason, b. 8/2/1904, m. St. Louis, Mo., to Virginia Fear.
3. Ruth Hannah Mason, b. 5/21/1907, m. E.A. Smith.

ESTHER MARYE (MASON) HEGGS was b. 4/12/1903; educated at St. Louis Grade and High Schools; Harris College and Washington University; taught in Webster School and Wyman Training School, St. Louis; m. 6/30/ 1926 to Kenneth Heggs, at the Church of the Redeemer, St. Louis. Kenneth Heggs, son of Thomas and Martha (Ilson) Heggs of St. Louis, b. in Kettering, England, 1/ 4/1902; emigrated to Mass. with his family when a boy, and later moved to St. Louis.

Both Kenneth and Esther Heggs took an active part in the life of their community in St. Louis; they removed to Cincinnati, where Kenneth Heggs is a member of the Civil War Round Table, and serves on numerous other committees. He is internationally known in his field of shoe-last manufacture, and has instructed in Mexico City. He has several important inventions in connection with shoe manufacturing patented in his name. Esther Heggs is Vice-Regent of Cincinnati D.A.R.; Ohio State Trustee, Waldschmidt Museum; and belongs to several National Societies. Children:
1. Marye Jane E. Heggs, (Torchy), b. St. Louis, Mo., 7/22/1928; educated in Webster Groves; Brockton, Mass.; and Missouri University; m. at Calvary Episcopal Church, Columbia, Mo., 3/24/1948,

Chester Wm. McNamara, elder son of William and Violet McNamara of University City, Mo. Chester McNamara is in the Army as a career. Children:
  (1) Mary Katherine McNamara (Kathy), b. Columbia, Mo., 11/9/1948.
  (2) Susan Nancy McNamara, b. 11/16/1955.
  (3) Patricia Ann McNamara, b. El Paso, Texas, 11/16/1960.
  (4) Barbara Jean McNamara, b. 11/12/1961.
2. David Kenneth Heggs, b. St. Louis, Mo., 10/16/1936; educated Mo. and Cincinnati; graduated from Texas A. and M. College with a distinguished record. He m. 6/26/1959 at White Rock Methodist Church, Dallas, Texas, Nita Sue Sandel, dau of Clarence and Juanita Sandel of Dallas. Sue was b. Dallas 4/8/1939, educated in Dallas, and Texas University. Child:
  (1) Heather Avery Heggs, b. 9/4/1963, Dallas, Texas.

****

SMITH LINEAGE

HENRY SMITH: b. 1714, d. 1780; m. 1736 Sarah Crosby (b. 1718, d. 1756 in Va.) They had William.

WILLIAM SMITH: b. 10/28/1742, Stafford Co., Va. m. (1) Joice Humphrey on 12/16/1746, d. 9/20/1774 in Va. Chn:

HENRY, George, David, William and Enoch. William Smith m. (2) Mary Eleanor _____, who d. at Mt. Sterling, Ky. Children: Sarah, Elizabeth, Mary, Ann, John, Robert, Lydia, and Elkanah. Capt. William Smith served in the Rev. War under Col. Dan Morgan, 11th and 15th Regt., 1775-1777. He d. 11/11/1816, Mt. Sterling, Montgomery Co., Ky. His will is in W. B. A., p. 173. (Ref: Va. Soldiers in the Rev. War, Vol. 8, p. 408; Saffrell's Records of the Rev. War, p. 261; Overwharton Parish Records, p. 157.)

HENRY SMITH, son of William and Joice (Humphrey) Smith, b. Va. 8/26/1770, m. in Clark Co., Ky., 2/22/1797, Nancy Davis, dau of Ignatius Davis. Henry Smith's will dated 9/17/1841, filed 10/24/1857, on record in Warrenton, Mo., where he died. Children: John, George,

Owen, William, Mary, Sarah, Elizabeth, Nancy, Maria and Rebecca.

JOHN D. SMITH, son of Henry and Nancy (Davis) Smith, was b. 5/21/1815, d. 10/17/1857 in Warrensburg, Mo., m. in Lincoln Co., Mo., Susan Oldham Geiger, dau of John and Caroline (Ross) Geiger. (see Ross Lineage). Children: Ann Mariah, James Montgomery, William Henry, and Mary Elizabeth.

ANN MARIAH SMITH, b. 1842, Lincoln Co., Mo., m. in Warrensburg, Mo., 10/17/1858 William George Collins, son of Richard Collins and his wife Catherine (Ennis) Collins. (See Collins lineage.)

****

ROSS LINEAGE

LAWRENCE ROSS, b. Ross-shire, Scotland, 5/15/1722 (Bible record), d. in Jefferson Co., Ky., 8/8/1818; m. ca. 1762 in Va. to Susannah Oldham, b. 1/1/1746 in Va., d. 1819 in Jefferson Co., Ky. (Record of Service of Lawrence Ross: Pa. Archives, Vol. 23, 3rd. Series, p. 303, Northampton Co. Also listed among soldiers who served as "Rangers on the Frontier", 1778-1783.) Children:
1. SHAPLEY ROSS, b. 2/12/1763 in Va.; d. 1823 in Linc. Co., Mo.; m. Mary Prince (b. in Va. 1767, d. in Iowa 1837) on 2/19/1790. Shapleigh was an "original settler" of Louisville, Ky. (Ref: Va. State Papers, "Calendar of State Papers", p. 161.)
2. Nancy Ross, b. 11/29/1771. m. Jacob Owens 3/17/1789.
3. Susannah Ross, b. 9/13/1773. m. 8/12/1794 to Matthew Love.
4. Anne Ross, m. 11/3/1798 to Thomas Prince.
5. Mary Ross, m. 2/22/1786 to William Peyton.
6. Elizabeth Ross, m. 1/6/1791 to Samuel Phillips.
7. Sarah Ross, m. 7/2/1794 to Nathan Sullivan.
8. Milly Ross, m. 9/15/1803 to Jesse Carter.
9. Fanny Ross, m. 1/1/1801 to Conway Oldham.
10. Presley Neville Ross, d. 1821. m. Martha Covington 8/19/1813.

Children of SHAPLEY ROSS,(son of Lawrence) and Mary (Prince) Ross:
1. Mervin Ross, m. Elizabeth Wright.
2. William Oldham Ross, m. Lucinda Taylor 12/1/1817.
3. Lawrence Ross, m. Sarah Ross, nee Sarah Taylor.
4. Presley Neville Ross, m. Susan Wright.
5. Caroline M. Ross, m. John Geiger 4/4/1815. (see Scott descent)
6. ELIZABETH WAKEFIELD ROSS, b. in Ky. 10/17/1807. m. John Allen Woolfolk 3/17/1823 in Mo., (who was b. 6/16/1798 in Shelby Co., Ky., d. 10/26/1854 in Troy Co., Mo.) Elizabeth d. in Troy 3/8/1852.
7. Susan Ross, m. Austin Woolfolk 7/26/1812.
8. Nancy Ross.
9. Shapleigh Prince Ross, b. 1/18/1811, d. 9/17/1889. m. Catherine Fulkerson.

Children of ELIZABETH WAKEFIELD ROSS and John Allen Woolfolk: (Bible records):
1. Susan Ann Woolfolk, b. 1/11/1824.
2. Shapleigh Ross Woolfolk, b. 6/23/1825.
3. Mary Jane Woolfolk, b. 5/27/1827.
4. Rebecca Alice Woolfolk, b. 2/8/1829.
5. Robert Woolfolk, b. 2/7/1832.
6. Richard Oscar Woolfolk, b. 3/22/1834, d. 1/25/1905.
7. Austin Coleman Woolfolk, b. 10/20/1837.
8. Martha Caroline Woolfolk, b. 12/9/1839.
9. Helen B. Woolfolk, b. 5/1/1842.
10. Georgia Cowan Woolfolk, b. 5/31/1844.
11. Louisa Woolfolk.
12. Elizabeth Woolfolk.

****

Ref: - Jefferson County, Kentucky DEED BOOK #4, page 91, item 180 -

> "Indenture July 7, 1795, - between SHAPLEY ROSS and MARY his wife of Jefferson Co., Ky. and Leonard Harpool, etc. for money consideration, - 39 acres of land in Jefferson Co. beginning at a corner of Richard Finley's land; thence south in Alexander Breckinridge's line; then southeast to John Veech's."

Rec. July 7th, 1795. Pages 259-60, Book 4.

Item #35. -
Frederick Edwards, wife Mary. - August 1793, of Jeff. Co., Ky. and SHAPLEY ROSS, his heirs, etc., - one tract of land of 39 acres in Jefferson Co., Ky. for money - beginning at Rich'd Finley's corner; thence to Jno. Veech's land. Rec. p. 54, Bk. 4.

Item #407.
Referring to Indenture, Sept. 2, 1789 between John Stuart and Mourning, his wife, by Samuel Shackleford, their Atty. and LAWRENCE ROSS for sale of 38 acres of land; -
"The Commonwealth of Kentucky orders Peachy Bledsoe and James Thomas to examine the sd. Mourning Stuart as to her consent to this sale, Dec. 9th, 1796.
Jan. 10, 1797, Oglethorpe County, Georgia. S'd. examination made, and Dower Rights relinquished by Sd. Mourning Stuart.
Rec. Aug. 1, 1797. Original delivered to Lawrence Ross on June 20th, 1809. Ref:-Bk. #4, pages 509-510.

DEED BOOK 2. --
Item #21. ----

LAWRENCE ROSS, - John Stewart and wife Mourning of Amherst Co., Va. --
"To LAWRENCE ROSS of Jefferson County, Sept. 2, 1789, -for 350 pounds paid, -for 328 acres on Beargrass, being a part of Col. John Floyd's, including HOUGHLAND'S OLD STATION, - beginning on the southeast bank of Beargrass below Breckinridge's Still-House; thence to the corner of William Meriwether's field."
Signed Oct. 6th, 1789. Rec. Bk. 2, p. 27.

****

SOME LINEAGES SHOWING THE DESCENT OF ESTHER MASON HEGGS

WYATT DESCENT THROUGH EDMUND, EARL OF LANCASTER:

KING HENRY 3rd. of England, m. Eleanor of Provence. They had Edmund.
EDMUND "Crouchback", Earl of Lancaster (d. 1296), m. Blanche, daughter of Robert 1st of Artois. They had Henry Plantagenet.
HENRY PLANTAGENET, (d. 1345), Earl of Leicester, m. Maud, daughter and heiress of Sir Patrick Chaworth. They had Joane.
    JOANE PLANTAGENET, m. John, 3rd. Lord Mowbray (d. 1361). They had John Mowbray.
    JOHN, 4th LORD MOWBRAY (slain 1368), m. Elizabeth, daughter and heiress of John, 3rd. Lord Segrave, and his wife, Margaret, Duchess of Norfolk. They had Thomas Mowbray.
    THOMAS MOWBRAY, Duke of Norfolk, (d. 1400), m. Elizabeth Fitzalan, daughter and heiress of Richard Fitzalan, 10th Earl of Arundel (beheaded 1397) and his wife Elizabeth De Bohun, dau. of William, 1st Earl of Northampton. They had Margaret Mowbray.
    MARGARET MOWBRAY, Daughter and co-heiress of her father, m. Sir Robert Howard. They had Catherine Howard.
    CATHERINE HOWARD m. (as his second wife) Edward Neville, 1st. Lord Abergavenny. They had Margaret Neville.
    MARGARET NEVILLE m. John Brooke, Lord Cobham (d. 1506). They had Thomas Brooke.
    THOMAS BROOKE, Lord Cobham (d. 1529), m. Dorothy, dau of Sir Henry Heyden by his first wife. They had Elizabeth Brooke.
    ELIZABETH BROOKE m. (1) Sir Thomas Wyatt, poet, of Allington Castle. (A picture of this castle may be seen in "Va. Magazine of History and Biography", Vol. 31, p. 237.) Sir Thomas Wyatt, b. 1503, m. 1520, d. 1544, is buried at Sherborne, Dorset. They had Thomas Wyatt.
    SIR THOMAS WYATT, of Allington Castle, Kent, b.

1521, m. 1536, executed 4/11/1554 for attempting to put Lady Grey on the throne, m. Jane, daughter and co-heiress of Sir William Hawte of Bourne, Kent. (See Hawte descent). They had Jane Wyatt.

 JANE WYATT, aunt of Governor Wyatt of Va., m. Charles Scott of Egerton, who d. 1617. (See Scott descent). They had Deborah Scott.

 DEBORAH SCOTT m. Sir William Fleete, the largest stock-holder in the Third Va. Company. Their son was Capt. Henry Fleete of Maryland and Virginia. (See Fleete descent)

****

WYATT DESCENT FROM HENRY 3RD AND ELEANOR OF PROVENCE:

Henry 3rd. and Eleanor of Provence had Edward 1st of England.

 EDWARD 1st. m. Eleanor of Castile, dau of King Ferdinand. They had

 EDWARD 2nd. m. Isabella, dau of Phillip. They had

 EDWARD 3rd. m. Philippa, dau of William, Count of Hainault. They had

 JOHN OF GAUNT, Duke of Lancaster, Knight of the Garter, (d. 1399). He m. Catherine, dau of Sir Payn Roelt, Guienne King at Arms. They had

 JOAN DE BEAUFORT, who m. Ralph Neville, 1st Lord of Westmoreland, Knight of the Garter (d. 1425). They had

 EDWARD NEVILLE, 1st Lord Abergavenny, who m. as his second wife Catherine Howard. They had

 MARGARET NEVILLE, m. John Brooke, Lord Cobham (d. 1506). They had

 THOMAS BROOKE, Lord Cobham (d. 1529) m. Dorothy Heyden, dau of Sir Henry Heyden by his first wife. They had ELIZABETH BROOKE. (see previous lineage.)

****

WYATT DESCENT THROUGH ELIZABETH PLANTAGENET

EDWARD 1st, King of England, son of Henry 3rd and Eleanor of Provence, m. Eleanor, dau of Ferdinand 3rd., King of Castile (d. 1290). Their dau:
ELIZABETH PLANTAGENET, m. Humphrey De Bohun, 4th Earl of Hereford, who was slain at Borough Bridge, 1322. Their daughter:
MARGARET, m. Hugh Courtney, 2nd. Earl of Devon (d. 1377). Their daughter:
MARGARET, m. John, 3rd. Lord Cobham. Their daughter:
JOANE, heiress of Lord Cobham, m. Sir John de la Pole. Thier daughter:
JOANE de la POLE, m. Sir Reginald Braybrooke. Their daughter:
JOANE, m. Sir Thomas Brooke, Lord Cobham, their son:
SIR EDWARD BROOKE, Lord Cobham (d. 1464), m. Elizabeth, dau. of James, Lord Audley. Their son:
JOHN BROOKE, Lord Cobham (d. 1506) m. Margaret, dau of Edward Neville, 1st. Lord Abergavenny and Catherine (2nd wife). Their son:
THOMAS BROOKE, Lord Cobham (d. 1529). m. Dorothy, dau of Sir Henry Heyden. They had Elizabeth Brooke who m. Sir Thomas Wyatt. (see previously.)
(Ref: "Virginia Genealogies", by Hayden, p.p. 231-234.)

****

SCOTT AND FLEETE DESCENT

Henry 3rd of England and Eleanor of Provence had
EDWARD 1st, who m. Eleanor of Castile. They had
JOAN OF ACRE, m. Gilbert Clare (d. 1295), 7th Earl of Hertford and 3rd Earl of Gloucester. They had
ALIANORE (d. July 1337), m. Hugh de la Despencer the younger, Earl of Winchester, executed 1326. They had
ISABEL, first wife of Richard Fitzalan, (d. 1375), 9th Earl of Arundel. Their only child
PHILIPPA, m. Sir Richard Sergeaux, Knight, of Ser-

geaux, Cornwall. They had
  PHILIPPA, m. Sir Robert Pashley, Knight. They had
SIR JOHN PASHLEY, m. Lowys, dau and heiress of
Thomas Gower. They had
  ELIZABETH PASHLEY, dau and heiress, m. Reginald
Pympe (or de Pympa), and old Saxon family. They had
  ANNE PYMPE, dau and heiress, m. Sir John Scott,
of Scott's Hall and Nettlested.

****

WILLIAM BALIOL le SCOTT. He had
  JOHN le SCOTT, of Brabourne, Kent, d. ca. 1348.
He had
  SIR WILLIAM SCOTT, of Brabourne, Knighted by
Edward 3rd, 1337; Lord Chief Justice 1/8/1341; Knight
Marshall of England before 1347; buried in the Church at
Brabourne. He had
  MICHAEL SCOTT, taken prisoner at the Battle of
Dunsene; m. Emma _____ and had
  WILLIAM SCOTT, buried at Brabourne. m. Matilda
_____. They had
  JOHN SCOTT, Member of Parliament for Hythe, Kent,
1399-1413; Lt. of Dover Castle, temp. Henry 4th; Buried
in Brabourne Church, 1413; m. the heiress of Cumbe,
(Brabourne), dau of William de Cumbe. They had
  WILLIAM SCOTT, of Scott's Hall, Kent; Sheriff of
Kent, 1413-1429; Sword-bearer to Henry 5th; m. (1)
Joane de Orlastone. They had
  SIR JOHN SCOTTE, of Scott's Hall, Kent; High Sheriff
of Kent; Lord Warden of the Cinque Ports and Governor
of Dover Castle; Marshall of Calais; Ambassador to the
Duke of Burgundy and Bretagne; buried at Brabourne 10/
17/1485; m. Agnes Beaufitz. They had
  SIR WILLIAM SCOTT, High Sheriff of Kent 1491, 1502,
1515, 1517; Lord Warden of the Cinque Ports and Constable
of Dover Castle; Knight of the Bath; rebuilt Scott's Hall
ca. 1491; m. Sybilla Lewknor who d. 1528. They had
  SIR JOHN SCOTT, of Scott's Hall and Nettlested;
Sheriff of Kent, 1528; m. Anne Pympe. (see previously).
They had
  SIR REGINALD SCOTT, of Scott's Hall, Kent; Captain
of the Castles of Calais and Sangatte; High Sheriff of Kent

1541-42; was principally engaged abroad in military service; d. 12/16/1554; m. (1) Emmiline Kempe, dau of Sir William Kempe of Ollantigh, Kent; he m. (2) Mary, dau of Sir Bryan Tuke of Layer Marney in Essex, who was Secretary to Cardinal Wolsey; their chn. included Mary, who m. Richard Argyll; they had three other daus and five sons, including

CHARLES SCOTT of Egerton, Kent, d. 1617, m. Jane Wyatt, dau of Sir Thomas Wyatt of Allington Castle, Kent, (see Wyatt descent), and his wife Jane, dau of Sir William Hawte (see Hawte descent). Their eldest daughter

DEBORAH SCOTT, m. Sir William Fleete, of Chartham, Kent. They had seven sons and one daughter, viz: George, William, Henry, Brian, Edward, Reynolds, John, and Catherine. Their son

HENRY FLEETE, Captain, was the progenitor of this line in America. He lived in Maryland and Lancaster Co., Va., and owned many vessels plying between England, the Barbadoes and other islands, and the coast of America. He settled first in Maryland, where there can be seen today the manors of the Scotts and the Wyatts. He removed to Lancaster Co., Va., and represented it in 1652. (Ref: Va. Magazine of History, Vol. 8, p. 174.) He ma. Sarah _____ and had

SARAH FLEETE, who m. Edwin Conway the 2nd., Gentleman, of Lancaster Co., Va. They had

EDWIN CONWAY 3rd, Colonel, who m. Anne Ball, dau of Col. Joseph Ball and his wife Elizabeth (Romney) Ball. Anne Ball Conway was half sister to Mary Ball Washington, mother of George Washington. Edwin Conway and his wife had

ANNE CONWAY who m. Col. John Oldham of Va., a Huguenot. They had

SUSANNAH OLDHAM, who m. Lawrence Ross, Rev. War Ranger. (See Ross lineage.) They had

SHAPLEIGH ROSS, an "original settler" of Louisville, Ky., (see Va. State Papers, "Calendar of State Papers", p. 161), who m. Mary Prince, dau of Sylvannus Prince (Rev. War) of Va. and Ky. They had

CAROLINE MARY ROSS, who ma. John Geiger, War of 1812. (Ky. and Mo. Records.) They had

SUSAN OLDHAM GEIGER, who m. John Davis Smith.

(see Smith lineage). They had
ANN MARIAH SMITH, who m. William George Collins.
(see Collins lineage). They had
KATE EMMA COLLINS, who m. Samuel Robinson Avery, son of Edward and Sarah Avery. They had
MARY COLLINS AVERY, who m. Charles Henry Mason Jr., of St. Louis. They had
ESTHER MARYE MASON, m. Kenneth Heggs, son of Thomas and Martha Heggs. They had
MARY JANE HEGGS and DAVID KENNETH HEGGS.
(see previously.)
(Refs: "Conway Family History", by Conway, pp. 231-233. "Virginia Genealogies" by Rev. Horace Hayden, p. 234; "Genesis of the United States", by Brown, pp. 996-7.)

Scott Arms and Crest:
Arms: Argent, three Catherine Wheels, sable, a bordure engrailed, gules.
Crest: A demi-griffin, segreant, sable, beaked and legged, or.
Motto: AMO. (I love).

****

HAUTE (HAWTE) DESCENT

From Hugh de Haut; his son Richard de Haute m. the heiress of Waddenhall; their son was William de Haute; his son Henry de Haute, d. before 1321, m. Margery de Marynes; their son Henry de Haute, b. ca. 1300, m. Annabel atte Halle; their son Sir Edmund de Haute m. Bennet de Shelving; their son Sir Nicholas de Haute, b. 1358, d. 1416, m. Alice de Covan; their son William Haute, b. 1390, d. 1462, m. (1) Margaret Berwick, (2) Joan Wydville; son by second marriage was Sir William Hawte, who m. Joan Horne; their son Sir Thomas Hawte, d. 1502, m. Isabel Frowick; their son Sir William Hawte, d. 1539, m. (1) Mary Guildford (2) Margaret Wood; daughter by the first marriage was Jane Hawte, b. 1522, who m. Sir Thomas Wyatt of Allington, m. 1537.

HAWTE - WYATT CRESTS:
Azure, crusilly or, a lion rampant argent, a fesse gules over all. (Used by Sir William Haute in the 13th century.)

Argent, crusilly, a lion rampant sable. (Used by William's grandson Henry.)

Azure, crusilly or, a lion rampant ermine, a fesse gules over all. (Used by William's grandson James, younger brother of the above Henry).

Gules, a cross engrailed or, impaling azure, crusilly or, a lion rampant argent, a fesse gules over all. (Used by Henry 3rd. de Haute, who m. 1290 Margery de Marynes).

By 1395 the above were all discarded, and the new "Arms" were beautifully carved on bosses in the roof of the cloisters of Canterbury Cathedral. These "Arms" were used until the middle of the 16th century.

Crest: Head and wings of a dragon.

In 1530, possibly because of the marriage with the House of York, a new Crest was used - "a bushe of whytte roses stalked vert, standing on a wreath silver and gules." (This was used by the last Sir William Hawte.)

    Elizabeth Wydville, dau of Richard, m. Edward IV, King of England. Her sister Joan Wydville (Woodville) m. William Haute. A series of crests shows the marriages with the Haute family. (Ref: Harleian MS. #1421): Haute-Wydville, Haute-Horne, Haute-Frowick, Haute-Guildford, Haute-Wyatt.

    NOTE: Sir William Hawte, Knight, of Bishopsbourne, aged 49, made his will 1/12/1539, leaving "to Alexander Culpepper, and to Thomas Wyatt, son-in-law, and his wife my daughter." His surviving children were: Elizabeth, widow of Thomas Culpepper, son and heir of Sir Alexander Culpepper, and Jane, wife of Thomas Wyatt. Jane and Thomas Wyatt had ten children; the second child Jane, m. Charles Scott of Egerton. (see Wyatt descent). The above is to be found in "The Ancestry of Mary Isaac." in the Library of Congress.

                              ****

          Contributed by: Esther Mason Heggs
                                      6222 Orchard Lane
                                       Cincinnati, Ohio.

    (Member of D. A. R., D. A. C., Magna Charta Dames, Americans of Royal Descent, Knights of the Garter, the Huguenot Society, etc.)

RAGAN OF GEORGIA WITH RELATED FAMILIES SPENCE, HILLIARD, TIMMONS, SHEFFIELD, SINGLETON, FITZGERALD

This lineage traces the Irish Ragan family back to eighteenth century North Carolina, where the name is often recorded as Regan. (Ref: Wheeler's History of N. C., Vol. 3, p. 353; "Memoirs of Ga.", Vol. 2.) Robert Alexander Ragan was b. in Robeson Co., N. C., in 1798. He married Mary Evans, b. 1/1/1792 in N. C. They came to Ga., settling first in Houston Co., 1835, and removing to Hawkinsville, Pulaski Co., in 1836. Robert d. in Pulaski Co. 6/15/1853, and his wife d. there 3/4/1893 at the age of 101 years. (Ref: D. A. R. History of Pulaski Co., Ga.) Children:
1. Robert A. Ragan Jr., b. 1827 in Ga., d. Hawkinsville 12/12/1912. (see later)
2. Mary Ragan, b. 1834 in N. C., m. James Rozar 8/3/1856. (Pulaski Co. Records.)
3. Julia Ragan, m. James M. Lancaster, 1/24/1843, Pulaski Co.
4. Jane Ragan, m. W. M. Anderson.
5. James Ragan, b. 1838 in Ga. Killed in Battle of Garrett's Farm 6/23/1862. Buried at Hawkinsville. (Will recorded, W. Bk. A, Pulaski Co.)
6. Dorothy Ragan.
7. Nancy Ragan.

Robert Alexander Ragan Jr., m. Sophia Elizabeth Davis in Hawkinsville 12/14/1852. She was the dau. of Hosiah L. Davis, who was b. in Laurens Co., S. C., in 1793, and his wife Mary, b. in S. C. 1797. Sophia Davis was b. 1/1/1830 and d. 2/11/1889 in Hawkinsville. Her father Hosiah was a Justice of the Inferior Court of the 14th District of Ga., 1840-1845. Hosiah's other children included Zion Davis, b. 1828, James Davis, b. 1834, E. A. P. Davis, b. 1836. (Pulaski Co. Wills; D. A. R. "History of Pulaski Co.")

Children of Robert Alexander Jr. and wife Sophia:
1. LaFayette H. Ragan, b. 10/16/1853 Hawkinsville, Ga. d. 1924. m. Mary E. Daniel (1853-1929) on 12/30/1875.

Children:
- (1) Ida Ragan (1876-1924) m. W.J. Ferguson (1866-1946)
- (2) O'Bena Ragan. d. s. p.
- (3) Leniaus C. Ragan (1879-1943) m. Mamie Wall (1874-1943.) Children:
  - i. Julian Ragan, m. Virginia Johnston. They had Julie Ragan.
  - ii. Elizabeth Ragan. Unmarried.
  - iii. Henry Ragan, m. Edith Elder. no issue
  - iv. Willard Ragan, m. James Pope Pate. They had Willard Pate.
2. Robert Timothy Ragan, b. 3/10/1855, d. Sept. 1890. (see later)
3. Mary Elizabeth Ragan, b. 10/2/1858, m. H. L. Lowery of Eastman, Ga., 10/18/1876.
4. James Monroe Ragan, b. 1/22/1861, d. s. p. 7/11/1887.
5. Thomas Barlow Ragan, b. 11/28/1862, d. 1931. m. 10/9/1881 Belle Wimberly of Macon Ga., dau of Lewis and Julia Wimberly. Belle was b. 3/16/1867, d. 11/13/1961. Children:
   - (1) Grace Ragan, m. Stephen Pace of Americus. They have Stephen and Mary Pace.
   - (2) Estelle Ragan. Unmarried.
   - (3) Elsie Ragan. Unmarried.
6. Alexander Ragan Jr., b. 11/10/1864, d. 1914, m. Nannie Lowery of Eastman, Ga. Children: Robert, Willie, Herman, Chester and Ruth Ragan.
7. Sophia Eudora Ragan, b. 11/1/1866, d. 4/20/1921, m. C. C. Atkinson (b. 1/3/1862, d. 12/14/1945) on 7/20/1889. Children: Leonard, Christopher, Arthur, Myrtle, Cecil, Eudora Atkinson.
8. Daniel Lamar Ragan, b. 4/20/1869, d. 4/6/1925, m. Ida Anderson. They had Marian, Pearl and Ruth Ragan.
9. Needham Rufus Ragan, b. 4/11/1871, d. 11/1/1948. m. Mina Lee Lancaster (b. 1/14/1870) on 12/23/1894. No issue.
10. William Pester Ragan, b. 8/2/1874, d. 1912. m. Grace Warren of Abbeville, Ga. They had Grace Ragan.

After the death of his first wife, Robert Alexander Ragan m. Frances Dunn in 1890. They had three children:

Joseph, John, and Curtis. The Ragan section of the Hawkinsville cemetery is the final resting place of many of these early Georgia Ragans. (Ref: Tombstone records, and Bible records in the possession of Miss Estelle Ragan.) Robert Timothy Ragan was b. in Hawkinsville. He m. Susan Underwood Spence of Camilla, Ga. 10/5/1881. (See Spence later.) He d. 1890 at the height of his business career, and Ragan and Company was taken over by his brother Thomas. Susan Spence Ragan d. in Camilla in 1910. Children:
1. Elizabeth Hilliard Ragan, b. 12/6/1886, m. Lawrence Washington Murphy, b. 1882, d. 1953, of Magnolia, Ark. She was a writer, and her husband taught at Georgia Technical School, and later at the Hotchkiss School, Lakeville, Conn. He was one of the country's foremost educators. Mrs. Murphy lives in Atlanta, Ga.
2. Roberta M. Ragan, m. Cleve Evins, a member of an old Atlanta family. Their dau. Harriet m. ____ Sinclair. Thier child: Susan Sinclair.
3. Alexander Timothy Ragan, b. 10/6/1890 in Hawkinsville, a few weeks after his father's death. He attended Locus Grove Institute and Mercer University. He was associated with the Pullman Company, and d. 1957. He m. 3/11/1920 in Blakely, Ga., Ela Lucille Timmons, b. 8/12/1897 in Early Co. (See Timmons lineage.) Children:
    (1) Alexander Timothy Ragan Jr., b. 12/8/1920 at Savannah, Ga. Graduated from Hotchkiss School, Lakeville, Conn., and from Ga. Technical School. m. Lucille Franklin. Living (1966) in Victoria, Texas. Children: Alexander, Sherry and Sandra Ragan.
    (2) Ethel Lucille Ragan, b. 10/22/1926 at Lakeland, Fla. Attended Agnes Scott College; m. 9/13/1947 Louis Millard Wood. Reside (1966) in East Point, Ga. Children: Millard, Susan, Christopher and Nancy Wood.
    (3) Seaborn Bryant Timmons Ragan, b. 4/28/1929 in Augusta, Ga. Graduated from Salisbury School, Salisbury, Conn; attended Emory University, University of Ga., and Ga. State College. Resides

(1966) in Macon, Ga. m. 9/5/1958 Sandra Glyn Farris of Atlanta. She attended University of Tenn. and Ga. State College. Children: S. Bryant T. Ragan Jr., b. 2/16/1960 in Atlanta, and Sandra Leigh Ragan, b. 10/14/1964 in Jacksonville, Fla.

SPENCE

The Spence line is one of the oldest in the country. William Spence arrived in James Citte, Va., in 1619. His nephew, Robert Spence, settled in New Kent County, Va., in 1654 and m. Mary Blank. Their son, William Spence, m. Mary Green. William and Mary Green Spence had a son James, b. 1748 in Augusta Co., Va. James Spence m. Jane Bluford, b. 1751, d. 1795; he served in the Revolution. (DAR "History of Stewart Co., Ga."; "Va. State Library Report", Vol. Vlll, p. 412; "Abstracts of Augusta Co., Va.," Vol. 1, pp 388-404; Spence family Bible.)

The children of James and Jane Bluford Spence were: William Spence, b. 1772, m. Mary Anderson; James Spence Jr., b. 1776, m. _____ Palmer; Bluford Thorpe Spence, b. 1774.

Bluford Thorpe Spence m. 1795 Charity Smith, in Burke Co., Ga., relocated Emanuel Co., Ga. Charity was an orphan who had been reared by William Hinds of Burke or Emanuel Co. Children: Joseph, Greene, Leaston (who m. Elizabeth Costow), and Bluford Thorpe Spence Jr.

Bluford Thorpe Spence Jr., b. 1801 in Emanuel Co., m. (1) Polly Faun. Child:
1. Susan Spence, m. 1838 James Adams.

Bluford Thorpe Spence Jr. m. (2) in 1822 Elizabeth Fitzgerald (see Fitzgerald lineage). Children:
2. Joe T. Spence, m. his cousin Jane Hilliard. (see Hilliard later)
3. Sarah Spence m. J.A. Collins.
4. Mary Spence m. _____ Walker.
5. Ann Spence, m. _____ Metcalf.
6. Greene Spence, m. his cousin Mary Hilliard.
7. Martha Spence, m. _____ Thompson.

8. William Spence.
William Spence, b. 11/29/1823 in Stewart Co., Ga.,
d. 2/28/1885 in Hawkinsville; m. Susan Hilliard in 1846.
She was b. 1830 in Stewart Co. and d. June 1863. They
had ten children.

HILLIARD

Four Hilliard brothers came to Georgia from Cumberland Co., N.C. in the early part of the nineteenth century.
They were:
1. Henry Hilliard. His son was
   James Hilliard, who served in the Ga. Senate 1861-63.
   He m. (1) Irene Middleton (b. 12/8/1804, d. 8/15/1852)
   on 3/23/1823. She was the dau of Samuel Middleton
   (1778-1855) and his wife Elizabeth Dow Middleton (1782-1825). Parents of Samuel Middleton were Charles
   Middleton (b. 1750 Westmoreland Co., Va., d. 1780
   Dooley Co., Ga.,) and Margaret Middleton.
   Children of James and Irene Middleton Hilliard:
   i. Andrew J.B. Hilliard, m. Laura Fitzgerald.
   ii. James K. Hilliard, b. 1825, m. and had Helen,
       Susan, and Henry Hilliard. (1850 Census, Appling
       Co., Ga.)
   iii. Jane Hilliard, m. Joe Spence, son of Bluford
        Spence, Jr.
   iv. Susan Hilliard, m. William Spence, brother of
       Joe Spence.
   James Hilliard m. (2) in 1852 Elizabeth Fitzgerald
   Spence, widow of Bluford Thorpe Spence, Jr. He m.
   (3) Clara Clark of Florida.
2. Frank Hilliard, of whom nothing is known.
3. Kinchen Hilliard, m. Mary Broach; two daus: Anne
   and Laura Hilliard.
4. Major Hilliard, m. _____ Hayes. Children:
   i. Martin Hilliard, m. Nancy Daniel.
   ii. Celia Hilliard, m. James Powell.
   iii. Tempe Hilliard, m. Alan Calhoun.
   iv. William Hilliard, m. Polly Daniel (b. 1790, d.
       1864). 13 children.
       Elizabeth Hilliard, dau. of William and Polly
       Hilliard, m. James Spence, who d. 1847. He was

the son of James Spence (b. 1776) who was the brother of Bluford Thorpe Spence. Elizabeth and James Spence left a son, Hiram Warner Spence, b. Stewart Co. 12/30/1836. This child was reared, after the deaths of his parents, by his aunt and uncle, Nancy and James Fitzgerald. Hiram m. Susan Jane Clyatt, and removed to Mitchell Co., where they raised a large family.

TIMMONS & SHEFFIELD

Levi Timmons Sr. appears in the 1790 census of George town District, Prince Frederick Province, S.C. He had two sons; Levi Timmons Jr., b. 1800, and J.M. Timmons, b. 1801. Levi m. Martha _____, of Emanuel Co., Ga. Nothing is known of her except that she was born 1807, and was living in 1850 after the death of Levi Jr., between 1847 and 1850. She was then one of the largest landowners in South Georgia, owning acreage in Baker, Early, and Calhoun Counties. Levi Jr. drew land in his father's name in District 4, Capt. Johnson unit, Pulaski Co., in the 1820's. Further information is being sought. (Ref: 1850 Census, Baker Co., Ga., and Bible and cemetery records.)

John Aubrey Timmons, son of Martha and Levi Timmons, was b. in Baker Co., 9/30/1830, and d. 5/1/1888. He m. Prussia Sheffield (b. 3/28/1831, d. 6/18/1922) dau of Bryan Sheffield (1781-1847) and his wife Nancy Paine Sheffield (1794-1858). (Ref: W. Bk. A, Early Co. Wills, Blakely, Ga.) Bryan and Nancy Paine Sheffield were married 10/5/1820 in Early Co. Nancy was orphaned by the deaths of her parents, who were on their way to Georgia in a different wagon train from the one which was bringing Nancy. The train of her parents was wiped out in an Indian raid. She then became the ward of Richard Grimsley of Early Co. Bryan Sheffield was either a son or grandson of John Sheffield (Shuffield) who died in Duplin Co., N.C., 1791. (Ref: Olds' Abstracts of Wills in Duplin Co., N.C., p. 103.) Bryan and Nancy Sheffield are buried in the Timmons-Mayes cemetery in Arlington, Ga. Children:
1. Seaborn Sheffield, 1821-1886.

2. Russia Sheffield, 1829-1891, m. Wm. Sasser (1824-1874).
3. Prussia Sheffield, b. 3/28/1831. m. John Aubrey Timmons. He acquired large land holdings in Early and Calhoun Counties, and his wife Prussia also inherited many hundreds of acres of adjoining land. (Ref: Early Co. D. Bks.) Children: (Bible records)
   (1) Martha Timmons, (1844-1866).
   (2) Seaborn Bryant Timmons, b. 6/11/1852, d. 12/7/1919 (see later).
   (3) Delilah Timmons, d. 1957, m. Jimmy Johnson (1859-1937) of Emanuel Co. (Ref: "History of Bethel Association.")
Bryan and Nancy Sheffield had twelve other children, of whom little is known.
Seaborn Bryant Timmons and his brother-in-law Jimmy Johnson purchased an additional 2240 acres of land in Early Co. and built their homes amid the large plantations. (D. Bk., Early Co., Ga.) Seaborn deeded land for a cemetery which is now known as the Timmons-Mayes cemetery near Arlington. He likewise gave land for Timmons church. Many of the family now lie in this cemetery, and outside the fence lie former slaves and present-day negro neighbours. From the vast plantations of the past, the only land left with the Timmons name is the cemetery and the church.
Seaborn Timmons m. 1875 Frances Eudora Johnson (b. 3/12/1857, d. 12/11/1927) dau of Thomas Johnson of Bluffton, Ga., and his wife Mahala Singleton Johnson. (see Singleton lineage). Children:
(a) Julius Edgar Timmons, b. 8/19/1876, d. 12/20/1955, m. Nebraska Brown. Children: Doyle and Murris Timmons.
(b) John Aubrey Timmons, b. 1878, m. Clara Pierce, who lived in Bainbridge, Ga. Children: Thelma, Christine, Harris, Lee, and Mary Timmons.
(c) Joseph P. Timmons, b. 1880, d. 1927, m. Lovie Sheffield. Children: Laura, Lucille, and Clyde Timmons.
(d) Ethel Mae Timmons, b. 4/21/1882, d. 2/7/1950, m. Robert Thompson. Children: Eunice and Roy Thompson.

(e) Mamie Timmons, b. 1884, m. _____ Sasser of Arlington. Children: Dora, Frances, George, Weldon, Felix and Inez Sasser.
(f) Annie Pearl Timmons, b. 1886, d. 1964, m. J. B. Johnson. Children: Evelyn, Hazel, Gladys, Faye, J. B. Jr., and Gloria Johnson.
(g) Dr. Carl C. Timmons, b. 11/15/1889, d. 1955, m. Catherine Corley, a descendant of one of the pioneer families of Edgefield, S.C. Children: Carl Jr., and Miriam Timmons.
(h) Thomas George Timmons, b. 1893, d. 1934, m. Julia deSmith. Children: Margaret, Mildred, and Helen Timmons.
(i) Ela Lucille Timmons, b. 8/12/1897 at Arlington, m. Alexander Timothy Ragan. Of the large Timmons clan, only Mrs. Ragan survives. She lives (1966) at East Point, Ga.
(j) Vera Eudora Timmons, b. 12/28/1898, m. Tom Pickron. Children: Ruth and Ruby Pickron.

J. B. Timmons, second son of Levi Timmons Sr., b. 1801, m. Elizabeth _____, b. 1809. He appears in the 1850 Census of Darlington Co., S.C., with nine children.

SINGLETON

Of this line, the two oldest known members were the brothers William and Richard Singleton. Richard's daughter Angelica became the daughter-in-law of President Van Buren, and acted as his hostess.

William Singleton m. Pamela Parsons of Charleston, S.C. He served as colonel in the N.C. Line during the Revolution. Their children included James, b. 9/2/1767, who m. on 5/29/1793 Margaret Northcutt (b. 11/23/1768) whom one source shows ".... of English nobility." (Ref: Singleton family records.) Their children: William (see later); Mary, b. 2/5/1797; John, b. 1/23/1800; James, b. 2/17/1802; Elizabeth, b. 1/16/1803; Daniel, b. 3/12/1805 (m. Charlotte Patrick); Solomon, b. 8/6/1807; Margaret, b. 5/8/1809.

William Northcutt Singleton was b. in N.C. 7/20/1795 and came to Macon Co., Ga., in 1831. He is mentioned

in many land transactions recorded in Clay Co. Courthouse. He d. in Early Co. 9/27/1866. He m. 11/22/1822 Mary Patrick, sister of Daniel's wife Charlotte. Mary was b. in S.C. 9/25/1808 and d. in Bluffton, Ga., 11/11/1890. (see Patrick lineage). Children of William and Mary Singleton:
1. Harriet Singleton, b. 10/23/1823, m. Robert Thompson.
2. Catherine Singleton, b. 7/31/1825, m. William Sheffield.
3. Franklin Singleton, b. 7/10/1827, m. Mildred Greer.
4. Mary Ann Singleton, b. 1/21/1829, m. Philip Tinsley.
5. Mahala Singleton, b. 9/27/1830, m. Thomas J. Johnson. Their dau Frances m. S.B. Timmons.
6. Eliza Singleton, b. 3/14/1832, m. J.S. Garrett.
7. Ellen Singleton, b. 10/10/1833, m. (1) Wm. Lindsay (2) L.L. Monk.
8. Martha Singleton, b. 12/9/1835, d. in childhood.
9. George Singleton, b. 8/8/1838, m. Zilpha Hammack.
10, 11. Louise and Martha, twins, b. 1841, d. in childhood.
12. Patrick H. Singleton, b. 4/28/1843 in Arlington, Ga., d. 1924 in Edison, Ga. He m. 1/9/1866 Mary Ann Hammack (1847-1905) at Coleman, Ga. Children:
   (1) Lena Singleton (1866-1931) m. W.F. Davis. Children: Felix, Fanny, Amis, Daniel and Joshua Davis.
   (2) William H. Singleton, m. Fannie Smith.
   (3) Rillie K. Singleton, b. 1870. m. (1) Bennie Mills. Children: John and Bennie Mills. She m. (2) Robert Bryant. Children: Milton and Robert Bryant.
   (4) Mary M. Singleton, b. 1873, m. 1900 E.B. Hudspeth. Their son John Hudspeth, b. 1903.
   (5) George Harbin Singleton, b. 1874, m. Mary Allen. Children: George Jr., Anna, and Zemma Singleton.
   (6) Lula Graves Singleton, b. 1877, m. J.A. Poindexter. Children: Jennie Poindexter, b. 1905, m. Edwin A. Richardson; Allene Poindexter, b. 1908, Mary Poindexter, b. 1911.
   (7) Frank P. Singleton, b. 1879, m. Pope Thurman.
   (8) Winnie Singleton, b. 1882, m. R.L. Jenkins.
   (9) Henry Singleton, b. 1885, m. Mary Pearce.

(10) Gordon G. Singleton, b. 1890, m. Hallie Jenkins. In 1965 he was named Elder Statesman of the Year by the Texas Baptist Convention. He was formerly Porfessor of History at Baylor University.

FITZGERALD

James Fitzgerald was born in County Kildare, Ireland, 1740. He m. Christian Fields there in 1763, and they left for America and landed at Yamacrow, near Savannah, Ga., in 1765. Children:
1. Edward Fitzgerald, who died at sea on the way to America.
2. Mary Fitzgerald, b. 1767, m. James Stewart.
3. James Fitzgerald Jr., b. Burke Co., Ga., 2/12/1769, d. Emanuel Co. 2/18/1818; m. Mary Fenn, b. 4/22/1780, of Montgomery Co. Children:
    (1) Christian Fitzgerald, d. in infancy.
    (2) John Fitzgerald, b. 4/28/1802.
    (3) Mary Fitzgerald, b. 4/23/1805, m. Wiley Bullard in 1840, who had been m. previously to Mary Talbot of Pulaski Co. Children: Marthenie, Allen, Cassius, Wiley Jr., Polly, Georgia, and Laura Bullard.
4. James Fitzgerald 3rd., b. 3/10/1808 in Emanuel Co., d. 2/7/1880. He m. Nancy Hilliard in 1831. Eleven children.
5. David Fitzgerald, m. in 1793 in Burke Co., Ga., Sarah Spivey, b. 1773 in Burke Co. They had seven children including Elizabeth, b. 1802, who m. (1) Bluford Thorpe Spence Jr., (see Spence lineage.) Elizabeth m. (2) James Hilliard, whose wife Irene Middleton Hilliard had died. (Ref: DAR "History of Stewart Co., Ga.;" Personal Papers of Martha Culpepper, Ordinary, Mitchell Co., Ga; Georgia Records, 1850.)

****

Data contributed by: Bryant T. Ragan,
Macon, Georgia.

MATHEWS OF VIRGINIA AND GEORGIA

1. John Mathews emigrated from Ireland to Western Virginia ca. 1737. Mar. and had issue, including
2. George Mathews, who d. in Augusta, Georgia, March 1812. He was a General and twice Governor of Ga. (See later.) He m. (1) Anne Paul, daughter of John and Margaret (Linn) Paul. Children: John, William, George, Charles Lewis, Anne, and Rebekah Mathews. He m. (2) Mrs. Reed of Staunton, from whom he was divorced by the Legislature of Va. He m. (3) Mrs. Flowers of Mississippi, who may have been an aunt of Sarah Carpenter Mathews, and great-aunt of Harriet Carpenter Mathews, wives of Judge George Mathews.
3. George Mathews, third son of George and Anne (Paul) Mathews, was b. in 1774, probably in Va. Died 1836, buried at St. Francisville, La., in Grace Episcopal Church cemetery. He m. (1) Sarah Carpenter, dau. of Dr. Samuel and Mary (Flower) Carpenter, who lived near St. Francisville. One child: Anne Paul Mathews. He m. (2) Harriet Carpenter, niece of his first wife Sarah, who was b. 1799, d. St. Francisville. One child: Charles Lewis Mathews. (See later.)
4. Anne Paul Mathews, dau. of Judge George Mathews and Sarah his wife, b. 1809, d. Oct. 1863, buried in Grace Episcopal Church cemetery. She m. 6/28/1828 in New Orleans, La., Major William Henry Chase, son of Thomas and Sarah (Greenleaf) Chase of Boston, Mass., who was b. 1792, d. 1870, and buried beside his wife. He graduated from the U.S. Military Academy in 1815, and was Superintendent of that institute in 1856. One child of the marriage.
5. Anne Paul Chase, only child of Major William Henry Chase and his wife Anne Paul Mathews, was b. 2/19 1848 at Fort Barancas, Pensacola, Fla., and d. 2/16 1918 in Alexandria, Rapides Parish, La. Buried in Rapides Cemetery, Pineville, La. She m. 4/22/1868 in St. Francisville, her cousin Joel Early Mathews, son of Joel Early Mathews and his wife Ann (Glover) Mathews, b. 10/7/1842 at Cahaba, Dallas Co., Ala., and d. 12/17/1897 in Alexandria, La. Children: Anne

Paul, Ann Glover, Medora, Thomas, and William Chase.

6. Medora Mathews, third dau. of Joel and Ann Mathews, was b. 7/9/1872 in Pensacola, Fla., and d. 3/19/1919. She m. 4/14/1896 Robert Henry Jackson, son of Robert Henry Jackson and his second wife Sarah Maria (Baillio) Jackson, born 7/16/1863 in Cheneyville, Rapides Parish, La., and d. 3/9/1942 at LeCompte, La. Children: Joel Early Mathews Jackson, Elizabeth Carter Marshall Jackson, Robert Davenport Slaughter Jackson, and Anne Paul Chase Jackson.
7. Joel Early Mathews Jackson, eldest child of Robert Henry Jackson and his wife Medora, was b. 1/3/1898 in Cheneyville, La., and d. 1/4/1966 at Lake Charles, La. He m. 3/7/1926 in Alexandria, La., Corinne Kendall, fourth child and second dau. of Dr. William Samuel Kendall and his second wife Mary Burt (Tooke) Kendall, b. 11/25/1901 in Lincoln Parish, La., d. 3/12/1957 in Alexandria; buried with her husband in Trinity Episcopal Church Cemetery, Cheneyville, La. Children: Joel Early Mathews Jackson Jr., and Mary Jeanne Jackson.
8. Mary Jeanne Jackson, dau. of Joel Early Mathews Jackson and his wife Corinne, was b. 12/21/1929 in LeCompte, La., m. 10/8/1949 at Baton Rouge, La., Francis Joseph D'Autremont 3rd., only child of Francis Joseph D'Autremont Jr., and his wife Daisy Ruth (Olsen) D'Autremont, b. 2/20/1926 in Joplin, Mo. Children: (all born LeCompte, La.)
   1. Sarah Baillio D'Autremont, b. 8/15/1950.
   2. Ann Glover D'Autremont, b. 10/23/1951.
   3. Francis Joseph D'Autremont 4th, b. 5/18/1954.

****

Ref: "First Settlers of Upper Georgia", by Dr. George Gilmer; Records taken from Grace Episcopal Church, St. Francisville, La.; personal letters and papers.

GOVERNOR GEORGE MATHEWS, General, son of the immigrant John Mathews, lived with his father in Western Virginia, in the neighborhood of Staunton. The Indians west of the Ohio River were the most warlike of all the tribes, and carried on a predatory campaign against the British from 1754 to 1763. George Mathews became familiar with danger and fighting. Soon after the commencement of the Revolutionary War, he was appointed Lieut. Colonel of the Ninth Regiment of Va. troops, and soon after 1775 was placed with his regiment by Congress on the continental establishment. For nearly two years they were stationed on Chesapeake Bay under the command of Gen. Andrew Lewis. Gen. Washington recognized the worth of Col. Mathews as an officer; he ordered him to join the main army, and Col. Mathews distinguished himself in the Battle of Brandywine. He was wounded and taken prisoner at the Battle of Germantown, and was not exchanged until the end of the war. He was one of the original holders of the Order of Cincinnati.

General Mathews purchased the Goosepond tract of land on Broad River, and removed there with his family in 1784. He was elected Governor of Georgia in 1786, and was the first representative for Ga. in Congress under the present Constitution. He was again Governor of Ga. in 1795. He d. in Augusta, Ga., in March 1812.

CHARLES LEWIS MATHEWS, youngest son of General George Mathews, b. probably in Va., married Lucy Early, sister of Governor Peter Early, and of Eleazer Early. He owned and lived at Goosepond, Ga., until his wife's death, and some years later he removed to Cahaba, Dallas Co., Alabama, where he died in the 1840's. He was one of the richest planters in the South. His son JOEL EARLY MATHEWS, was b. probably in Ga., and d. at Cahaba, Dallas Co., Ala.; he m. Ann Glover of Marengo Co., Ala., and had issue: Joel, Charles, Eli, Wiley, and Medora Mathews. JOEL EARLY MATHEWS, JR., was b. 10/7/1842 in Cahaba, Ala., and d. 12/17/1897 in Alexandria, Rapides Parish, La. He m. 4.22/1868 in St. Francisville, La., his cousin Anne Paul Chase. (See previously).

****

Data contributed by: Mrs. F. J. D'Autremont, Chaseland Plantation, LeCompte, La.

Lineage of Margarett Butler Lawrason,
Cherokee Plantation, St. Francisville, Louisiana.

Tobias Mathews, Archbishop of York, b. 1546. Buried in Wellington Chapel, York Minster, England. His son

Samuel Mathews, Governor of Virginia 1657-1659, m. Elizabeth Taverner. His son

John Mathews. His son

Samuel Mathews, b. ca. 1675. His son

John Mathews, settled near Borden's Grant, 1734, m. Ann Archer. d. 1757. His son

General George Mathews, Governor of Georgia for two terms, one of the original members of the Society of Cincinnati. m. Ann Paul. His son

Judge George Mathews. m. Harriet Flower. His son

Charles Lewis Mathews, m. Penelope Stewart. Their daughter

Harriet Mathews, m. Samuel McCutchon Lawrason. Their daughter

Margarett Butler Lawrason.

****

COX AND HUTCHENS (HUTCHINS) OF VIRGINIA & NORTH CAROLINA

William Cox, b. 1598, d. before 1656, came to America in the "Goodspeed", 1610, and is believed to be the immigrant ancestor in Virginia. Descendants of this family concur in this statement. Mrs. Ella Foy O'Gorman, Washington, D. C., a descendant of Richard Cox through his son Henry, after years of patient investigation, agrees. So also does Judge Edwin P. Cox, of Richmond, Va., a student of the family records, who descends through George Cox, son of John Cox.

WILLIAM COX was granted 100 acres in Elizabeth City County on 9/20/1628. He had a grand of 150 acres in Henrico Co., on the James River, 11/29/1636, two and a half miles above Harroe Addocks, with wife Elizabeth. On 9/1/1642, he bought 250 acres in partnership with Isaac Hutchins, at the mouth of Falling Creek, along the James River. On 8/5/1665 Thomas Cox, son and heir of William Cox, sold half of this 250 acres. Harroe Addocks, or Arrohateck, was five or six miles above Dutch Gap. The grant in 1636 was possibly not far from the mouth of Falling Creek. William Cox was the father of JOHN COX, who was the father of RICHARD COX. John Cox's will, dated 2/10/1691, Henrico Co., named as his heirs his six sons: John, William, Bartholomew, Richard, Henry, George, and wife Mary. One 4/1/1685, John Cox., of Harroe Addocks, had made a deed to his son William. (Ref: "Four Generations of Strangeman Hutchins and his wife Elizabeth Cox", by Mrs. E.C. Crider.)

RICHARD COX, son of John Cox, m. Mary Trent, dau. of Henry Trent and his wife Elizabeth. Elizabeth Trent, b. ca. 1657, was the dau. of Henry and Cisly Sherman. Cisly Sherman was previously married to Isaac Hutchins, whose will made in Henrico Co. 2/23/1656, named as his heirs his minor son Robert Hutchins and his wife Cisly, (Sisely). Henry Trent, in his will made in Henrico Co. 1/8/1700, named as his heirs Alexander Trent, Henry Trent, John Trent, William Trent, Mary Cox, wife of Richard Cox, Rebecca Trent,

Susanna Trent, and his wife Elizabeth.
Richard Cox and his wife Mary (Trent) Cox had a daughter Elizabeth, who m. STRANGEMAN HUTCHINS. Richard made his will in Henrico Co., Va., 7/13/1734, in which he named his heirs, John Cox, Henry Cox, Mary Ford, Elizabeth Hutchins, Richard Cox, Obedience Perkins, Edith Whitloe, a grandson Hickenson Cox, and his wife Mary. (Ref. as above.) A deed made previous to the will shows that he also had a daughter Martha.

WILL OF RICHARD COX: (Henrico Co., Va., Deeds and Wills, #2, part 1, 1725-1737)
In the name of God, Amen. I, Richard Cox Sr., of the Parish and County of Henrico, being sick and weak, but in perfect sense and memory, I thank Almighty God for it, do make this my last Will and Testament in the manner following:

Item: I give and bequeath to my son, John Cox, and his heirs and assigns forever all my outward land it being one hundred and five acres where I now liveth.

Item: I give devise and bequeath to my son Henry Cox all my land lying and being on the Northside of Cornelius Creek containing four hundred acres to the said Henry Cox and his heirs forever, only I give to my loving wife, Mary Cox, one hundred acres of it during her lifetime where the house is.

Item: I give and bequeath to my daughter, Mary, for and to her heirs one Bell Mettle skillet and small iron pot.

Item: I give and bequeath to my daughter Elizabeth Hutchens one (?) cow and all her increase to her and her heirs forever.

Item: I give and bequeath to my grandson Hickenson Cox, one hundred and five acres of land where my son, Richard Cox, now liveth, bynding upon Will Farmer and Michael Turpin lines, to him and said Hickenson and his heirs forever.

Item: I give and bequeath to my son, Richard Cox, one shilling sterling.

Item: I give and bequeath to my daughter, Obedience Perkins, one shilling.

Item: I give and bequeath to my daughter, Edith Whirtler,

my book and spectells.

Item: I give and bequeath unto my loving wife, Mary Cox, all my hogs and sheep and my mare, bridle and saddle, and all the rest of my estate and lastly constitute and appoint my loving wife, Mary Cox, whole and sole Executor of this my last will and testament. Disannulling and making void all other wills hereunto by me made. In witness whereof I have hereunto set my hand and affixed my seal this 13 day of July 1734. I also give to my said wife Mary, my Negro man, Daniel, during her life and then to return to my son, John Cox.

his
RICHARD   X   COX
mark

In the presence of us
Michael Turpin
    ?   Turpin
James Whitler

At a court held for Henrico County on ye third day of February 1735 Mary Cox presented this will upon oath and being proved by the oaths of the other witnesses thereto it was thereupon directed to record.

CHESTER BOWLER COCKE, CC

****

HUTCHINS LINEAGE

The following is taken from Henrico Co., Va., Monthly Meeting Records, 1699-1756, p. 12.
Whereas <u>Nicholas Hutchins</u>, of the County of Henrico, and <u>Mary Watkins</u>, daughter of Henry Watkins, of the same County, have proposed their intentions of marriage before several meetings of the people to scorn called Quakers, which after due inquiry of their clearness, and it appearing that the relations of the said Mary were consenting to their marriage, did give consent that the said parties might accomplish their said intentions.

We, therefore, whose names are underwritten do certify all whom it may concern, that said NICHOLAS HUTCHINS and the said MARY WATKINS did at the meeting house of the aforesaid people in the County aforesaid, the 9th day of the 8th month, 1701, then and there take each other for wife and husband. He, the said NICHOLAS HUTCHINS, taking the said MARY by the hand, and declaring that in the presence of the Lord, and before this congregation, " I take MARY WATKINS to be my lawful wife, promising to be to her a true and loving husband till death." And the said MARY WATKINS then and there declaring "that I take NICHOLAS HUTCHINS to be my husband, promising to be a true and loving wife till death." In confirmation thereof the said NICHOLAS and MARY did set their hands.

                    NICHOLAS HUTCHINS
                    MARY HUTCHINS

Those whose names are hereunto subscribed, being present as witnesses to the ceremony.

Henry Watkins, Jr.	Robert Crews
James Howard	Tarlton Woodson
Edward Mosby	Benja. Woodson
Robert Gate	Edw. Good, Jr.
Wm. Lead	Joseph Woodson, Jr.
Eph. Gartrite	Mary Howard
Saml. Gartrite	Mary Watkins
John Pleasants	Elija Crype
Robert Boyes	Sarah Crype
Thos. Watkins	Jane Pleasants
Wm. Porter, Jr.	Huldah Lea
Joseph Pleasants	Martha Pleasants
Mary Woodson, Sr.	Judith Woodson

Note: Nicholas Hutchins b. ca. 1645 - died 1729-30, Mary Hutchins nee Watkins b. ca 1662 -died after 1736.

Children of Nicholas Hutchins and Mary Watkins Hutchins:
1. Catherine Hutchins, m. James Stanley 3/6/1728.
2. Mary Hutchins. She declared her intention to marry 10/14/1729 Daniel Harris, son of John Harris of

Hanover Co. This announcement stated that Nicholas Hutchins was deceased.
3. STRANGEMAN HUTCHENS. (See later)
4. Martha Hutchins, m. John Stanley, son of Thomas Stanley, as his second wife. (Ref: "Four Generations of Strangeman Hutchins"; Quaker Records.)

STRANGEMAN HUTCHENS, son of Nicholas and Mary Watkins Hutchens (Hutchins), was b. in Va. 1707, and d. in Surry Co. (now Yadkin Co.) North Carolina, 2/10/1792. He probably lived in Henrico Co. until his marriage ca 1731 to Elizabeth Cox, (see previously). Elizabeth was b. 2/25/1713 in Va. and d., according to Thomas W. Barnett, in North Carolina at the age of 103 years. (Also shown in Wade Hinshaw's Quaker Encyclopedia.) Goochland Co. D.Bk. 5, 1745-49, shows deed mady by Strangeman Hutchens and wife Elizabeth dated 8/16/1748.

Some time after his marriage, Strangeman moved up the James River to Goochland Co., along Genito Creek. Here he bought and occasionally sold land. In 1782-85, when preparing to remove to North Carolina, he disposed of land, showing that he owned about 750 acres, of which his son John had an interest in 250 acres. Goochland Co. D.Bk, 3, 1779-84, shows Strangeman Hutchens freed 11 slaves by a deed of Manumission. Strangeman was a prominent member of the Friends Church, and a man of remarkable ability. There was a small Meeting at Genito Creek, but his principal activity was at the great central Meeting at Cedar Creek, in Hanover Co. His name is first found on the Cedar Creek records in 1741; from that time, until 1786 when he removed to N.C., his name appears continually on the records as a witness, on committees, and as representative, overseer, clerk, and elder. (Ref: Quaker Encyclopedia). His will, Surry Co., N.C., W.Bk. 3, p. 5, dated 11/23/1791, probated 1792, names his son JOHN.

Children of Strangeman Hutchens and Elizabeth (Cox) Hutchens:
1. Mary Hutchens, b. 10/17/1733, m. Samuel Robert Brooks 5/8/1762.
2. Edith Hutchens, b. 11/15/1736, m. John Stanley 10/16/1754.

3. John Hutchens, b. 12/23/1738, m. (1) Alice Stanley 12/11/1757
   (2) Jane Braswell 3/26/1792
4. Nicholas Hutchens, b. 1/9/1740, m. (1) Sarah Ladd 7/1/1765
   (2) Lydia Carter 10/20/1809
5. Elizabeth Hutchens, b. 12/13/1742, m. John Barnett 9/12/1767.
6. Obedience Hutchens, b. 12/3/1744, m. William Harding 10/16/1773.
7. Thomas Hutchens, b. 7/20/1746, m. (1) Patty Chiles 3/9/1757
   (2) Susannah Ladd 4/1/1780
8. Jane Hutchens, b. 6/10/1743, m. Arthanacious Barnett 12/12/1767.
9. Milly Hutchens, b. 10/5/1750. Married.
10. Lydia Hutchens, b. 2/15/1752, m. John Johnson 4/15/1770.
11. Benjamin Hutchens, b. 5/8/1756, m. (1) Judith McGehee 1775
    (2) Mary Jenkins 2/9/1815

****

DESCENT OF NELL BOLES, Greensboro, N.C., from Strangeman Hutchens:
John Hutchens b. 12/23/1738, Va., m. (2) Jane Braswell, N.C., 3/26/1792. Chn:
1. John Hutchens, b. ca. 1793, m. Elizabeth McCollum, Surry Co., N.C., 1/21/1814. (Surry Co. W. Bk. 3, p. 162, 9/18/1824, names John.)
2. Jesse Hutchens, m. Lydia Clark, 6/25/1813, Surry Co.
3. Alexander Balis Hutchens, m. Margaret Pruett 10/28/1814.
4. Quintalla Hutchens, m. George Branson 7/1/1815.
5. Elkanah Hutchens, b. 11/20/1803, m. Frances Pilcher 4/10/1822, Surry Co.
6. Ellis Hutchens, b. 1805, m. Mary Shore.

John Hutchens, b. ca. 1793, m. Elizabeth McCollum.
1. Ellis Hutchens, b. 1814, m. (1) Eliza Dixon (2) Sarah Maynard.

2. Alexander Hutchens, b. 1815, m. Catherine Wishon ca. 1837. (Yadkin Co. D. Bk. E, p. 428, dated 9/26/1879, mentions McCollum tract of land from Alexander Hutchens).
Alexander Hutchens, b. 1815, m. Catherine Wishon. Children:
1. Joseph Ellis Hutchens, b. 1838, m. Nancy Shermer 10/2/1858.
2. Barbara Elizabeth Hutchens, b. 11/7/1842, m. John Shermer 9/16/1865.
3. Lucy S. Hutchens, b. 1/13/1844, m. Isaac Atwood.
4. Alexander Hutchens, Jr., b. 6/1/1847, m. Jeanette Baity.
5. Theophilus Hutchens, b. 1/19/1849, m. Eliza Caroline Groce 3/20/1887.
6. Andrew Barton Hutchens, b. 1/28/1853, m. Mollie Whitaker 5/30/1880.
7. Giles Hutchens, b. 1859, m. Nancy Meyers 3/7/1876.

Joseph Ellis Hutchens, b. 1838, m. Nancy Shermer 10/2/1858. Chn:
(1) Wylie Lafayette Hutchens, b. 7/14/1859, m. Rebecca Alice Mitchell.
(2) John Ellis Hutchens, b. 3/25/1862, m. Mary Allgood.

Wylie Lafayette Hutchens, b. 7/14/1859, m. Rebecca A. Mitchell 12/20/1876. Children:
(1) Ulysses Hayes Hutchens, b. 6/15/1878, m. Mary Ann Coley 8/13/1899.
(2) Ellis Garfield Hutchens, b. 12/20/1881, m. (1) Alice Cline 1/16/1901, (2) Stella Clapp 6/27/1909.
(3) Mittie Ella Hutchens, b. 2/3/1888, m. James Nelson Reele 11/24/1905.
(4) Hattie Belle Hutchens, b. 8/8/1883, m. John Columbus Medlin 1/17/1901.
(5) Sarah Hutchens, b. 4/15/1893, m. Charles Fogleman 7/4/1911.
(6) Wylie Lafayette Hutchens, Jr., b. 3/18/1896, d. s. p. 3/25/1914.
(7) Nancy Anne Hutchens, b. 9/11/1899, m. John Arthur Forlines 12/25/1919.

Ellis Garfield Hutchens and his first wife Alice Cline had the following children:

(1) Ella Hutchens, b. 10/18/1901, m. Earl Archie Landon 9/26/1922.
  (2) Desiree Hutchens, b. ca. 1903, d. in infancy.
  (3) Kathleen Hutchens, b. 1/22/1905, m. (1) Henry Pendergraph 7/5/1922 (2) Jack Gonsalves 8/2/1936.
  (4) Nell Hutchens, b. 2/2/1907, m. John Reuben Boles Jr., 6/16/1928. Children:
    (a) John Hutchins Boles, b. 6/14/1929, m. Peggy Tucker 8/8/1959.
    Child:
    (i) John Calvin Boles, b. 4/15/1965.

    Data contributed by: Mrs. J.R. Boles Jr.
    Greensboro, N.C.
    DAR National No. 506956

****

DESCENT OF LOUALLEN FINE FROM STRANGEMAN HUTCHENS:

Strangeman Hutchens, b. 1707 in Va., son of Nicholas and Mary (Watkins) Hutchens, m. ca. 1731 Elizabeth Cox, (see previously). Their son:
John Hutchens, b. 12/23/1738 in Va., m. (1) Alice Stanley 12/11/1757 in Va. (2) Jane Braswell, 2/26/1792 in N.C.
  Children by first marriage: (all b. in Va.)
  1. Nancy Hutchens, m. Anselm George 5/7/1775.
  2. Jonathan Hutchens, b. 2/28/1763, m. _____ 2/21/1783.
  3. Agatha Hutchens, b. 1/21/1764, m. ___ Hudspeth.
  4. Susannah Hutchens, b. 1/15/1769, m. William Bills 5/4/1786, N.C.
  5. Mary Hutchens, b. 1/20/1771, m. Gersham Bills, 9/1/1788.
  6. Elizabeth Hutchens, b. 1/12/1772, m. ___ Cain.
  7. Thomas Hutchens, b. 11/23/1774, m. Rachael Wells 12/18/1795 N.C.
  8. Strangeman Hutchens, b. 9/15/1776, m. Charity

Williams 7/17/1799 N.C.
9. William Hutchens, b. 8/14/1778, m. Elizabeth King 7/11/1799 N.C.
10. Patrick Hutchens, b. 3/10/1781, m. ca. 1800.

Strangeman Hutchens, b. 9/15/1776, Goochland Co., Va., m. Charity Williams. Children: (all b. in Surry Co., N.C.):
1. William Hutchens, m. _____ Gilmore.
2. Polly Hutchens, m. Calvin Kelly.
3. Aquilla Hutchens, b. 12/18/1804, m. Winney Winn.
4. Anderson Hutchens, b. 7/23/1807, m. Jane Winn.
5. Caroline Hutchens, m. James Dodd.
6. Elizabeth Hutchens, b. 10/23/1812, m. William D. Shores.
7. Charity Hutchens, b. 4/12/1815, m. (1) _____ Moore; (2) John Robinson, Nov. 1847; (3) Wm. Woolsey 10/18/1855.
8. Alice Hutchens, m. Henry Heaton.

Aquilla Hutchens, b. 12/18/1804, Surry Co., N.C. m. Winney Winn 1836. Children: (all b. in Ark.)
1. James A. Hutchens, b. 6/1/1837.
2. Anderson Hutchens, b. 12/1/1839, m. Adeline _____.
3. William Miles Hutchens, b. 9/1/1842, m. Adeline Hutchens, widow of his brother Anderson.
4. Dicey Hutchens, b. 4/12/1845.
5. Silvannus Hutchens, b. 4/24/1848.
6. Eliza Jane Hutchens, b. 2/23/1851, m. Zachariah Fine.
7. Aquilla Green Hutchens, b. 4/16/1854, m. Fanny Palmer 11/17/1872.
8. Ambrose W. Hutchens, b. 12/14/1858.
9. Nancy Irene Hutchens, b. 1865.

Eliza Jane Hutchens, b. 2/23/1851, m. Zachariah Fine 5/23/1869. Children: (all born in Washington Co., Ark.):
1. Sarah Elizabeth Fine, b. 4/14/1870, m. James A. Brown 12/26/1886.
2. Child d. in infancy 1873.
3. Millie Winifred Fine, b. 1/8/1875, m. William Patterson 5/8/1894.
4. Belle Fine, b. 6/1/1877, m. Charles W. Black

7/21/1892.
5. Ella Fine, b. 3/4/1880, m. Charles W. Ross, 12/24/1899.
6. Anna Fine, b. 5/7/1883, m. Ebb B. Jett 11/29/1903.
7. Albert Bluford Fine, b. 2/3/1885, m. Mae Ellen Skelton 2/10/1910.
8. Myrtle Daphne Fine, b. 8/11/1889, m. Oral A. Pridemore 7/27/1910.
9. C. Louallen Fine, b. 7/28/1894, m. Emmerrett G. Goff 5/2/1923.

C. Louallen Fine, b. 7/28/1894, m. Emmerrett Goff.
Child:
1. Carmel Eleanor Fine, b. 12/11/1924, in Okla., m. Wm. F. Voscinar 10/11/1947.

****

This descent contributed by: Louallen Fine
Rt. 2, Box 174
Lincoln, Ark.

LAND, ARRINGTON, and BRIDGER
of GEORGIA, NORTH CAROLINA and VIRGINIA
showing DUDLEY descent.

The first known ancestor of this lineage in America was John Land, b. ca. 1760. He lived in either Edgefield or Nash County, N. C. (Nash Co. was separated from Edgefield in 1777). The Land family came originally from Va. John Land m. Elizabeth Fountain in 1781. Their children:
1. Mildred Land, b. 12/27/1781.
2. Thomas Land, b. 3/26/1783.
3. Henry Land, b. 12/25/1784.
4. John Land, b. 12/20/1786. (see later.)
5. Judith Land, b. 10/22/1788.
6. William Land, b. 12/7/1790.
7. James Land, b. 10/14/1792.
8. Nancy Land, b. 10/2/1793.
9. Fountain Land, b. 2/7/1803.
10. Cecelia Land, b. 12/15/1804.

John Land, Jr., b. 12/20/1786 in Nash or Edgefield Co., N. C., d. 1815 in Twiggs Co., Georgia. He removed to Ga. at the age of 19 years, and settled first in Wilkinson Co., later in Twiggs Co. He married 3/24/1806 in Twiggs Co. Delilah Solomon (b. 9/12/1789 in Washington Co., N. C., d. 2/25/1875 in Twiggs Co., Ga.) She married as her second husband Freeman Finch of Twiggs Co.

Children of John Land Jr. and his wife Delilah:
1. Henry Land, b. 4/15/1807, d. 1/16/1859. See later.
2. James Land, b. 11/22/1808.
3. Elisha Land, b. 8/21/1809, d. 5/10/1827.
4. Nathan Land, b. 5/12/1812, d. 8/2/1880.
5. Elizabeth Land, b. 6/10/1813, d. 6/18/1815.

Henry Land was born and died in Twiggs Co. He m. Elizabeth Mary Arrington (b. 3/14/1816, d. 10/20/1846). They had one child, Henry Freeman Land.

Henry Freeman Land was b. 9/27/1846 in Twiggs Co. and d. 2/17/1924 in Vienna, Ga. He m. 6/18/1871 at Cassville, Bartow Co., Ga., Mona (Mourning) Arrington Land, his first cousin (b. 9/18/1846 in Twiggs Co., d. 2/16/1924, Vienna, G.) Both buried Sunnyside Cemetery,

Cordele, Ga. Their children:
1. Judge Max Emmel Land, b. 4/3/1872, Twiggs Co., Ga., d. 4/8/1942 Atlanta Ga. (See later).
2. Grace Neome Land, b. 8/24/1873, d. 2/19/1924, m. ca. 1898 at Rochelle, Ga., Perry Green Busbee, born and died in Vienna, Ga.
3. Paul Clayton Land, b. 1876, d. in infancy.
4. Fort Elmo Land, State Commissioner of Education in Ga., b. 6/3/1878 Twiggs Co., Ga., d. August 1927 Atlanta. m. ca. 1926 at Dawson, Ga., Mrs. Susan Barrow Gurr, who was b. in Madison, Ga., widow of Edward Gurr. She d. 1950. Their son Lt. Col. Fort E. Land Jr. died in action, WW2.
5. Vallie Vale Land, d. in infancy.
6. Carl Gordon Land, b. 5/25/1884, d. in Arizona, ca. 1946. Married.
7. Mona May Land, b. 6/22/1887, m. ca. 1920 in Macon, Ga., Ellison C. Anchors, b. Macon, d. Augusta, Ga. (Refs: Family Bible Records; "Southside Va. Families", Vol. 2, Boddie).

LAND DESCENT THROUGH DUDLEY AND PREWITT (PRUETT)

1. Edward 1st. of England (1239-1307) m. 1254 Eleanor of Castile.
2. Joan Plantagenet, b. Acre 1272, d. 4/23/1307. m. 4/30/1290 Sir Gilbert de Clare, 1243-1299, Earl of Clare, Hereford and Gloucester.
3. Margaret de Clare, b. 1292, d. 4/13/1342. m. (2) 4/28/1317 Hugh de Audley, d. 11/10/1347, Lord Audley, 8th Earl of Gloucester, Ambassador to France 1341.
4. Margaret de Audley, d. 9/7/1349. m. before 7/6/1336 Sir Ralph de Stafford, K.G., d. 8/1/1372, Earl of Stafford, Steward of the Royal Household.
5. Catherine de Stafford, m. as his first wife 1361, John de Sutton, Lord Dudley, son of John de Sutton, Lord Dudley of Dudley Castle, Stafford.
6. Sir John Sutton, 4th Baron Dudley, of Dudley Castle, m. Joan _____.

7. Sir John Sutton, 5th Baron Dudley of Dudley Castle (1370-1407), m. Constance Blout, d. 1412, dau of Sir Walter Blount of Barton.
8. Sir John Sutton, K.G., b. 12/25/1400, (will dated 8/17/1487), Baron Dudley, Lord Lieutenant of Ireland, 1428-30; M.P. 1440-1487; wounded at Bloreheath 1459; m. after 1422 Elizabeth Berkeley, dau of Sir John Berkeley of Beverstone.
9. Sir Edmund Sutton, Lord Dudley, d. after 7/6/1483 but prior to 1487; m. (2) Matilda Clifford, dau of Thomas de Clifford, 8th Lord de Clifford.
10. Thomas Sutton, d. 1530. m. Grace Trekeld, dau of Launcelot Trekeld, Esq., of Yeanwith.
11. Richard Sutton of Yeanwith, assumed the name of Dudley, d. 1/1/1593; m. Dorothy Sanford, dau of Edward Sanford of Ashem.
12. John Dudley of Newcastle-on-Tyne, Northumberland. m. Bridget Carre, dau of William Carre. (Tyler's Quarterly, Vol. XV, p. 176)
13. Sir Robert Dudley, Kt., Collector of the Port of Newcastle, 1603. Mayor of Newcastle, knighted by James 1st; m. Anne Wood, dau of Christopher Wood.
14. Robert Dudley of Bristol; m. a sister of Edward and Robert Green.
15. Edward Dudley of Bristol, England. Emigrated to Virginia and was the progenitor of the Dudley families of Va., North and South Carolina, Ga., and other southern states. He was persuaded to come to Va. in Feb. 1637 by Rev. Thomas Hampton, Rector of Wilmington Parish, Jamestown. He resided first in New Norfolk, Va., later in York Co., where he purchased land 2/6/1661. He m. Elizabeth Pritchard of Bristol, England, dau of Robert Pritchard and Hester his wife.
16. Col. Richard Dudley, b. 1623 in Bristol, England, d. ca. 1687 in Gloucester Co., Va.; m. Mary Seawell (Sewell) in 1645, dau of Henry Seawell (Sewell) and his wife Lady Jane (Lowe) Seawell. Henry Seawell was Secretary to Lord Baltimore. Col. Dudley was summoned to the Orphan's Court, York Co., 1646 and was granted more than 1,000 acres of land in Gloucester Co. He was High Sheriff of Gloucester Co. 1675, patented land on Mobjock Bay 1659; was vestry-

man of Kingston Parish 1667-1677. Col. of Militia 1679.
17. Col. Ambrose Dudley, b. 1649 Gloucester Co., Va. He was a member of the Vestry of Kingston Parish; Justice of Gloucester Co. 1698, ("Va. Mag. of History", Vol. 1.); Burgess of Gloucester Co., and Speaker of the House of Burgesses 1710-1712. ("Colonial Va. Register", by Stanard.)
18. Ambrose Dudley Jr., lived in St. Peter's Parish, New Kent Co., Va., m. Judith Scott, dau of Capt. John Scott.
19. Dorcus Dudley, b. New Kent Co., Va., m. William Rowntree 1st., of New Kent Co. (Vestry Bk. of St. Peter's Parish, New Kent and James Counties states: "Dudley, son of William and Dorcus Dudley Rowntree, b. 1/14/1728, d. 3/2/1728, was baptized.")
20. William Rowntree Jr., m. Elizabeth Turner, dau of James Turner; William Jr. d. 1766. (Will in D. Bk. 9, p. 38, Goochland Co., Va. Many of Goochland Co. records were destroyed by fire.)
21. Capt. Richardson Rowntree, eldest son of William Jr., was b. Goochland Co., Va., ca. 1747, m. Mildred (Mary) Hart, b. 1752, Hopewell, N.J., dau of Hon. John Hart, signer of the Declaration of Independence and Speaker of the House, and his wife Deborah Scudder. Richardson and Mary Rowntree settled in Edgefield Co., S.C. He served in the War of Independence. (S.C. Stub Entries to Indents, Bk. X, part 1, p. 178; Bk. Y - Z, p. 258; also Estate Papers.)
22. Mary Rowntree (Rountree), b. Va. 1772, m. 1790-1791 (census report), Major Elijah Wellborn (Wilbourne), b. Randolph Co., N.C. ca. 1763, son of Thomas Wellborn (Wilbourne) and his wife Esther. Settled in Union District, S.C. after their marriage. Major Wellborn served in the War of 1812 and d., according to his estate papers, Feb. 1819, after which Mary removed to Panola Co., Miss., with her youngest daughter's family, and d. 6/10/1857. (Ref: Estate papers; census records.)
23. Mildred Rowntree Wellborn, b. 2/10/1801, m. 2/15/1818 Alexander Prewitt (Pruett) b. 4/14/1794, Union Co., S.C., son of Obediah Prewitt (Pruett) of Va.

and S.C. and his wife Mary Palmer of Va. Alexander
Prewitt served in the War of 1812, from S.C. He
removed with his family to Newton Co., Ga., ca. 1830.
In his latter years he removed to Ashland, Ala., so
that he with his wife might be near their two sons and
their families. In Ga. he was appointed Commissioner
of Pensions by the Federal Government, and was also
appointed to serve in the same capacity for the State
of Ga. (Ref: Bible Records; War Dept. Records.)
24. Jeffrey Wellborn (Wilbourne) (Prewitt) Pruett, b. 12/
20/1822, Union Co., S.C., d. 9/17/1903 Calhoun Co.,
Ga., m. 1/2/1847 Mary Ann Riley, b. 12/12/1824,
d. 3/28/1862, dau of Abraham Riley and Hannah
Garner of S.C. and Ga. (Mary Ann's grandfather,
Patrick Riley, served in the War of Independence.
After his death, his wife Ann Riley continued to give
service by providing food and other assistance, so
that both their records are documented. Their graves
have been marked by the D.A.R. with their emblem
of service, and a thriving town in Laurens Co., S.C.
now marks the site of their home place.) Jeffrey
Pruett was a schoolmaster, later becoming a land-
owner and planter. His home was the meeting place
for intellectual and religious groups. He served in
the War Between the States. (Ref: Bible records; his
will.)
25. Lucretia Pruett, dau of Jeffrey and Mary Ann Pruett,
b. 1/26/1849, d. 12/24/1929 at Atlanta, Ga., buried
in Bethel Cemetery, Randolph Co., Ga. Graduated
Bethel College, Cuthbert, Ga., m. 12/1/1872 Judge
Columbus Taylor, b. 10/12/1844, Randolph Co., Ga.,
d. 11/1/1912 Cuthbert, Ga., son of William Taylor
of S.C. and Ga., and Matilda Bass, of N.C. and Ga.,
and grandson of Francis Taylor of N.C. and S.C.
Judge Taylor served in the War Between the States;
Representative of his County in the Ga. Legislature;
Clerk of the Court of Randolph Co. for eighteen years;
managed his large landholdings. (Ref: Bible Records;
his will.)
26. Gertrude Taylor, b. 4/24/1878 in Cuthbert, Ga., m.
Judge Max E. Land 8/19/1903. Judge Land was b. 4/
3/1872 in Twiggs Co., Ga., d. 4/7/1942 in Atlanta,

Ga. He was a son of Henry Freeman Land, b. 9/27/1846, Twiggs Co., and his wife Mona Arrington Land, b. 9/18/1846, Cass Co., Ga. (See Land lineage previously.) They were descendants of the Hon. Joseph Bridger of Va. and his wife Hester Pitt. (See Bridger lineage later.) Judge Land served in the Spanish-American War as First Lieut. and as Captain. He later settled in Cordele, Ga., where he was Representative to the Ga. Legislature for Crisp Co. Later became Mayor of Cordele; owner and editor of the "Cordele Dispatch", subsequently Judge of Crisp Co. Court. Solicitor-General of the Judicial Circuit. Appointed by the Governor as one of three members of the Ga. State Industrial Relations Board. Later removed to Atlanta. Mrs. Land, now living (1966) in Dallas, Texas, is a graduate of Andrew College, Cuthbert, and Ga. State College for Women, and took post-graduate work at Chicago University. She is a member of the National Society of Colonial Dames of America, Magna Charta Dames, Descendants of Knights of the Garter, and many other clubs and societies. Children:

27. (a) Gertrude Land, b. in Cordele, Ga., attended Ga. State College for Women, Milledgeville, and Wesleyan College in Macon, Ga., where she specialized in music and literature. She is active in many societies. She m. 5/22/1938 Fletcher Brown Quillian Jr., of Atlanta, a descendant of the Scottish clan of MacQuillians; he attended Emory University, Atlanta, Ga. Executive of the Hartford Fire Insurance Co., Ga. Later removed to Charlotte, N.C. Their son, Fletcher Brown Quillian 3rd., is a graduate of Industrial Engineering, Ga. Technical School, and is associated with Lockheed of Ga. He m. 6/27/1965 Claire Burns, dau of Mr. and Mrs. Dane Burns of Decatur. They reside (1966) in Atlanta.

(b) Maxine Grace Land, graduated in journalism and dramatic art and later became editor of the Druid's Hills section of "Dekalb New Era", Decatur. m. 6/30/1943 Earl Moore Holt of Dallas, graduate of University of Texas. They reside (1966) at Dallas, Texas. Both are active in civic affairs. Earl Holt is descended from Charles Carroll of Carrollton, Signer of the National Declaration of Independence, and from William Carroll Crawford, Signer of the Texas Declaration of Independence.

(c) Taylor Land, graduated from High School, Atlanta, and Emory University. Served in W. W. 2. m. 3/3/1935 Elizabeth Anne Treseder of New York, a graduate of Washington Seminary, Atlanta, and Miss Finch's School, New York. She is descended from the Treseder, Rundell, and Pace families, who have been prominent in the development of America. Their son, William Fort Treseder Land, b. 4/10/1942 in Indianapolis, is a graduate of Indiana University, where he worked on his Ph.D. while serving as assistant professor there; m. 8/12/1960 Joanne Behrens of Indianapolis, dau of Dr. and Mrs. Otto Behrens. They have Patricia and Susan Land. Reside (1966) Indianapolis, Ind.

LAND DESCENT FROM JOSEPH BRIDGER

The Hon. Joseph Bridger was the third son of Samuel Bridger, who died in Gloucester, England, 1650, and his wife Mary Bridger. Samuel owned the Manor of Woodmancote in the Parish of Dursley, where Joseph was born ca. 1628. Mary Bridger was living in 1683 as she is mentioned in the will of her son Joseph dated 10/18/1683. Joseph Bridger came to Virginia prior to 1657, and was a member of the House of Burgesses 1657-58, also in 1663. (Journals of the House of Burgesses, XXIII.) His tombstone in the Old Brick Church, near Smithfield, Isle of Wight Co., Va. gives the date of his death as "April ye 15; A.D. 1686; Aged 58 years." Joseph Bridger m. Hester, dau. of Colonel Robert Pitt, who was also a member of the House of Burgesses and of the Governor's Council. (Ref: "Seventeenth Century Isle of Wight Co.", p. 425 by Boddie.) Their daughter Martha Bridger m. ca. 1679, Thomas Godwin of Nansemond, Speaker of the House of Burgesses. His family may have come from Somerset. (W. & M. Quarterly 13 (2), p. 131.) Their dau. Elizabeth Godwin, b. 1693, d. 2/13/1761 at Halifax, N.C., m. Capt. Barnaby Kearney. Their dau. Elizabeth Kearney, b. 6/17/1724, m. Carter Crafford, who d.

Surry Co., Va., ca. 1782. Their dau. Martha Crafford m. Joseph Arrington, who d. Nash Co., N.C., ca. 1819. Their dau. Martha Arrington, b. 6/9/1792 N.C., d. 4/23/1840 Twiggs Co., Ga., m. Thomas Arrington, b. 1/24/1793 Nash Co., N.C., d. 9/3/1828 Twiggs Co., Ga.; they were married 1/21/1812. Their dau. Elizabeth Mary Arrington, b. 3/14/1816 in Nash Co., d. 10/20/1846 Twiggs Co., Ga., m. 12/18/1834 Henry Land, b. 4/15/1807 Twiggs Co., d. 1/17/1859 Twiggs Co. Their son, Henry Freeman Land, b. 9/27/1846 in Twiggs Co., d. 2/17/1924 at Vienna, Ga. m. 6/8/1871 Mona (Mourning) Arrington Land, his first cousin, b. 9/18/1845 Twiggs Co., d. 2/16/1924 at Vienna, Ga. Their son was Max Emmel Land. (See previously.) (Ref: "Southside Va. Families", Vol. 2, p. 1 - 20, by Boddie. Records of the National Society of Colonial Dames in America.)

****

    Data contributed by: Mrs. Max E. Land
                   6525 Oriolc Drive
                   Dallas, Texas

SOME ACCOUNT OF THE KNIGHT FAMILY OF BYBERRY, PHILADELPHIA COUNTY, PENNSYLVANIA

Written by

ISAAC COMLY, April 24, 1838

In Bailey's etymological dictionary published upwards of a hundred years ago, we are informed that the word Knight is derived from the Saxon word cniht which signifies a servant; and that in ancient times the King's servants or his lifeguards were called Knights. It seems to have been adopted as a title of honor which the King bestowed on such as he chose to single out from the common class of gentlemen. Those characters called Knights make a great figure in the ancient history of England, being remarkable for warlike exercises and daring adventures. Various orders of Knighthood in most of the European nations are enumerated, English, Scotch, French, German, Spanish, Danish, Swedish, and Italian. Those most conspicious in England were the Knights of St. George, commonly called Knights of the most noble order of the Garter.

As a surname, Knight was common in some parts of England near two hundred years ago. In 1663, Sir John Knight was Mayor of Bristol; and a few years after we find another John Knight who was vicar of Banbury. Divers persons of the name of Knight were among the early converts to the principle of truth promulgated by George Fox. In the record of Friends sufferings during the reign of Charles II, we find notices of Thomas Knight of Cirenchester, William Knight of Hampshire, George Knight and Mary Knight of London or Middlesex, Robert Knight of Oxford, and Giles Knight of Chisselborough in Somersetshire. Most of these were apprehended at religious meetings, and for refusing to take the oath of allegiance, were committed to prison. Friends, being subject to great difficulties and embarrassments through the intolerance and persecuting spirit of those times, when William Penn opened a prospect of a peaceful settlement in Pennsylvania, many gladly embraced the opportunity to remove with their families to a country where they might freely enjoy the unmolested exercise of their conscientious sensations.

Giles Knight of Gloucestershire was among the first adventurers who came with William Penn in 1682. His wife was Mary English and at the time of their removal they had one child, Joseph Knight, then aged about two years. Some of their relatives, it is said, were not altogether favorable to their prospect, and urged that at least, Joseph might be left behind, under an apprehension that he would be in danger from bears, wolves, or panthers. Mary Knight was sick on the passage, so that her recovery was doubtful: on their arrival in Delaware, she was carried ashore in a blanket and laid on the river bank: she then observed, she had been fully persuaded during her illness, she should live to see America: her prospect being now realized, she could not tell how it might go with her. She, however, after recovering had twelve children.

It is said that English, the father of Mary Knight, purchased from William Penn about 500 acres of land that was located in Byberry, and that he authorized Giles Knight to settle thereon, with the understanding that if his son Henry English should come hither, the tract was to be equally divided between them. Giles Knight on receiving the property, fixed upon a spot where he formed a cave by the side of an old log near Poquessing Creek, where he dwelt about six weeks. By this time he became acquainted with some of the neighboring Indians who instructed him how to build a wigwam. This seems to have been quite an improvement in his domestic accommodations, and sheltered him and his family from the inclemencies of the weather until he was able to erect a small log house. This building, we are told, stood near the run eastward from where David Comfort now lives. As the family increased, it became necessary to provide more house room and Giles put up a long frame building, one story high, for a dwelling, about the place where Comfort's house now stands. Giles Knight is reported to have been one of the first settler's in Byberry: some accounts say, the Walton's had previously settled further down the

Poquessing but this is doubtful. Giles had a neighbor
Josiah Ellis who settled on land adjoining southwestward.
Ellis first had his habitation on the lowlands of Poquessing
below the present Knight's mill; but being annoyed by the
freshets he moved his quarters to more rising ground,
to what is called Gingerbread or Gingerbaker field. He
died there and was buried in his garden. His widow was
buried there also. Old Jacob Walton told me he remembered seeing holes in the ground near Poquessing that
Ellis had dug for wolf traps; and that formerly there was
a large pine tree growing near the place where he and
his wife were buried. Josiah Ellis was not a Friend by
profession; but he and Giles Knight are reported to have
lived in great harmony and mutual good will and associated together in the true spirit of excellent neighbors. Provisions were very scarce at first, and once they went
five miles to an Indian settlement for half a bushel of
peas: another time they both set out to seek for game, and
fortunately surprised a deer, who in his haste for escape
became entangled in the branches of a fallen tree, where
they dispatched him with clubs. The Indians instructed
them how to raise pumpkins; about the time they were
ripening, Giles Knight procured some fresh fish from
the river, and invited Ellis to dine with him on fish and
pumpkins. While partaking of their repast, the discourse
turned upon the wheat bread and roast beef of old England,
and a query presented whether such fare would ever come
within their reach again. Joseph Knight was then a very
little boy; he had no recollection of the bread and beef
they alluded to but he though to himself, whatever they
might be, fish and pumpkins were good enough for him.
In relating the circumstance, when quite an old man,
he observed that in process of time his father had those
articles of provision in great plenty. The first season
these new settlers raised a small quantity of Indian corn,
and while it was in the milky state, there came a storm
which they apprehended would ruin it; so they husked and
gathered it as fast as they could and most of it was rendered useless. Those little incidents serve to show some
of the difficulties and privations of the original settlers.
But we are told that their circumstances soon began to
wear a better aspect and gradually improved, till some

of them are represented to have had plenty of everything necessary. Giles Knight carried on the family business successfully, and also kept a store for the sale of groceries and other goods. Three of his children died in their infancy, two of them were buried on his ground near where Knight's mill dam now is, and the other one was the first that was interred in the burial grounds belonging to Byberry Meeting. For several years, friends were preserved in much harmony at Byberry; they had meetings mostly at John Hart's house but sometimes at Giles Knight's house and also at Henry English's and it is said a small meeting house was built on John Hart's land near the Red Lion. In 1692, the dissensions raised by George Keith were introduced among them principally by John Hart, their preacher, taking a warm part with Keith which resulted in a division so that each party held meetings separate from the other. Giles Knight was a prominent character among those who adhered to the principles and doctrines of Friends in opposition to the Kethians. They abandoned their former meeting place and held their religious assemblies at Henry English's house. In 1694, English gave one acre of ground for the Meeting's use. A meeting house was soon after built on it and the Byberry Meeting became settled. We are told the Keithian Meeting in the south end of Byberry was of but a few years continuance probably not more than two or three. They evidently abandoned that bond of union which is inseparable from a devout adherance to the fundamental principles of the Christian Religion as professed and practiced originally by the society of Friends, they fell into disputes concerning baptism and other outward ceremonies and the lateral acceptation of the Holy Scripture and finally dispered: some to the Baptists, some to the Episcopalians, and some to nothing at all.

 Among those who sustained the principles of Friends and the meeting at Byberry, we find Giles Knight, John Gilbert, John Carver, Daniel Walton, William Walton, Thomas Walton, William Hibbs, Thomas Knight, Thomas Groom, Henry English, and John Brock. These with their wives and children assembled twice in the week, to manifest their devotion and gratitude to a bountiful providence for the favors which they were daily receiving, and it is probable many an acceptable aspiration was breathed to the Father of mercies for preservation in the harmony and happiness of the unchangeable truth.

In 1717, Giles Knight went to England. The following is a copy of the certificate furnished him on that occasion:

"To our well beloved friends and Brethern in the truth at Nailswarte in Gloucestershire, or elsewhere, we send greeting.

Signifieing that our Ancient friend Giles Knight having some occasion to see his native country, and his outward business requiring his personal appearance, doth induce him as well as affection, to undertake his voyage to see his old friends. Now having made application to our Monthly Meeting in order to have a certificate and persons appointed to make inquiry how he leaves his family. And with all if the ship could not stay until our next Monthly Meeting he might have a certificate signed by the particular meeting where he belongs, to witt Byberry.

There may certify that enquiry being made and no objection found, we recommend him, as an Elder, and one well esteemed by us for many years having left his family with a great deal of love; he has had the great comfort of sober and well inclined children, and the Lord has blest him with outward substance which we hope may be well disposed of to his hopeful offspring. We heartily wish the Lord may spare his life to see his friends and family again, having left us in unity and love. We wish and pray for his preservation in the truth with all the faithful through out the world. We salute you and bid you farewell in the Lord Jesus Christ. Signed at Biberry, 7 month, 8th, 1717, by order of the Abington Meeting."

William Walton, Thomas Walton, Thomas Knight, Henry English, George James, Gocrard Bolton, Alexander Mode, Thomas Martin, James Cooper, Henry Cornly, James Duncan, John Carver, James Carver, Edmond Dunkan, John Brock, Joseph Gilbert, Thomas Knight, Daniel Knight, Jonathan Knight.

Thomas Knight, whose signature is third in this list, is understood to have been a half brother of Giles Knight and the three last appear to have been Giles' sons: his eldest son Joseph probably resided at that time in New Jersey. In the records of Byberry preparative meeting in 1721, mention is made of Thomas Knight, Junior and Thomas Knight son of Giles Knight. I believe none of the descendants of Thomas Knight, Junior or Senior remain in the neighborhood of Byberry, some of them removed to New Jersey and others in Buckingham many years ago.

Giles Knight died the 20th of the 8th month, 1726, in the 73rd year of his age. Mary, his wife died 24th of 7th month, 1732, in her 77th year. Her son, Thomas Knight then resided in New Jersey on a place belonging to Litar Leeds, the almanac Maker, and had just returned from a voyage with Thomas Chalkly to Barbadoes, and being informed of the illness of his mother, he concluded to go to see her the next day. In the night his mind became impressed with the persuasion that he must go as soon as he could or it would be too late, in accordance with which he set out as soon as he could, and on his arrival, he found his mother sitting in a chair: she directed her grand-daughters who waited on her to prepare breakfast for him and before he had finished eating she died. Giles and Mary Knight left several daughters but no particular account of them has come to my knowledge. They probably married and settled in other neighborhoods. Some account of their four sons, Joseph, Thomas, Daniel, and Jonathan as follows:

Joseph Knight appears to have been an honest, well-meaning man, not remarkable for brilliant talents, but habitually industrious, and always careful to suffer nothing that was valuable to be wasted or lost. At the age of 37 he married Abigail Antill who came from England about three years before. Her sentiments of economy appear to have coincided with those of her husband. The objects of their solicitude were the necessaries of life, the guarded and prudent education of their children and the fulfillment of their own social and religious duties. When I fancy to myself the figure of the old man with a coat upon his back that was darned all over with threads of different colors so that the original texture was scarcely discernible or see him trudging to market with his wallet on his shoulder and his shoes in his hand, or notice his tending the meeting house for 20 and 25 shillings a a year and the old woman making one candle serve her a whole winter, eating roasted apples and soaking crusts of bread in the creek to favor their decayed teeth, in the decline of life - what a contrast is presented to the modern style of living and what an evidence of the authenticity of the report that although Joseph Knight did not know as well as some people how to make money, he had learned to perfection the art of keeping it. He first settled in Jersey but returned to Byberry about the year 1728. The remainder of his time he dwelt on his farm, the same one that is now owned by his great grandson, James Thornton. He died there in 1762, aged 82 and Abigail his wife in 1764 at about the same age.

Thomas Knight married Sarah Clifton and it is said had only one child which died in infancy. He had no learning and could neither read nor write, yet, by the prudent exercise of a vigorous mind, he conducted his temporal business successfully. We find him at one time an overseer at Byberry Meeting; but apprehend he was not remarkable for his religious sensibility, as it is reported he declared in an argument on the Conestoga massacre that it is nonsense to talk of such creatures as the Indians having a future being. He was careful to encourage industry both by his own example and by precept and to maintain the necessity and expediency of a strict observance of moral obligations --- as he had no children of his own upon whom he might direct the exercise of his affectionate solicitude --- his benevolent feelings appear to have been occasionally extended to such young people as he considered meritorious; and he directed his estate to be divided equally among his relations. He died in 1774 in the 89th year of his age. Some years previous to his decease he was desirous to be buried on his own farm, but afterwards disposing of his real estate, he was interred in the usual burial ground at Byberry.

Daniel Knight married Elizabeth Walker in 1719. In 1728, he married a second wife, Esther Walton, and in advanced life he had as his third wife, Mary Wilson. He is reported to have been a man of good understanding and sound judgment and was many years one of the meeting committee for the superintendence of funerals, and sometimes was placed on other appointments. He died in 1782, age 85 years.

Jonathan Knight is supposed to have been the youngest of the three brothers. It is believed he settled where Ebenezer Knight now lives. He died the first of the fifth month, 1745, and his wife Jane the seventh of the same month, both with the flu. In the burying ground at Byberry, is a small gravestone, marked J.K. 1745, said to be for Jane Knight.

Of the succeeding or third generation of the Knight family of Byberry, a few notices may suffice.

Giles Knight, son of Joseph, married at the age of eighteen years and three months. Notwithstanding the commercial system of his parents, he appeared to have had a good chance of school learning and possessing a strong and vigorous mind, he carried on his business with energy and being in comfortable circumstances his attention was directed to measures of a political character and the promotion of public good. His upright standing, known integrity and sound judgment naturally brought him into the notice of his fellow citizens as a man qualified for public service and he was elected for several years successively a member of the General Assembly of Pennsylvania. He was afterwards commissioner of the county of Bucks. In 1766, while in the Assembly in Philadelphia, his wife died very suddenly: the same night he dreamed three times he had lost the mainspring of his watch, and when a messenger came to inform him of the circumstance, he observed his dreams were realized. His wife is said to have had a presentiment of her decease by an extraordinary sermon delivered at Byberry meeting a short time before by Isaac Child.

Giles Knight married a second wife much younger than himself. By his two wives he had sixteen children. I retain in my mind's eye, a view of the venerable patriarch in full dress of velvet and broadcloth with buckles and buttons of silver, a full-bottomed wig and first rate beaver hat turned up behind and on each side, before all of which seemed to belong to a class that did not mix with ordinary characters. And together with a commanding countenance, and dignity of manners and deportment induced an apprehension and belief that Giles Knight was one of the great men of his day and generation. He died

in 1799 at eighty years of age.
William Knight, son of Daniel, died in 1782, age 53 years. His general characteristics were not beyond mediocrity and had it not been for several striking incidents which occurred when in a state of mental derangement in the latter part of his time, he would have passed this life unheeded and his name by this time would have been nearly lost in oblivion. It was an age when the marvelous had more credit than it has in this generation; but the facts were reported and believed that William Knight during this mental aberation, uttered predictions which were afterwards strikingly fulfilled, so that many people believed that notwithstanding he was insane, he had some uncommon knowledge of future events, in one instance, he mentioned the death of his sister which happened nearly fifteen miles distant, nearly at the time it occurred. His prophecies related to the burning of his father's house and barn, and the derangement of his brothers and sisters. The latter was not, however, realized. William, in his first days was not considered a very religious man but went to meetings on first days and when matters of importance as he conceived, were the subject of his consideration, he endeavored to weigh them well. It is reproted that he walked to and fro all one night in his father's barn, pondering a matrimonial concern which eventually settled in a satisfactory result.

Mary Knight, daughter of Jonathan, died in 1759, aged 25 years. In an attempt to delineate her character written in verse by one of her contemporaries, she is described as one who loved the truth --- that she was of a sweet temper, always mild, meek, and modest; plain and neat in her apparel, prudent in her conduct, and that she was held in high esteem among her neighbors, and friends.

Jonathan Knight, the second, was a man of pleasant and agreeable manners, graceful in his movements, nice in his personal appearance --- fine sense combined with ease and polish and a social liberality, made him generally esteemed, beloved, and respected. He was frequently called Gentleman Jonathan to distinguish him from another of that name. He was several years Clerk of Byberry Meeting and took a lively interest in support of schools and other subjects of benefit to the meeting and township.

Thomas, his brother was also a very worthy man and was much respected for the regularity of his life and the consistency of his conduct and filled the stations of overseer and elder of Byberry Meeting to the satisfaction of his friends. The Knights at Byberry have been in comfortable circumstances as to property, with scarcely a single exception and in a general way have supported a respectability of character for moral rectitude.

****

GENEALOGY

Giles Knight, born about 1653--------died 1726, age 73
Mary, his wife, born about 1655----- died 1732, age 77
           Their Children
Joseph, born 1680, married Abigail
    Antil ------------------------- died 1762, age 82
Thomas, born 1685, married Sarah
    Clifton ------------------------died 1774, age 89
Daniel, born 1697, married
       (1) Elizabeth Walker
   m. (2) Esther Walton
   m. (3) Mary Wilson ----- he died 1782, age 85
Jonathan, married Jane Allen -------died 1745, age 45
Anne, married Atkins --------------died 1754
          Children of Joseph and Abigail
Giles, born 1719, married Eliza James
      m. (2) Phoebe Mather ----- died 1799, age 80
Mary, born 1723, married James
    Thornton ----------------------died 1793, age 70
         Children of Daniel by His two Wives
Mary, born 1719, married David
    Buchanan --------------------- died 1781, age 61
Joseph, born 1721
Jonathan, born 1722, married Grace
    Corasdale --------------------- died 1772, age 50
William, born 1729, married Anne -- died 1782, age 53
Daniel, born 1732 ---------------- died 1757, age 25
Martha, born 1736, married Henry
    Walmsby
Joseph, born 1739, mar. Eliza James-died 1807, age 68

Anne, born 1741, married
    (1) Daniel Walton
    (2) Alex Edwards ------ died 1825, age 83
Thomas, born 1744, married Sarah
    Walton ------------- died 1778, age 34

Children of Jonathan and Jane Knight

Jonathan, born 1730, married Anne Paul
    (2) Margaret Baldwin
    (3) Martha Lloyd ------ died 1802, age 72
Mary, born 1734 ----------------- died 1759, age 25
Thomas, born 1736, married Mary
    Walmsby ---------------------- died 1806, age 70

Children of Giles Knight, son of Joseph

Joseph, born 1739, married Rachel
    Townsend ---------------------died 1799, age 60
Susanna, born 1740, married James
    Paul --------------------------- died 1808, age 68
Abigail, born 1742, married William
    Walmsby --------------------- died 1820, age 78
Giles, born 1744, married Sarah
    Townsend --------------------- died 1783, age 39
Rebecca, born 1747, married Jonathan Parry   died 1824, age 77
Mary, born 1750, married William
    Satherhaite -------------------- died 1822, age 72
Elizabeth, born 1752, married Thomas
    Lamms ----------------------- died 1799, age 47
Abel, born 1755 ------------------ died 1777, age 22
Sarah, born 1757
Israel, born 1760, married Sarah
    Tyson ------------------------- died 1810, age 50
Asa, born 1770, married Ellen Paul
    m. (2) Grace Crowsdale ----died 1826, age 56
Evan L., born 1771, married
    Martha Comly
Phoebe, born 1773, married William
    Walmsby, Jr. ------------------ died 1808, age 35
Rachel, born 1775, married Samuel
    Paul
Jesse, born 1779, married Mary
    Stackhouse -------------------- died 1829, age 50
Anne, born 1781 ------------------died 1786, age 5

Children of Jonathan, son of Daniel
John, born 1748, married Margery
  Paxson -------------------------- died 1808, age 59
Abraham, born 1752, married Anne
  Croasdale ---------------------- died 1809, age 57
David, born 1757 ------------------ died 1821, age 64
Absalom, born 1754, married Anne
  Winder ------------------------ died 1818, age 64
Samuel, married Mary Paul -------- died 1796
English, married Martha Salleroth -- died 1824

William Knight, son of Daniel, had four children; Daniel, Joseph, Hannah, and Esther. Joseph, son of Daniel, had four sons; James, Joseph, Jesse, and Josiah. And Thomas, son of Daniel, left three children; Amous, Rebecca, and Esther.

Children of Jonathan, son of Jonathan
James, born 1753, married Gaynor
  Lukens ------------------------- died 1784, age 31
Jonathan, born 1755, married Eliza
  Thomas ------------------------ died 1830, age 75
Daniel, born 1757, married Rachel
  Walton ------------------------ died 1821, age 64
Sarah, married John Stackhouse ---- died 1838, age 81
Tacy, married Robert Croasdale
Mary, married Josiah Costell
Jane, married Joseph Bolton
Anne, born 1769, married Benjamin
  Albertson
Thomas, married Mary Worrell ----- died 1824
Paul, born 1772, married Eliza
  Boutcher ---------------------- died 1828, age 56

As most of the present generation of the Knight family may readily recognize their respective ancestors in the foregoing genealogy and continue as may suit their own taste and convenience, I will here close my part of the history. With observing that in compiling it I have had reference to Bipes history of Friends sufferings, the records of the Monthly Meeting of Abington and the preparative meeting of Byberry, to Giles Knight's family register, Henry Tomlinson's account of the decease of persons in and around Byberry - and to information received several years ago and then noted from my ancient Friends, Ann Edwards, Lydia Walton, and others whose recollections reached back as far as 1750 and who were intimately acquainted with Joseph, Thomas, and Daniel Knight, the sons of Giles Knight, the elder.

Isaac Comly

****

ALBERTSON OF PENNSYLVANIA AND NEW JERSEY

The first of this family of whom there is any definite record is William Albertson of Gloucester Co., N.J. He appeared in the records of Gloucester Co. for the first time in 1682, but his antecedents are not known. The surname Albertson was originally used to indicate "son of Albert", and is mentioned in O'Callahan's Register of New Netherlands as early as 1647. The coat of arms used by this family is described as: Azure, a lion, argent, crowned, or, with the motto "Probitas verus honens". (Hollowell-Paull Family History by M.P. Hough.) According to one authority, William Albertson was the son of Jan Albertson who came to New Netherlands from Steinwyck, Holland, in 1650, and together with his wife and one child was killed by the Indians in 1663. (Colonial and Revolutionary Families of Pa., 6-657). However, no record establishing this has been found. William Albertson was not the first person of the name to settle on the Delaware. In 1656 Hans Albertson purchased a tract of land at the Dutch settlement at Fort Casimir (on the site of the present Wilmington) and in 1672 Derrick Albertson built a mill near the same place. (Dutch Manuscripts: 350-383, New York Historical Society).

It is of interest that one Albert Albertson was an early settler in Perquimans Co., in the Albemarle section of North Carolina, and died there in 1701, leaving many descendants. It has been said that he was from the Dutch settlements in New York. However, it seems likely that he was the "Alberte Albatson" listed in the tithable lists in Surry Co., Va., in 1668. (Colonial Surry, Boddie). It is also of interest that there is a pedigree in East Anglian Pedigrees, Harleian Soc., showing a long line of Albert Albertsons. Hence the North Carolina Albertsons could be of English origin. Albert Albertson did not receive any land grants in Surry.

William Albertson[1] first appears in the New Jersey records 5/2/1682, when he located a tract in Newton Township (now Haddon), Camden Co., between the south and middle branches of Newton Creek, below the land of William Bates. In 1692 he deeded this land to his son

William, and purchased a tract within the town limits of Gloucester, N.J., on the south bank of Newton Creek. William Albertson was a Quaker, and was a trustee of the Newton Friends Meeting. He represented Gloucester Co. in the New Jersey Assembly in 1685. (Leaming and Spicer's Laws). There is a sketch of William Albertson in Sketches of the Emigrant Settlers in Newton Township - Old Gloucester, West N.J., pp. 101-109, by John Clement. In 1692 Walter Forrest, who married Albertson's daughter Ann, willed his widow "one half his mills and lands in Byberry", and the other half to her brothers and sister, William the younger, Abraham, and Rebecca Albertson. William Sr., "of West Jersey by Newton Creek," was executor of the will. This land was in Bucks Co., Pa., where the Poquessing Creek flows into the Delaware River. In some way William gained title to this property inherited by his children, and removed there, where he lived until in death in 1709.

William Albertson married twice. The name of his first wife is not known. He m. (2) ca 1694 Hannah, dau of Morgan and Cassandra Druet of the Colony of Delaware, and the widow of William Stockdale. After the death of Albertson, she m. (3) 5/11/1723 Hugh Dauberron in Philadelphia, and d. 7/17/1736. (Hinshaw's Enc. Quaker Genealogy, 2 - 451). Hannah Druet was b. 9/1/1669 in the Parish of Shadwell, Middlesex Co., England, and came to America with her parents in the ship "Kent" 1677. Morgan Druet eventually settled near the mouth of Bout Creek in New Castle Co., Del. In 1681 he was a member of Governor Markham's Council, and was a member of the Newark, Del., Monthly Meeting. His will, dated 7/27/1695, probated 3/16/1698, mentioned among others his dau Hannah Albertson, and appointed son-in-law William Albertson one of the executors. (Encyclopedia of Pa. Biography, John Jordan, 2-19.) Hannah Druet m. (1) William Stockdale, Aug. 1689. (Newark Monthly Meeting.) They later moved to Philadelphia, where he d. July 1693. They had issue Jervis and Ruth, who were mentioned in the will of their step-father, William Albertson.

The will of William Albertson of Bucks Co., dated Dec. 7, 1709, devised to wife Hannah the plantation, houses and mills where he lived at Poquessing, and then to son Benjamin, dau Cassandra, son Josiah "240 acres near Timber Creek and negro boy Dick", dau Anne "negro girl Betty", sons William and Abraham remainder of land in New Jersey, dau Rebecca Satterthwait, son-in-law John Kaighan, and the Stockdale step-children mentioned previously. The mention of the two slaves in the will indicates that slavery had not yet been ruled contrary to Quaker beliefs.

William Albertson[1] had issue by his first wife:
1. William Albertson[2], m. 1695 Esther Willis of Westbury, Long Island. His will was probated Gloucester Co. in 1720, mentioning 3 sons and 3 daus.
2. Rebecca Albertson, m. Joseph Satterthwait. No record.
3. Abraham Albertson, m. Hannah Medcalf. His will prob. Gloucester Co., N.J., 1730. 8 children.
4. Ann Albertson, m (1) Walter Forrest who came to America with Penn in 1682. He d. without issue in 1692 and she m. (2) John Kaighan by whom she had Ann Kaighan, d. s. p. 1715.

Issue of William Albertson by his second wife:
5. Benjamin Albertson, of whom later.
6. Ann Albertson, (second dau of that name) m. Jacob Duberrow, son of Hugh Duberrow, her step-father. No record.
7. Josiah Albertson, (1706-1784), m. 1727 Ann Austin. Resided in Gloucester, N.J.
8. Cassandra Albertson, m. Joshua Walton and d. 12/18/1759. Joshua committed suicide by hanging himself from a tree in front of his house, and for many years the premises were considered to be haunted. (Martindale's History of Byberry and Moreland). They had three sons, Joshua, Jonathan, and Albertson Walton, the last named being a Tory in the Revolution, who d. 1821 at the age of 90.

SECOND GENERATION:

Benjamin Albertson, son of William and Hannah Druet Albertson. The mill devised him by his father was burned in 1711, and ownership passed to John Swift who had a mortgage on the property. (Suit in Chancery, 1719). The will of John Swift, Bucks Co., 1722, mentions his property "Albertson's Mill". in 1724 Benjamin m. Sarah Walton, dau of William Walton and his wife Sarah Howell. (See Martindale's History of Byberry and Moreland for Walton family.) The will of Sarah Walton, dated 1749, left to dau Sarah Albertson "a warming pan, riding hood, and one blanket for life, then to her daughter Sarah". Sarah, the wife of Benjamin, d. 7/2/1757. (Records of Philadelphia MM).

In 1724 Joseph Ellis sold 80 acres of tract in Byberry known as "Old Sod" to Benjamin Albertson. In 1750, Benjamin sold 51 acres of this to his sons, and the balance to Richard Walton. At the orphan's Court, New Castle Co., Del., 7/17/1764, Benjamin petitioned that Cassandra Druet, widow of Morgan Druet, had been seized of 360 acres of land in Brandywine Hundred on the Delaware River, and had died leaving 2 sons and 4 daughters, of whom Hannah had married Wm. Albertson, father and mother of the petitioner. William died, and Hannah conveyed her interest in the land to her son Benjamin, being one-seventh, and he asks for a division. There is no record of the death of Benjamin Albertson. Issue:
1. Jacob Albertson, settled at Egg Harbor, N.J.
2. Josiah Albertson, of Egg Harbor, m. Ann Chew and had issue including Josiah Albertson Jr., (1770-1859), proprietor of the Blue Anchor Inn, Camden. (Col. and Rev. Families, Pa., Vol. Vl.)
3. Benjamin Albertson, of whom later.
4. Chalkey Albertson.
5. Marmaduke Albertson, no record.
6. Sarah Albertson.
7. Hannah Albertson.

The will of William Albertson of Newtown Township, grandson of Benj. Albertson and Sarah Walton, was dated 6/30/1815 and probated 7/26/1815 in Bucks Co., Pa. (W. Bk. 9-59). From the will, it would appear that he was the son of either Marmaduke or Chalkey Albertson. The will mentioned property of 126 acres on Neshaminy Creek, and made bequests to the following: sister Ann Severns; William Albertson, son of cousin Benjamin Albertson of Falls Township, Bucks; Elizabeth, wife of George Logan of Northampton, Bucks; Elizabeth, wife of Joshua Wiser of New Castle Co., Del.; William Vandegrift, son of Bernard Vandegrift of Northampton, Bucks; William, son of John Titus of Lamberton, N.J.; Sarah, wife of John Titus; the sons of Uncle Jacob Albertson, decd., late of Egg Harbor; the sons of uncle Josiah Albertson, decd., late of Egg Harbor; Elizabeth, the wife of Robert Bond of Newtown; Joseph Williard and wife Sarah of Newtown; the children of Jonathan Philips and Rachael his wife; Trustees of the Newtown Presbyterian Congregation, and the Trustees of the Congregation at Bensalem.

THIRD GENERATION:

Benjamin Albertson, son of Benjamin and Sarah (Walton) Albertson, m. Susanna Shoemaker of Abingdon, dau of George Shoemaker and Rebecca Dillworth. George Shoemaker was the son of Jacob Shoemaker, a native of Kreigsheim on the Rhine, who came to Pa. in 1683 in the ship "America" with Pastorius, the founder of Germantown. Rebecca Dillworth was the dau of James Dillworth, a Quaker from Lancashire, England, who arrived on board "The Lamb of Liverpool" in August 1682. He was a member of the Pa. Assembly in 1685, and died of yellow fever in 1699. The will of Jacob Shoemaker, "druggist of Philadelphia", dated Jan. 1, 1790, mentions among others his sister Susanna Albertson and her children - Jacob, Benj. Jr., Rebecca, Susanna, Jonathan, and Thomas. Benj. Albertson (third generation) died intestate, and letters of administration of his estate were granted Benjamin and Jonathan Albertson, Nov. 29, 1808, in Montgomery Co., Pa.

The will of Susanna Albertson "of Abington, Montgomery Co." dated 7/25/1809, probated 8/22/1810 Philadelphia Co. (W. Bk. 3 - 405) mentioned daughters Sarah Webster and Susanna Beans, sons Benjamin, Jonathan, and Jacob Albertson, the chn. of son Thomas Albertson, and Susan and Thomas Albertson, chn. of Benjamin. The will was witnessed by Nicholas Waln Sr., and Nicholas Waln, Jr.

FOURTH GENERATION:

Benjamin Albertson, son of Benj. and Susanna Albertson, was b. 1763, d. 10/8/1828, m. 1786 Anne Paul Knight (b. 1769, d. 10/10/1830) dau of Jonathan Knight of Byberry and his third wife Anne Paul. (See account of Knight family in this volume). Benj. Albertson was a farmer and removed to Falls Township, Bucks Co., Pa. According to the records of the Falls Monthly Meeting, in 1804, Benj. Albertson Jr. with his wife Anne and minor chn. Thompson and Chalkley were received on certificate from the Abington Monthly Meeting. In 1828, Benjamin and Anne were disowned for joining the Hicksites. (Enc. Quaker Genealogy, Vol. 2, by Hinshaw.) The will of Benj. Albertson, dated 11/6/1824, probated Oct. 1828 in Bucks Co., Pa. (W. Bk. 10-662) mentioned his wife and five chn. His three eldest sons were named executors, and the will was witnessed by Evan Knight and Joshua Woolston.

Issue of Benjamin (4th generation) Albertson: (from his will, and Quaker records)
1. Jonathan Knight Albertson, 1802-1859, m. Esta Carlisle.
2. Thompson Albertson, Adm. dated 1840, Bucks Co., Pa.
3. William Albertson, of whom later.
4. Susanna Albertson, m. 1830 at Falls M.M. to Charles Wildman.
5. Chalkley Albertson, b. 1800, d. 3/9/1846 Falls Township, m. Eliza, dau of Ebenezer Headley, in 1829. She d. 2/29/1844. (Bucks Co. "Intelligencer", 3/3/1844).

FIFTH GENERATION:

William Albertson, b. 5/13/1810, d. 10/27/1864, was the son of Benjamin and Anne (Knight) Albertson. He m. 6/1/1835 at the house of Mr. Ridge in Bensalem, Bucks Co., Pa., Asenath Strickland. She was b. 6/2/1815, d. 7/29/1894, daughter of Amous Strickland and Rebecca Van Buskirk of Newtown, Bucks Co. William received a legacy in the will of his cousin William Albertson of

Newton (see previously.) He lived near Fallsington, Bucks Co., and d. intestate. He and his wife are buried in the Friends' Cemetery, Fallsington, Pa. They had issue:
1. Amous Strickland Albertson, b. 11/30/1835, d. 4/23/1838.
2. Benjamin Albertson, b. 12/21/1837, d. 10/3/1911, m. (1) Edith Sickles and (2) Jennie Chevilier.
3. William Ridge Albertson, of whom later.
4. Rebecca Ann Albertson, b. 4/4/1844, d. 1/3/1851.
5. Charlotte W. Albertson, b. 2/28/1846, d. 3/12/1851.
6. Bushrod Knight Albertson, b. 11/23/1848, d. 1915 in California.
7. Caroline Strickland Albertson, b. 3/26/1852, d. 9/15/1904, m. 1876 John G. Shull.
8. Marion S. Albertson, b. 1/8/1855, d. 8/6/1879.
9. Asaneth Strickland Albertson, b. 11/27/1856, d. 1931 Philadelphia, Pa.

SIXTH GENERATION:

William Ridge Albertson, b. 8/17/1842, d. 9/2/1918 in Philadelphia, son of William and Asaneth Albertson, m. 8/30/1864 Anna Leah Thomson, who was b. 9/4/1842, d. 4/26/1935 in Rocky Mount, N.C., the dau of James Thomson (1808-1877), proprietor of the Fallsington Inn, Bucks Co., and his wife Phoebe Ann Skelton (1811-1877), dau of John and Leah Skelton of Bucks Co., and descendant of John Skelton (1688-1760), a Quaker from Cumberland, England, who settled in Solebury, Bucks Co. (Early Settlers of Solebury, p. 45). James Thomson was the son of Alexander Thomson, a Scotch Quaker who came to Pa. in 1800, and his wife Catherine Wharton. William R. Albertson moved to Worcester, Mass., where he manufactured shoe polish. He was fond of hunting, and acquired property in Halifax Co., N.C., on Roanoke River, for this purpose. On 5/10/1904 William R. Albertson and his wife Anna, of the city of Worcester, in the state of Mass., devised to son Charles W. Albertson of Halifax Co., N.C., for ten dollars, two tracts of land - "Edwards Ferry" and "The Looking Glass". W.R. Albertson, his wife, and chn. with the exception of Charles W. Albertson, are buried in the public cemetery at

WILLIAM RIDGE ALBERTSON (1842-1918) with wife ANNA THOMSON (1942-1935) and sons CHARLES WILLIAM, and FRANK

WILLIAM ALBERTSON ASENATH STRICKLAND
(1810-1864)   (1815-1894)

Claiborne Smith, Jr., Bertha Albertson Smith, Claiborne T. Smith, M.D., Maybelle Smith Chipley, Elizabeth Smith Miller, Elizabeth Smith Chipley, Anne Claiborne Chipley.

Morrisville, Pa. They had issue:
1. Herbert W. Albertson, b. 2/28/1868, d. s. p.
2. Ernest Albertson, d. s. p. 1877.
3. Charles William Albertson, of whom later.
4. Frank Albertson, (1876-1941), graduated from Harvard Dental School and practiced in Pittsburg and Philadelphia. He m. twice, but had no issue.

SEVENTH GENERATION:

Charles William Albertson, b. 11/24/1873, d. 1/31/1925, m. 4/4/1897 Maybelle Ida Sears, b. 6/26/1876 in Barnet, Vt., d. 6/1/1945 Rocky Mount, N.C., the dau. of Alfred Albert Sears, alias Cyr, b. in Sherbrooke, Canada, and his wife Ida Charlotte Ellis, b. Vermont, d. 12/5/1926 Los Angeles, Calif. Charles W. Albertson was graduated from the Worcester Polytechnic Institute, and was a chemist by profession. However, ca 1902 he removed to Scotland Neck, Halifax Co., N.C., and became a farmer. He and his wife are buried in Trinity Episcopal Cemetery, Scotland Neck, N.C. Issue: one child.

EIGHTH GENERATION:

Bertha Sears Albertson, dau of above, b. 10/9/1898, d. 7/17/1966, m. 11/22/1923 Claiborne Thweatt Smith, M.D., in Trinity Church, Scotland Neck. He was b. in Scotland Neck, N.C., 11/13/1893, son of William Edward Smith and Virginia Peterson Cocke. Bertha graduated from St. Mary's School, Raleigh, N.C., and was a member of the Nash Co. Chapter, N.C. Society of Colonial Dames. She is buried in Trinity Churchyard, Scotland Neck, N.C. They had issue:

NINTH GENERATION:

1. Claiborne Thweatt Smith Jr., M.D., Philadelphia,Pa.
2. Maybelle Albertson Smith, b. 5/12/1926, m. Flake B. Chipley Jr., Rocky Mount, N.C. (See Chipley lineage)
3. Elizabeth Herbert Smith, b. 1/4/1937, m. John M. Miller Jr., M.D., Norfolk, Va.

CHIPLEY OF MARYLAND, VIRGINIA, and
NORTH CAROLINA

The family and name are of English origin. In 1327 the Bishop of Winchester reported a holding "Chappeleghe" in Taunton Hundred, Somersetshire, which is probably the same location as "Chipleigh" shown on Greenwood's map of Somersetshire, north of Milverton and west of Bishop's Lydeard. This map also shows a village, "Chipley" in Taunton Hundred, south of Mynehead and northwest of Willington.

In 1337 Robert de Chippelegh sued Richard Gyvernay for the manor of Lynington, which he claimed as greatgrandson of Avice de Welyngton who married a de Chippelegh. They had a son Robert, father of John, who in turn was the father of the above Robert, plaintiff in this suit. (The Genealogist, Vol. 1X - 80). This would show the family to have been established in Somerset as early as 1200. The will of Robert Chappeleghe is recorded at Milverton in 1406. In 1623 a record was made of the genealogy of Thomas Warre of Hesterly, the greatgrandson of Thomas Warre and Thomazine, daughter and heiress of Thomas Chipley. (Harleian Soc., Vol. 1X - 115). The same record shows the genealogy of the family of Warre of Chapleigh and lists John Warr of Chipley, Esq. It would seem from these records that the estate of De Chippelegh passed through Thomazine Chipley to the Warre family. In 1582 Henry Chipley was witness in a suit, and John Chipley of Donnyet in Somerset appeared as a witness in the trial of Phillippe Gamon for heresy. The will of a Katherine Chipley was recorded in 1623 at Ashill, Somerset, and the will of Joshua Chipley was recorded at Yeovil in the same county in 1640. Collinson's History of Somersetshire gives the coat-of-arms of Chipley: Azure, a chevron, between three stags' heads cabossed, or. Suffolk Records and Mss. by Coppinger gives various spellings of the name of Chipley as Chippelegh, Chippeleye, Chepeleghe, Chipeleye, Chippleygh, Chypley, and Chyppeleye. The name is not to be confused with Shipley, which is a separate and distinct family of Yorkshire origin. No authentic connection has been dis-

149

covered between the Chipley family of Somerset, England, and one William Chipley who first appears in the Maryland records of 1709.

William Chipley, first of the name in America, witnessed a will in Talbot Co., Maryland, in 1709. This date places his birth not later than 1688. His origin or the date of his arrival in Maryland are not known. He arrived later than 1683, as his name is not listed among those who received land grants which were given to all who settled in the province before that date. In 1719 he bought from Isaac Nicholls a plantation called "Richardson's Choyce" in Dorchester County, for 3500 pounds of tobacco. The deed describes it as containing 120 acres. The same land was deeded back to Isaac Nicholls on March 18, 1731, for 3000 pounds of tobacco. In the early days of Maryland, leaf tobacco was legal currency, and one pound seems to have been the equivalent of one English shilling. This last deed was signed by William Chipley only, probably indicating that his wife was not living. His name appears as witness to various wills probated in Dorchester Co., Maryland, from 1722-1730.

On Dec. 20th, 1737, John and Eleanor Chipley, as administrators of the estate of William Chipley, filed an account of his estate in Kent Co., Maryland. He died intestate. He met with an accidental or unexpected death, as according to the administrator's accounts, the sum of one pound, five shillings was paid to "John Sherwood, Coroner, for an inquest held on the body of the deceased." The total value of William Chipley's estate was 98 pounds. According to tradition, William Chipley had issue John, the administrator of his estate, and Edward Chipley, of whom later. There is no further record of John Chipley. Two daughters of John and Rachael Chipley are listed in the Shrewsbury Parish Records, Kent Co., Maryland, in 1739.

Edward Chipley, planter, of Dorchester Co., Md., is the earliest ancestor from whom any of the present family can prove descent by legal records. It is believed that he was the son of William Chipley, discussed above. Edward Chipley married Rebecca, daughter of Stephen Fleaharty or Fluharty, and widow of Samuel Chezum. Her first husband died between 1-21-1753, on which date

his will was made, and 3-13-1754, the date of probate. On 3-12-1755 the accounting of Chezum's estate was made by "Edward Chipley and Rebecca, his wife, executrix." Edward Chipley died relatively young, for on 12-2-1756 bond was filed by Rebecca Chipley, administratrix of Edward Chipley. It is unlikely that she was the mother of any of Edward Chipley's children.
1. Ann Chipley.
2. William Chipley, of whom later.
3. John Chipley, of whom later.
4. Elijah, no record.

William Chipley was b. 1739. He m. Sarah, daughter of James and Hannah Bell of Queen Anne Co., Md. The will of James Bell, dated 1-29-1738 and probated 7-25-1739, devised to his children James and Sarah a property known as "Turner's Plains Addition". On 2-18-1769 William Chipley, cordwainer, and wife Lydia, sold 188 acres known as "Turner's Plains" to James Ricks for 222 pounds. (Queen Anne Co. Records). William Chipley became active in the Rev. War, and on 9-27-1776 he was listed as ensign of the militia company raised in Caroline Co., Md. (Archives of Md., Xl -48). On 6-19-1777 he was listed as 2nd Lt., and later as Captain. (Ibid: 294). On 11-20-1774 William Chipley "of Queen Anne Co., province of Maryland", bought from Robert Wilson a plantation lying on both sides of Opeckon Creek for 400 pounds, in Frederick Co. in the colony of Virginia. (Frederick Co. D. Bk. 16 - 594.) However, he did not remove to Virginia until he had resigned from the militia in Maryland in 1780. The following record, dated 12-20-1780 (Frederick Co. D. Bk. 25 - 315) shows the date of removal:

"Winchester, Virginia. This day came before me the subscriber, a justice of the peace for the county aforesaid, and made oath pursuant to the act of the assembly - entitled an act to prevent the further importation of slaves - that his removal to this Commonwealth was with no intention to evade the said act, that he neither brought nor caused to be brought any slaves with an intent of selling them nor have any of the slaves now in the deponent's possession been imported from Africa or any of the West India Islands since the first

day of November, 1778, and that he came from the state of Maryland within ten days last. WILLIAM CHIPLEY.
Sworn before me JAMES BARNETT ...."
Capt. William Chipley died 5-8-1811, in his 72nd year, after a short illness. An obituary appeared in the Winchester, Va., Republican Constellation, 5/11/1811. His will dated 8-18-1808, probated 6-4-1811 in Frederick Co., Va., mentioned sons William, James, Jonathan (who was deceased), George Washington Chipley, grand-daughter Priscilla(daughter of son Jonathan), and daughters Elizabeth Kerfoot, Mary Hardesty, Hannah Buckels and Sarah Hoge.

Cartmell's History of the Shenandoah Valley, p. 492, refers to the Chipleys as follows:

"This was one of the pioneer families. They were on this ground long before the first deed was recorded in 1775. Several lines started from the original stock and descendants bearing the name are found in several states. The ancestors of James and L. J. Chipley who took part in the affairs of the county were buried at Opecquon in a small lot on the south side of the old stone church. Prior to the Civil War, this lot was surrounded by a stone wall, and graves were marked by marble slabs, all of which went, along with other devastation. The only mark now (1909) is the wall foundation under the shade of old aspen trees ...."

Dr. William Chipley, eldest son of Capt. William Chipley, was b. in Maryland 5-13-1771. He moved with his father to Frederick Co., Va., where he lived until ca. 1799. In 1800 he m. Abigail, daughter of William Herring. (Marriages of Rockingham Co., Va.) They removed to Statesville, N.C., where his wife died prior to 1806. Chalkley's Records of Augusta Co., Va., gives reference to a suit for partition of the estate of William Herring, and names his grandchildren William and Elizabeth Chipley, infant children of Wm. Herring's daughter Abigail "who m. William Chipley and had died in Carolina in William Herring's lifetime." On 3-4-1808 he m. Isabella Sharpe of Iredell Co., N.C., who was b. 7-22-1776. About 1820 they moved to Old Cambridge, S.C., where they lived until his death 10-8-1823. His wife and child-

ren returned to N.C. where she died on 4-4-1765.
Children: (1st marriage)
1. William Benton Chipley, M.D., b. 3-6-1801, d. 3-16-1884, settled in St. Louis. 8 children.
2. Elizabeth Chipley, of whom no record.
Children: (2nd marriage)
3. Neil Chipley, 1809 - 1823.
4. George Washington Chipley, of whom later.
5. Jonathan Marshall Chipley, 1812-1822.
6. Jane Chipley, 1813-1886, m. Mr. Ramsaur.
7. Jonathan S. Chipley, 1815-1886, m. Mary Hutchinson and moved to Greenwood, S.C. 5 children.
8. James Sharp Chipley, 1816-1876, m. Nancy Hunt and settled in Georgia. 10 children.
9. Sarah Isabella Chipley, m. Mr. Weaver.

George Washington Chipley, son of Dr. William Chipley and his second wife Isabella Sharpe, was b. 5-5-1810 near Statesville, N.C. He m. 7-12-1836 Sarah Adlin Sharpe, who was b. 8-17-1816 and d. 12-22-1891. He d. 4-21-1890 and is buried in Snow Creek Cemetery near Statesville. Their chn:
1. Sarah Isabella Chipley, b. 1-1-1839, d. 12-19-1890, m. (1) 11-22-1860 William H. Watts and had issue Nina Alice Watts. She m. (2) 5-16-1871 Dr. Daniel Bradwell of Bainbridge, Ga., by whom she had Derr Chipley Bradwell.
2. Mary L. Chipley, b. 3/28/1840, m. Mr. Woods.
3. Marshall William Chipley, b. 6-17-1843, killed at Gettysburg.
4. Simpson Davidson Chipley, of whom later.
5. Courtney A. Chipley, b. 4-3-1848.
6. Roxanna Chipley, b. 7-28-1851.
7. Milton F. Chipley, 6-25-1854.

Simpson Davidson Chipley, b. 3-11-1846 in Iredell Co., N.C., son of George Washington Chipley, m. in March 1866 Margaret A. Feimster. He d. 1867 and is buried in Snow Creek Cemetery, near Statesville.

Simpson Davidson Chipley Jr., only child of Simpson Davidson Chipley, b. 3-10-1867, m. 11-14-1889 Lela Bell Bailey, b. 3-20-1860. Issue:
1. Isla May Chipley, b. 10-19-1890, m. Robert F. Northey.

2. Roy Marshall Chipley, b. 8-3-1893 in Statesville, m. Agatha Knox of Raleigh, N.C. Issue: Agatha Heritage Chipley, b. 10-29-1924, and Roy Marshall Chipley, Jr., b. 3-25-1927.
3. Flake Bailey Chipley, of whom later.
4. George S. Chipley, b. 6-11-1898.

Flake Bailey Chipley, b. 4-18-1898 at Statesville, m. Luta Spann, b. 4-3-1896 at Washington, D.C. Issue:
1. Flake Bailey Chipley Jr., b. 9-2-1925, m. Maybelle Albertson Smith 10-21-1950.
2. Ann Lela Chipley, b. 5-14-1928.
3. Luta Spann Chipley, b. 12-7-1930.

JOHN CHIPLEY, seemingly the son of Edward Chipley (see previously) and brother of Capt. William Chipley of the Revolution, is recorded in the first census of Maryland in 1790 with his household, consisting of one adult male, two males under age, and two females under age. Annapolis land records show that in 1788 he was owner of "Rock Hall", 16 1/2 acres in Caroline County. The records of Caroline show that on 5-25-1795 for a consideration of 10 shillings, James and Mary Murphy sold to John Chipley 78 1/2 acres known as "Moore's Addition". This same property was sold in 1796 by John Chipley and Mary his wife to Lemuel Davis. These records indicate that John Chipley married Mary Murphy and they received the property as a gift from her parents, the nominal consideration being to bind the transaction. There is no legal record of the names of the children, but he probably had a son named Stephen, whose descendants have a tradition that his father's name was John. Records of the cemetery in Lexington, Ky., show that he was born in Maryland in 1779. This would fit him into John's family as reported in the 1790 census.

Stephen Chipley, by deduction the son of John above, was b. in Maryland in 1779. He moved to Lexington, Ky., and m. Amelia Stout of Cincinnati, Ohio, who was b. in Feb. 1784. He is mentioned several times in Ranck's History of Lexington as being a member of the Methodist Church in 1822; as a member of the building committee of Fayette Hospital in 1832; and as a member of the first City Council of Lexington. He d. in 1857, and his wife d. in 1882. Both are buried in Lexington. Issue:

1. William Stout Chipley, of whom later.
2. Adeline Chipley, m. Dr. Wilson of Quincy, Ill.
3. Eloise Chipley, m. Dr. Singleton. No issue.
4. Elinor Chipley, m. Mr. Huey.
5. Amanda Chipley, m. (1) Dr. Conyers (2) Dr. Slaughter, both of Marietta, Ga.

William Stout Chipley was b. 10-10-1810 at Lexington, Ky. He was graduated in medicine from Transylvania University in 1832 and moved to Columbus, Ga., where he m. in April 1837 Elizabeth Fannin, niece and ward of Col. James Fannin of Alamo fame. He served as Mayor of Columbus and was one of the commissioners appointed by the Government to supervise the removal of the Indians from Georgia. He returned to Lexington to be a member of the faculty of Transylvania University, and a member of the staff of Fayette Hospital, which had been purchased by the state of Kentucky to be used an asylum for the insane. In 1857 Dr. Chipley went to France to study the treatment of mental diseases, and after his return was recognized as one of the leaders in his branch of the profession. He was one of the first in this country to apply modern methods to the treatment and cure of insanity. He was in charge of the Asylum in Lexington until 1872, when he resigned to operate a private sanitarium. This burned soon after, and he was offered reappointment as head of the State Asylum but he declined. He died 2-11-1880, and is buried in Lexington. (American Medical Biographies, Vol. 1.)

Dr. William Stout Chipley and his wife Elizabeth Fannin(g) had issue:
1. Stephen Fanning Chipley, of whom later.
2. William Dudley Chipley, of whom later.
3. Charles Chipley, 1842-1868, Gen. Morgan's Cavalry - C.S.A.
4. Emily Chipley, m. Boykin Jones, and had William C. Jones of Tampa, Fla., who d. 1926.
5. Slaughter Bell Chipley, b. 3-8-1859, m. Nettie Pool of Memphis, Tenn. 4 children.

Stephen Fanning Chipley was b. Columbus, Ga., in 1828. He m. Elizabeth, dau of Norborne Alexander Galt of Louisville, Ky., and great-grand-daughter of John Minson Galt, surgeon-General for Marine Forces of

Virginia in the Revolution. Stephen was Capt., 1st Ky. Regiment, C.S.A., and later Lt. Col. on the Staff of Gen. S.B. Buckner. He died at Pensacola, Fla., in 1898. Issue:
1. William Galt Chipley
2. Anita Galt Chipley
3. Fanning Chipley, d. 1927
4. Alexina Galt, m. Isaac Aiken of Pensacola, Fla.
5. Buckner Chipley, m. Bessie Devlin.
6. Mary Elizabeth Chipley, m. Robert C.H. Tumler.

William Dudley Chipley, son of Dr. William S. Chipley, b. 6-6-1840, graduated Transylvania University 1858, and was Mayor of Pensacola, Fla., 1887. He was a railroad builder and pioneer in western Fla. Pensacola erected a monument in its public square in appreciation of the work he did in developing that city. Two towns, one in Ga. and another in Fla., are named for him. He was Lieutenant, Major, and Adjutant, 9th Ky. Regiment, C.S.A. (National Cyclopedia of American Biography, Vol. lX, p. 439). He m. 12-13-1866 Ann Elizabeth Billups of Columbus, Ga. He died ca. 1900 and is buried in Columbus. Issue:
1. Hunt Chipley, m. Sarah Walk of Norfolk, Va.
2. Clara Chipley, m. John E. Maxwell of Columbus, Ga.
3. Dudley Chipley, m. Louise Covington.

****

Contributed by: Dr. Claiborne Smith, Jr.
111 N. 49th Street
Philadelphia, Pa.

KEMP OF ENGLAND AND VIRGINIA

Since the publication of H.S.F., Vol. X, a copy of the following letter was secured from the British Museum. (Additional MSS 19-185, Harleian.) This letter tends to prove the following facts:

Col. Mathew Kemp, d. 1683 (H.S.F. X, p. 168) was the son of Sir Robert Kemp, Bart., and his wife Jane, dau. of Sir Mathew Brown. Col. Mathew Kemp had issue, sons Thomas and Peter and a daughter. Thomas Kemp married and left issue; Peter Kemp married and had ten children, of whom three married daughters survived him, including Mrs. Dorothy Seaton, writer of the letter. The original spelling has been retained in the letter. It was dated "Pianketank" 7-21-1730 and addressed to "Sir Robert Kemp, Bart., at Urbston Hall, near Yoxford in Suffolk by way of London." A notation on the inside envelope shows that it was read by Robert Kemp 10-26-1730.

"No doubt but you will be surprised when you see the name at the bottom of this letter that is entirely strange to you and withall from so remote a place as Virginia - therefore shall not trouble you with any long preamble but come immediately to the matter in hand which is this. There came in with our Govenour Spotswood, a gentleman who was a physician by profession, his name was Cock. This gentleman was for his porbity and worth made Secretary of this province. After he had been for some time in this country he went again to England about some affairs of his own which having finished he returned and soon after called me and told me of one Ladye Baycon, wife if I don't forget to Sir Edmund Bacon enquired of him if he knew of any of the family of the Kemps in Virginia and expressed a great desire to be informed whether any of them was living and in what circumstances. Dr. Cock did not know at that time I was of that family so could not satisfie the Lady. He told me that he was very sorry that he did not know that I was of that family before he left Virginia and advised me to rite to her

but he dying I did not know how to direct, till now
hearing of you by a gentleman one Mr. Mayhew, lately
come into these parts - I thought none so proper to
direct by as yourself - being I suppose either her
brother or very nearly related and this Sir, is the
reason of my giving you this trouble which I hope will
not be ungreatfull to you or at least that your cander
will excuse. The state of our family in these parts is
this: Col. Mathew Kemp, which was the head of this
branch - was my grandfather and as I think brother to
your father. He dying left two sons and one daughter.
The youngest son which was Peter was my father - he
had 10 children, 4 sons and 6 daughters but lived to
see them all go before him, only three daughters of
which I am the eldest - the first that dyed, living to
any age, was my brother Mathew which dyed in the
26th year of his age - whose death was lamented not
only by his friends but by every one that knew him.
Soon after was my brother Robert which was so called
in Honor to your father. He dyed in the 14th year of
his age. The next great tryall that I met with was the
Death of Dear Husbern who dyed the 16th Day of September in the year 1721 whose widdo I still remaind,
he left me with 3 small children and since that I have
lost both Father and Mother and had for three years
together almost an entire sickness in my famerly and
lost a great many brave slaves with it. Indeed to say
in short my troubles has been so many that if any one
had told me that I should have subsisted under them I
should not a beleaved them. My sisters is both married and have children and I thank God lives very well.
Hear is many more of the famurley which all in generally lives in credit and esteem but one daughter of
my uncle Thomas Kemp which married unadvisely.
She has many children and finds a hard matter to
maintain them. She has one comfort in her poverty.
She has got a very kind ingenious husband - tho not
much besides his labour to live by and this Sir is the
chief of what I have to say of our famerley which my
request is you would communicate to the Lady Baycon
if now living with my most humble service, tho unknown, and withall I should be proud of her correspon-

dence if pleases to honor me so far and I desire that if we have anything in our poor countrey worth your honour or the Layde's, expecting you will please to let me know if none shall be more forward in serving of you both than myself if in my power.

Sir, I am tho unknown your most humble servant - Dorothy Seaton. If you please to honor me with a line please to direct it for me at Seaton's Ferry on Pianketank, Virginia. ------"

In addition to the above letter, information was received showing that Edward Kemp, mentioned as brother in the will of Sec. Richard Kemp, and a headright in the landgrant of Edmund Kemp in 1653, resided in Virginia, and according to tradition was the father of Anne who m. (1) Edmund Kemp and (2) Sir Grey Skipwith, (H. S. F. Vol. X, p. 166). It is likely that this Edward Kemp was the father of Richard Kemp of Middlesex, otherwise unplaced. (Ibid - 169). Sec. Richard Kemp married Elizabeth, dau of Sir Henry Wormeley (1584 - 1658).

****

McNULTY and KLINE FAMILIES
in
PENNSYLVANIA and MISSISSIPPI

The McNulty (McAnulty) family is descended from Milesius, King of Spain, through his son Heremon. The founder of this family was Eogan, ancestor of the Northern Hy Nialls, and son of Nyall of the Nine Hostages, King of Ireland A.D. 397. The ancient name was Mc-NULTY, signifying "son of noble". The possessions of this clan were located in the present counties of Donegal and Caven (part of Ulster). There are many of this family in Ireland and in America today.

Ref: "Genealogical History of Irish Families in the North of Ireland in the 17th Century", by John Rooney, p. 383: Crest No. 239, plate 53. Description of McNulty (McAnulty) crest: - red hand (right) on white shield. Motto in Gaelic (Latin translation): "Manu et Corde Patria". The oldest and most renowned of Irish amorial symbols is the Red Hand of Ulster.

Ref: "Irish and Anglo-Irish Landed Gentry", p. 568; and "Irish Pedigree or the Origin and Stem of the Irish Nation", both by John O'Hart. The latter book gives another description of the McNulty Crest, Vol. 1, plate 18, No. 45: - A lion rampant argent, three crosses, two fesse gules. Motto - "Mirior Invictus." It is possible that this crest was bestowed upon a younger brother.

Ref: "The Scottish Macs, Their Derivations and Origin", by James B. Johnston: "A good many Scottish Macs were first recorded in Ireland, where there are more records." "Mac means 'son' and is also quite common in Irish surnames." "M'Nulty - Root, M'Inulty." "Ultach, an Ulsterman; his son, MacAnultigh, later Mc-Nulty, Nulty."

From Files of Columban Fathers, St. Columbans, Nebraska - Father Wolf, an authority on Irish names and who has at his disposal a most complete record of the Old Irish Families says: "There is no doubt that the O'-Donnell and McNulty Families belonged to the same original clan back in the days of Niall of the Nine Hostages.

There is no doubt whatever that the McNultys were a prominent Donegal Family in Ireland and were closely related to the Donleaveys who were also a prominent Donegal Family of Olde Eire - the Magic Land - Ireland."

In his book on Irish History (Newberry Library, Chicago, Illinois), John O'Hart tells of an incident: "The chief of the O'Donnell Clan went up into McNulty territory and stole cattle; in retaliation, the chief of the McNulty Clan descended into O'Donnell territory, and killed the Chieftain." There was desperate rivalry between these two clans in the early history of Ireland. The battle cry of the O'Donnell Clan was "O'Donnell Aboo," meaning "Victory to O'Donnell."

> Paper: State Times of Baton Rouge, Louisiana, on each 17th day of March, publishes a Shamrock shaped chart of the Counties of Ireland, - entitled "Erin Go Braugh," giving the family names of the "True Sons of the Auld Sod" who migrated to America. In these charts, the origin of the McNulty Family is found in the Counties of Donegal, Cavan and Mayo. In the early history of Ireland, the O'Donnell Clan was also found in the County of Donegal, so evidently the clan feud between these two families began in that county.

The McNulty Family left Donegal County, Ireland, at the time when Prince Charles, called Charles, "The Pretender," made a bid for the English Throne. As the McNulty Clan had followed the unsuccessful fortune of The Pretender, they were forced to flee Ireland and went into Holland under the leadership of Hannah McNulty, the Matriach of the Clan.

After a lengthy stay in Holland, the McNulty Family joined the exodus of many Hollanders to America and settled in "New Amsterdam" (now Westchester County, New York), during the reign of Queen Anne of England - prior to year 1709. The British grew intolerant of the Dutch, however. The Pennsylvania Colony, founded by William Penn, offered to the Dutch settlers more privileges than did the English, such as owning their own land; the Dutch settlers (this branch of the McNulty Family among them) moved to that Colony, thence the term

"Pennsylvania Dutch". Reference: Book: "Thirty Thousand Names of Immigrants," by Professor I. Daniel Rupp, Appendix No. X, Page 452.

Book: Genealogy of McNulty Family, by David Liggett McNulty: The McNulty Family came from the north of Ireland. John[1] McNulty and two grandsons settled in York County, Pennsylvania. John McNulty was the son of Daniel McNulty of Donegal County, Ireland.

Book: Memoirs of Mississippi, Volume 2, by Goodspeed Publishing Company, Chicago: "Among the early settlers of McGee's Creek was James McNulty."

Book: Spanish Records, Court House, Natchez, Adams County, Mississippi - Page 52: "Suit regarding theft of 2 horses - lasted for years, unsettled: James McNulty vs Robert Patton et al - Year 1796 - Book "G", Page 268 - James McNulty of Avoyelles Parish, Louisiana, (Arkansas River District) came to Natchez, Miss., in 1791."

According to letter from C.S. McNulty of Roanoke, Virginia, to Mrs. James E. O'Donnell, Woodville, Miss. - four McNulty brothers came over to America from Ireland. One brother settled in Virginia; one brother settled in New York; another brother settled in Illinois, while still another brother (from whom the southern branch descended) settled first in Pennsylvania; thence sons migrated into Mississippi, finally settling in Wilkinson, Pike, Amite and Claiborne Counties, Mississippi.

John[1] McNulty of York County, Pennsylvania, the emigrant, was the son of Daniel McNulty of Donegal County Ireland. His will is probated in Chanceford Township, York County, Province of Pennsylvania - dated Febuary 16, 1774 - recorded June 25, 1774 - Will Book "C", Page 234, naming wife, Mary, and sons, James Richard, William, John, Michael, Joseph and Caleb - last two minors.

Reference: <u>Letter from Historical Society of York County</u>, Pennsylvania, City of York: "John McNulty, granted a warrant for 25 acres of land in Chanceford Township, York County, Pennsylvania, 29 July 1772."

Census Records: York County, Pennsylvania - John McNulty - Nicholas Kline - Year 1790. History of Franklin County, Pennsylvania - Michael McNulty acquired 334 acres of land on May 24, 1753, in Antrim Township - page 556.
Pennsylvania Archives - Third Series, Volume 20, Page 538 - Assessment List - Antrim Township - Cumberland County, Pennsylvania - 1782: "John^3 McNulty - 130 acres - 3 horses and 4 cattle; Michael^2 McNulty - 301 acres - 1 horse and 2 cattle."
History of Franklin County, Antrim twp. - Penn. Michael^2 McNulty acquired 334 acres, p. 556.
Cumberland County, Penn-Tax List, Volume 20, P. 120, Antrim Township - 1779: James^2 McNulty - 3 horses - 3 cattle; John^3 McNulty - 1 horse - 1 cow; Michael^2 McNulty - 135 acres; - 3 horses - 3 cattle.
Cumberland County, Antrim twp., Penn. - James McNulty - 100 acres pp. 243-408 - yrs. 1780-81.

Revolutionary War Records:
Pennsylvania Archives - Third Series - Volume 23 - Page 714 - Cumberland County Militia - 1780 - Return of Captain William Long's Company, 4th Co. -8th Battalion- John Mc^{3}Nulty - private.
Pennsylvania Archives - Fifth Series - Volume 6 - Pages 80, 102: (Taken from book "American Revolutionary Soldiers of Franklin County, Pennsylvania", by Mrs. Virginia S. Fendrick, Mercersburg, Pa., Page 138.) Book "Caldwell History of Indiana Co., Penn.", gives this John McNulty as being born in Franklin County, Penn., and married Isabella McLane of Chambersburg, Pa. - Antrim twp. (Deed Book Vol. 3, -Page 314) - 1783 - sale of property by John McNulty, Westmoreland Co., Penn., which later became Indiana County, Pennsylvania.
Pennsylvania Archives - Fifth Series - Volume 6 - Page 143 - Return of full company enlisted for campaign in lower counties of Pennsylvania by Captain McClughan, delivered Wednesday 16th of May 1778 - Province of Penn. - John McNulty - farmer - enlisted April 22, 1778.
Pennsylvania Archives - Fifth Series - Volume 6 - Page 524 - John McNulty - 4th class private - October 1777 - Captain William Long's Company 8th Battalion,

Cumberland County, Pa., Militia.
>Pennsylvania Archives - Fifth Series - Volume 3 - Page 982 - Michael[2] McNulty - State Regiment of Artillery - April 1779 - gunner - born in Ireland - commissioned May 13, 1777. Franklin County.
>Pennsylvania Archives - Fifth Series - Volume 6, Page 72 - James[2] McNulty - 7th class private - First Battalion - called to a tour of duty August 1, 1780 - fined but remitted on appeal to First Company - First Battalion.
>>Pennsylvania Archives - Fifth Series - Volume 6, Page 94 - James[2] McNulty - Class roll of Male White inhabitants of Daniel Clapsadler's Company of First Battalion of Cumberland County Militia, commanded by James Johnston - August 20, 1880.
>Franklin County, Pennsylvania - Will Book B, P. 81 - Will of Michael[2] McNulty, dated September 4, 1794- probated May 7, 1799 - wife Mary; sons, John, Robert, Hugh - daughter, Mary Stuard - property in Chambersburg, Penn. John[3] McNulty, son of Michael[2] McNulty m. Rachel Templeton.
>Franklin County, Pennsylvania - Deed Book 3, Page 314 - October 27, 1783 - John[3] McNulty of Antrim Township sold a tract of land of 130 acres, which said John[3] McNulty had purchased from his father, Michael[2] McNulty on January 8, 1781, and said Michael[2] McNulty (his father) had acquired from Moses Liddle on March 24, 1760.
>Brumbaugh History of Maryland Records - Volume II, Page 528 - Washington County, Maryland Marriage Records - August 27, 1779 - JAMES McNULTY married SARAH GERRARD.

PROOF OF CONNECTION BETWEEN McNULTY AND KLINE FAMILIES:
>Both families originally of Pennsylvania (York and Franklin Counties); thence into Mississippi (Wilkinson, Pike, Amite and Claiborne Counties, Mississippi).
>Ref: Orphans' Court Records, Franklin County, Pennsylvania -Book A-Page 298-December 11, 1810- Petition of John Kline, eldest son of Nicholas Kline, deceased, of Green Village, states that his father,

deceased Oct. 23, 1805, died intestate, leaving a
widow, Elizabeth, and nine children-all living-
Susanna, John (the petitioner), Michael, George,
Dorothy, Nicholas, William, Jacob and CATHERINE,
married to JAMES[3] McNULTY.
ALSO: Same Book, Page 387 (Book A) - Petition repeated October 14, 1812.
ALSO: Same Book A, Page 420 - March 2, 1812 - Petition approved.
Book: Franklin County, Pennsylvania - Will Book B - Page 273 - November 6, 1805 - John Kline and John Wallace administrators of Estate of Nicholas Kline, Green Village, who died intestate:
Book: Orphans' Court Records, Franklin County, Pennsylvania - Book B - Page 337 - March 4, 1820 - Susanna Staley, daughter of Nicholas Kline, late of Green Village, deceased, petitioned Court, stating her father died intestate, leaving a widow, Elizabeth, and nine children; John, Michael, George, Dorothy married to John Wallace. Nicholas, Jacob, William, CATHERINE married to JAMES[3] McNULTY, and the petitioner, married to Jacob Staley, since deceased.
Book: Records of Deeds - Franklin County, Pennsylvania - Deed Book 16 - Page 590, November 12, 1834 - James[3] McNulty, Sr., and wife, Catherine, of Greene Township, gave Power of Attorney to John Radebaugh and John Embich to act as assignees for James[3] McNulty and his wife, Catherine, of the property described in the following deed: Same book - same page - as preceding date - April 16, 1835 - John Radebaugh and John Embich, assignees of James[3] McNulty, Sr., and wife, Catherine, of Greene Township, Franklin County, sold to John Wallace of Lancaster County, property acquired by Jacob Staley on April 27, 1805; then by Jacob Staley to John Wallace on April 11, 1806, and then to James[3] McNulty, Sr; and a second tract of land acquired by James[3] McNulty, Sr., on March 29, 1826, and sold to Radebaugh and Embich on November 12, 1834. Recorded April 16, 1835.
Found: In Uraine Cemetery in Somerset County - "John

McNulty" (vet. 61-65) stone buried deep in frozen ground, one-eighth mile from Rt. 83 on Jersey Church Road in lower Turkeyfoot Township - no other inscription legible.

Proof of Connection: Mississippi Branch of McNulty Family with Pennsylvania Branch of McNulty Family and with Kline Family.

Book: Minutes - Mississippi Baptist Association - 1806-1847, -Introduction by T. M. Bond:

"In spring of 1780 (about time James[2] McNulty appeared in Natchez from South Carolina) a number of emigrants left South Carolina for the Country of the Natchez. On arriving at the Holston River in Tennessee, they provided themselves with boats - three in number, and undertook the perilous task of passing down the waters of the Tennessee, Ohio and Mississippi Rivers to their place of destination. Two of the boats succeeded in escaping the Indians; the third boat was striken with smallpox - it was captured by the Indians."

Ref: History of the Valley of the Mississippi, Volume 2, Page 347, by John W. Monette: "In 1803, emigration from Georgia, Tennessee and Kentucky, as well as from western Pennsylvania, had begun to increase the population of this section. A large portion of land was claimed and occupied by virtue of grants. This was about the period that the McNulty Family appeared in Pike, Amite, Wilkinson and Claiborne Counties, Mississippi.

"Pike County, Mississippi, and Her People," by Luke Ward Connerly (Pike County lies next to Amite County, and Amite County lies next to Wilkinson County - all three counties are very close to each other).

"Michael McNulty settled in Clear Creek (Bogue Chitto) Mississippi in 1818. J. (John) McNulty came to Mississippi in 1811. William McNulty settled in Pike County in 1811. The first settlement in this County was made by William McNulty; he came to Mississippi by way of South Carolina in September 1811, and was accompanied by his father, Michael McNulty, Sr. Michael McNulty, Sr., had sons Samuel McNulty, William McNulty and Hugh McNulty. Samuel McNulty had a daughter, Mary McNulty, who married a Mr. Turner. Samuel W. Turner of Amite County, Mississippi, was the son of Mary (McNulty) Turner." Samuel W. Turner wrote to Mrs. J. E. O'Donnell, Woodville, Mississippi as follows:"dated December 13, 1949: John McNulty from Pennsylvania came to this part of the country early; I do not know who he married. John McNulty had a sister who married a Kline - I do not know his name. However, the Klines are kin to the McNultys - I heard my grandfather (Samuel McNulty) speak of them often. Some years after the War Between the States, my grandfather (Samuel McNulty) visited among his McNulty relatives in Wilkinson County, near Natchez (Fort Adams), and in Claiborne County, Mississippi, near Natchez."

 Will Book - Wilkinson County, Mississippi - Book 2 - Page 163 - Will of Abba (Mercer) DeLoach - dated Nov. 1, 1843. One of the witnesses to said will of Abba (Mercer) DeLoach was SAMUEL McNULTY, a close relative of John^3 McNulty who came to Wilkinson County, Miss., from Franklin County, Pennsylvania; he married Evalina DeLoach Orr, granddaughter of Abba (Mercer) DeLoach.

 Tradition in our family: John McNulty came to Wilkinson County, Mississippi, from Pennsylvania; he was in the employ of the United States Government - doing work in connection with the Mississippi River.

Letter to: Mrs. O'Donnell from William Bates McNulty of Memphis, Tennessee; - son of the William McNulty, original settler to Mississippi: "Michael McNulty, my grand-father, came south from Pennsylvania; he had several sons, among them my father, William McNulty, and my uncle, Samuel McNulty. NOTE: This is the same Samuel McNulty who signed the will of Abba (Mercer) DeLoach in Wilkinson County, Mississippi, referred to above - dated Nov. 1, 1842 - Probated in County Court, July 1860.

 Deed Records - York County, Pennsylvania - Book 2-M - Page 168 - June 30, 1796 - Charles McNulty and wife, Mary, late of Mt. Joy twp., York County, now

167
of Franklin County, etc. This Charles McNulty evidently was son of James[2] McNulty and wife (presumably Sarah Harrard).

Genealogy of McNulty Family, by David Liggett McNulty, verified by his daughter, Virginia Felt (McNulty) Koch of Winnetka, Illinois, with whom Mrs. O'Donnell corresponded.

"Charles[3] McNulty, son of James[2] McNulty of Green Village, Pennsylvania, came with John[1] McNulty, the immigrant (the grand-father), who settled in York County, Pennsylvania with his family - wife, Mary, and seven sons. However, Charles[3] McNulty, son of James[2] McNulty eventually moved into Mississippi and settled in Claiborne County, Mississippi, (near Natchez). James[2] McNulty evidently accompanied his son, Charles[3] McNulty, to Mississippi, as he (James[2] McNulty) is of record in Natchez, Mississippi, year 1791 in a law suit."

"James McNulty and wife, Mary, lived in Green Village, Pennsylvania, where most of their children were born - children: JAMES[3] McNulty married Catherine Kline daughter of Nicholas Kline; Saran Ann m. Felix Doyle; Nancy m. Mr. Immel or Gemmell; Joseph m. Margaret Culberson; Charles m. Jane McCarrell; Samuel m. Mary Mooney; Hannah? - Mary Ida m. Mr. Redette. THERE WERE SAID TO HAVE BEEN THREE OTHER SONS WHO WENT SOUTH. Research shows these three sons as having come to Mississippi and settled in Pike, Amite, Wilkinson and Claiborne Counties, Mississippi."

Genealogy of McNulty Family, by David Liggett McNulty;

On February 10, 1804, James[3] McNulty, son of James[2] McNulty, married Catherine Kline, daughter of Nicholas Kline, formerly of York County but later of Franklin County, Pennsylvania. Children: Nicholas K. (presumably Kline) - Harriet - Samuel - James who m. Margaret Pugh; Mathilda; Elizabeth; George and Philip (twins); John, and ANN born January 26, 1826, married Dr. Richard Denning. (Note: Book on McNulty Family said "Deering", but DAR marriage Records said "Denning"); Ann McNulty and Dr. Denning had one daughter, presumably Mary Ann. James[3] McNulty, wife (Catherine Kline) and most of their family moved to Ashland, Ohio, about year 1830. Ann McNulty, their daughter, as youngest child, went to Ashland, Ohio, with them.

Ashland City Library - DAR Cemetery Records (Ashland City, Ohio), Volume 4 -
"James McNulty, Sen. - born April 28, 1788 - Died November 13, 1845
Catherine, wife of James McNulty - died July 29, 1849 - aged 66 yrs, 11 month, 17 days
John McNulty - born November 2, 1821 - died October 1, 1842
William McNulty - born March 27, 1824 - died November 29, 1890
Margaret Pugh, his wife - born April 1822 - died April 9, 1894
Isabelle McNulty - born October 2, 1849 - died December 3, 1910
Horace P. McNulty - born 1845 - died 1919."

DAR Marriage Records of Ashland, Ohio - (up to 1862)
"Ann McNulty married Richard M. Denning, November 30, 1853
William McNulty married Margaret A. McNulty, Nov. 26, 1855."

Census Records - Ashland County, Montgomery Township, Ohio - Years: 1850-1860 - Family (205):
James McNulty - age 38 - Place of Birth-Pennsylvania
Ann McNulty (after ch.) - age 21 - Place of Birth - Pennsylvania.

Court House Records: Woodville, Wilkinson County, Miss.:
Book: Record of Wills - Book D - Page 134 - Recorded April Court 1835:
"Will of John^3 McNulty - dated 29th day of Jan. 1835 - witnessed by Seth Kline and others, giving all his property to his wife, Evalina DeLoach (Orr) McNulty and to my children - share and share alike."
Children: Thomas McNulty - died in infancy - few months after birth
John Wall McNulty - killed in War Between the States - m. Augusta Pressley

Mary Ann McNulty - died at age of 17 years
Elizabeth Ellen McNulty - youngest - b. April
13, 1835 - married Benjamin Row (Rowe)."
Marriage Records, Woodville, Wilkinson County,Miss.
- Book "C" - Page 200:Dated 27th day of March 1827
- John McNulty and Evaline Orr. Marriage solemnized
- March 29, 1827.
Probate Court Records, Woodville, Wilkinson County,
Mississippi: February 12, 1844 - Evalina DeLoach
(Orr) McNulty was appointed guardian of the person
and estate of "Eliza Ellen McNulty", infant child of
John McNulty, deceased. Guardian Book 3, Page 56.
1830 Census of Wilkinson County, Mississippi -Depart.
of History and Archives, Jackson, Mississippi:
"John McNulty: Males - 1 male under 5 (son, John
Wall McNulty)
1 male between 20-30 years
(John McNulty, himself, the father)
Females - 1 female under 30 - Evalina
DeLoach (Orr) McNulty, wife of JOHN Mc-
NULTY.

FAMILY RECORDS - MISSISSIPPI BRANCH OF McNULTYS:

John McNulty who came to Wilkinson County, Mississippi, married Evalina DeLoach Orr, March 29, 1827; they were the parents (among others) of Eliza Ellen McNulty who married Benjamin Row (Rowe).

The Compiler has in her possession a letter, dated March 23, 1853, addressed to MRS. ELIZA E. ROW, Rose Hill Plantation, near Fort Adams, Mississippi. This letter begins: "Dear Cousin Eliza" and ends "Your affectionate Cousin Ann." Ann McNulty of Ashland, Ohio, was then in Fort Adams, Mississippi, visiting her cousins, the McNultys and Klines - she was then"waiting for the Mississippi River up boat" to go home - to Ashland, Ohio.

Also: On an old envelope in her mother's handwriting (Sarah Eliza (Row) Babers) are these words: "Ann McNulty, wife of Richard M. Denning of Geneseo, Illinois, formerly of Ashland, Ohio - 'departed this life' - 'The righteous hath hope in His death'." Notice sent to Sarah Eliza (Row) Babers by M. A. Sites, daughter of Ann (McNulty) Denning.

She also has a picture of Anna McNulty in her old McNulty Family Album, and a picture of Fannie E. Kline, first wife of Darling Babers - picture taken by a photographer in Evansville, Indiana, when she, Fannie Kline, was visiting her Cousin Ann McNulty. This picture is signed "Fannie E. Kline" in her own handwriting.

Marriage Records - Woodville, Wilkinson County, Miss:
"Book 1 - Page 96, Marriage license of Benjamin Rowe and Eliza Ellen McNulty - March 27, 1851."
"Book L - Page 57 - Marriage license of Darling Babers and Fannie E. (Elizabeth) Kline-March 26, 1868. Fannie E. Kline was first (1st) wife of Darling Babers."
"Book L - Page 345 - Marriage license of Darling Babers and Sarah Elizabeth Rowe - October 11, 1876. Sarah Elizabeth Rowe was second (2nd) wife of Darling Babers."
Darling Babers married cousins; the two families, McNulty and Kline, were reared together in Fort Adams, Mississippi.

Biographical and Historical Memoirs of Mississippi, by Dunbar Rowland:
"Seth Kline came to Mississippi with his uncle, JOHN McNULTY, his mother's brother, and settled at Fort Adams, Mississippi.

Tradition in the family of John McNulty - John McNulty was in employ of Government of the United States in connection with a Mississippi River Project at that time - to aid in preventing overflow of Mississippi River in this section. Seth Kline was also in the employ of the Government of the United States.

Reference: Catholic Church Records: Corpus Christi Catholic Church Rectory, 320 Philadelphia Avenue, Chambersburg, Pennsylvania - Code: 17201. Record of McNulty Family found.

****

DATA ON SETH KLINE

SETH KLINE, born in Chambersburg, Pennsylvania about 1810, came to Fort Adams just before 1836, married ELIZABETH BURGESS of Baton Rouge, Louisiana, about 1841; died August 18, 1882, in his seventy second year, buried in Kline family plot at old home site. They had seven (7) children:

Mathilda Evelina Kline, born September 12, 1842, died about 1913. d. s. p.

Fannie Elizabeth Kline, born August 1, 1844; married Darling Babers (his first wife) on March 26, 1868; died September 1875.

Hannah Emma Kline, born July 10, 1845; married Dr. Charles C. Cage on September 30, 1866; died April 13, 1901.

Agnes Lucretia Kline, born July 19, 1847; died young - single.

Mary Jane Kline, born March 13, 1849; married Henry H. Hays on November 17, 1875; died September 1907.

Seth Quitman Kline, born ca 1851-1852; married Eliza Jane Miles on November 20, 1883; died (?).

Martha Jane Burgess Kline, born ca 1855; married John J. Davis on July 5, 1882; died (?).

Above data furnished by Mrs. T. D. Mingledorff, Box 1421, Monroe, Louisiana, great grand-daughter of Seth Kline and his wife, Elizabeth Genette Burgess, sister of Judge John Wesley Burgess of Baton Rouge, Louisiana; family tradition has it that Elizabeth Burgess Kline was buried on the Burgess Cemetery plot in Baton Rouge.

Kline Family tradition also has it that Seth Kline, before coming to Fort Adams, Mississippi, resided in Tyrone, Pennsylvania, although research has developed that Seth Kline was born in Chambersburg, Franklin County, Pennsylvania, while Tyrone is in Blair County, Pennsylvania.

Letter: St. Joseph's Church, P.O. Box 283, Rev. James B. Taylor, Pastor: "The baptismal records of St. Joseph's Church, Woodville, Wilkinson County, Miss., show: 'On the 3rd of March 1843, Matilda

Evelina, born September 12, 1842 to Seth Kline and Elizabeth Gennette Burgess, was baptized. On (Illegible), 1849, Bishop Chance baptized:
Hannah Emma, born July 10, 1845
Agnes Lucretia, born July 30, 1847
Mary Jane, born March 13, 1849 - children of Seth and Elizabeth Kline.'"

Ref: <u>Biographical and Historical Memoirs of Mississippi,</u> by Dunbar Rowland:
Seth Kline came to Natchez with his Uncle, John McNulty, his mother's brother, and settled at Fort Adams, Mississippi; he was from Tyrone, Pennsylvania. He married Elizabeth Burgess of Baton Rouge, Louisiana, sister to Judge J. Wesley Burgess; they had children - Matilda (never married); Agnes (died young - never married); Fannie, married; Jennie Kline married Henry H. Hays, Fort Adams, Miss., Emma Kline, married Dr. Charles C. Cage, on September 30, 1866, certificate signed by Vincent Row - Book records in Book "K", Page 429; Mattie Kline married John J. Davis, and Seth Quitman Kline married Eliza Jane Miles of Vicksburg, born in Natchez - daughter of Dr. John Davis Miles and Harriet Paine.

Seth Kline of Fort Adams followed occupation of Shipping Merchant.

<u>Memoirs of Mississippi</u> - Published by Goodspeed Publishing Company, Volume I, Page 324:
"Darling Babers was born in South Carolina in 1840; he was brought to Bienville Parish, Louisiana, by his parents when he was nine years old.

He served in the Civil War and was taken prisoner, was released and came home to Fort Adams. He was first married to Fannie Kline, a native of Fort Adams and a daughter of Seth Kline, one of the early settled of this place (Fort Adams) and his wife, Elizabeth Gwennette Burgess; he followed the occupation of planter and shipping merchant.

This marriage took place in 1868, but in 1875, his wife died at the age of 31 years. She was a member of the Catholic Church. By this union were born four daughters - Isabell, the first child, died an infant; Jenny

Darling, the second child, graduated from the Visitation Convent in Mobile, Alabama in July 1890; Lucy Lee and Fanny Sheppard were both students at St. Mary's Dominican Convent in New Orleans.

Mr. Babers was married a second time in 1876 to Miss Sarah Eliza Row, daughter of Benjamin Row, an old and respected settler of Wilkinson County, Mississippi, and his wife, Eliza Ellen McNulty, daughter of John McNulty and Evelina DeLoach Orr, -Mr. Babers was the father of seven children by his second wife: John Elwyn; Eveline DeLoach McNulty; Bertram Ferman; Edith Alpha; Lenore leBaron; George Darling, and Sarah Elise."

Court Records - West Baton Rouge Parish, Louisiana- Probate No. 2423, 22nd Judicial District Ct.

Judge Wesley Burgess was living in Baton Rouge in 1870, as he acquired a piece of property on that date. No marital status was given; his succession was opened in West Baton Rouge Parish; he is referred to as "Judge John Wesley Burgess". He died October 15, 1908; they had one son, George W. Burgess. A marriage license was issued to George W. Burgess and Keziah W. McHugh, November 27, 1867. A second marriage license was issued to George W. Burgess and Anna E. Willis, Feb. 1, 1875 - date of death of George W. Burgess, unknown, but his second wife, Anna, died March 27, 1926. Four children were born of the second marriage - Anna B. Willis; Mattie B. Burgess, Fannie B. Todd and George W. Burgess, Jr.

There is a family tradition that the name "Quitman" runs in the Burgess Family, as Seth Kline and Elizabeth Burgess named their only son, Seth Quitman Kline.

DATA ON McNULTY AND KLINE FAMILIES

Reference: Woodville, Wilkinson County, Mississippi:
    Will Book "D", Page 143 - Will of Ruffin
    DeLoach, naming among others:
    "Children of my deceased daughter, Elizabeth Orr, viz: Evelina McNulty - - and others."
Note: Ruffin DeLoach was husband of Abba (Mercer) De-

Loach, and they were grandparents of Evalina De-
Loach (Orr) McNulty, wife of John McNulty.

Also: Note the eldest daughter of Seth Kline and
his wife, Elizabeth Ginnett Burgess, was
named Matilda Evelina Kline, after Evelina
(Orr) McNulty, wife of John McNulty - John
McNulty was uncle of Seth Kline.

McNULTY LINE OF DESCENT:

1st Gen: John^1 McNulty, wife Mary; York County, Pennsylvania - from Donegal, Ireland.

2nd Gen: James^2 McNulty, wife Sarah Gerrard (and others) - Franklin County, Penn. (Chambersburg).

3rd Gen: James^3 McNulty, wife Catherine Kline (and others) - Franklin County, Pennsylvania; later moved to Ashland, Ohio.

4th Gen: Issue: Ann^4 McNulty (and others), b. January 26, 1825; m. Richard M. Denning, Nov. 30, 1853; visited her McNulty and Kline cousins in Ft. Adams, Miss.

3rd Gen: Daughter _____ of James ^{2} McNulty, m. ____ Kline; Issue; Seth^4 Kline and others. Seth Kline b. Chambersburg, Penn; moved to Ashland, Ohio; then to Ft. Adams, Miss.

3rd Gen: John^3 McNulty, Chambersburg, Franklin County, Pennsylvania, came to Wilkinson County, Miss., and settled at Fort Adams, Mississippi.

4th Gen: Issue: Eliza^4 Ellen McNulty, b. April 13, 1835; m. Benjamin Row, Mar. 27, 1851; Issue: (among others)

5th Gen: Sarah^5 Eliza Row, b. April 18, 1855; m. (2nd wife) Darling Babers, (see note below), March 11, 1876; Issue by 2nd marriage:
John Elwyn - died in infancy
Evelyn^6 DeLoach McNulty - married George
   Louis Roger
Bertram^6 Ferman - married Lucile Walsh
   Jackson
Edith^6 Alpha - married Joseph Charles St.
   Germain

Lenore[6] leBaron - married James Edward O'-
Donnell
Elise[6] - married Harold Beresford White.
(See H.S.F., II, P.16)

Note: Darling Babers married (1st) Fannie Elizabeth
Kline, March 26, 1868. Issue by 1st marriage:
Isabelle (died in infancy)
Jennie Darling - married (1st) Howard Newman;
(2nd) Judge William Thomas Tuggle
Lucile Lee - married St. John Richardson Liddell
Fannie Sheppard - married James W. Hammett.
(See H.S.F., II, P. 16)

****

Data compiled by: Lenore Babers O'Donnell
Box 282
Woodville, Mississippi

Member: D.A.R.; Colonial Dames XVll
Century;
United Daughters of the Con-
federacy;
National Society of Magna Charta
Dames;
Sovereign Society Americans of
Royal Descent; National Society
Daughters of Founders and
Patriots of America;
Colonial Order of the Crown.

WYNN - WYNNS - WYNNE of NORTH CAROLINA

Watkin William Wynns, b. Sept. 30, Old Style, 1742, d. 3/20/1812, m. (1) Mary _____, by whom he had two sons, Daniel and John. He m. (2) Ann Ward on 8/10/1769. Issue: 12 children, including Elizabeth, youngest daughter, b. 3/7/1792 in Martin Co., N. C., d. between 1840 - 1850. The above information is recorded in the Wynns Family Bible, discovered and restored in 1964, and corrects earlier data. A complete copy of the data in this Bible was published in the April-June, 1965, issue of "Ansearchin' News", published by the Memphis Genealogical Society, Tenn.

Elizabeth Wynns m. 3/1/1812 in Martin Co., N. C., Darling Cherry, b. 1787 in Martin Co., d. after 1850, son of Jesse Cherry of Martin Co. Elizabeth was named in her father's will. (W. Bk. 2, p. 220, Martin Co., N. C.)

Darling and Elizabeth Cherry had at least 6 children. (Census Records, Martin Co., 1830, 1840, 1850.)
1. Adeline (?) Cherry, b. 1813. (By deduction, she m. Bryant Buffaloe, and they are shown in Marshall Co., Miss., 1860.)
2. A son. No record. b. ca 1815.
3. WILEY P. CHERRY, b. 1818, see later.
4. A son. No record. b. ca. 1821.
5. A dau. No record. b. 1825.
6. Rufus Cherry, b. 1832.

WILEY P. CHERRY, b. 2/7/1818 in N. C., d. 11/24/1852 in Tenn., m. 1835 in N. C. Julia E. _____, who was b. 7/13/1815 in N. C. and d. 1873 in Tenn. (Family Bible records.)

Ref: D. Bk. L, p. 271, recorded at Haywood County Court House, Brownsville, Tenn., shows the following Power of Attorney:

> "Know all men by these presents that I Darling Cherry of the County of Martin and State of North Carolina, do hereby nominate, constitute and appoint my son Wiley Cherry, of the County of Haywood and State of Tennessee, my true and lawful attorney in fact

for me and in my name to sell ------------------.
In testimony whereof I have hereunto set my hand and
affixed my seal this 20th day of August, 1844.
        Darling Cherry. (SEAL)
Signed, sealed and acknowledged in the presence of
--------."

Wiley and Julia Cherry had ten children, whose births are recorded in the Cherry Bible:

1. Ann Elizabeth Cherry, b. 9/30/1836, N.C., d. ca 1922 in Tenn., m. William H. Ford, b. 1831 in Va. Issue:
    - i. Laura A. Ford, b. 1854, d.s.p.
    - ii. George R. Ford, b. 1856, m. Mary Williams Jones, b. 1863, d. 1935. Their son, Archer T. Ford.
    - iii. Nancy Adeline Ford, b. 1858, m. ____ Kilby. Chn: Farris, James, Frank, Elizabeth and Laura Kilby.
    - iv. Julia M. Ford, b. 1860, m. ____ Taylor.
    - v. James A. Ford, b. 1863. No issue.
    - vi. Robert W. Ford, b. 1865, d. 1949, m. Emma Walden, b. 1869, d. 1936. Chn: Lenna, Annie, Emma, and Robert Ford.
2. Andrew D. Cherry, b. 1839, Tenn., no issue. He served in the Confederate Army in the Civil and tradition says he was killed in the Battle of Shiloh, April 1862.
3. James P. Cherry, b. 1841, Tenn., no issue. He enlisted 5/23/1861 in the Confederate Army and fought in the Battle of Shiloh 1862. He was wounded in the engagement at Perryville, Ky., near Murfreesboro, Tenn., 10/8/1862, and was taken prisoner the next day. He was shipped to Illinois and tradition says he died from his wounds the following year.
4. Sarah Amanda Cherry, b. 11/12/1842, m. L.D. Marshall, b. 1838. Issue: John, Blanche, Anna, George, and Julia Marshall.
5. George Dallas Cherry, 1844-1872. No issue. He enlisted in the Confederate Army 11/4/1863 at Dancyville, Tenn, and served in Forrest's 14th Tenn. Cavalry, Capt. E.G. Green's Company.
6. Aurora Cherry, b. 8/18/1846, d. 1/30/1851. Twin

of
7. Augusta Cherry, b. 8/18/1846, d. 2/6/1906, m. 1/18/1870 Jubel A. Hodges, b. 12/4/1847, d. 5/3/1920. Issue:
- (1) George C. Hodges, b. 12/8/1870, d. s. p.
- (2) Aurora (Ora) Hodges, b. 2/10/1873, d. 8/18/1911, m. (1) Harold C. Barr, (2) Daniel McGrath. Issue: Pauline Barr, Mary and Thomas McGrath.
- (3) Oscar Hodges, b. 5/25/1875, m. Feb. 14, 1899 Alice T. Dailey.
- (4) Laura Hodges, b. 4/24/1877, m. Dec. 26, 1896 Thomas Sauerman. Issue: Vera, Agnes and John.
- (5) Anna T. Hodges, b. 11/1/1880. m. H. P. Jones. Issue: Harry, Lewis, and Rosamond.
- (6) Jubie Hodges, b. 11/14/1882, d. 12/13/1885.
- (7) Nonnie M. Hodges, b. 4/1/1892, m. Ellis Scates. Issue: Clifford and Ellise.

8. Louis Cass Cherry, b. 11/19/1848, d. 12/13/1940, m. 1/11/1875 in Haywood Co., Tenn., Statyra Isabella Coppedge, b. 11/19/1855, d. 11/12/1937. Issue:
- i. Walter Clarence Cherry, b. 11/28/1875, d. 10/18/1963, m. Edna Earl Austin. Issue: Clarence, Annie Belle, Martha, William, Walter Clarence Cherry Jr.
- ii. James Wiley Cherry, b. 3/20/1878, d. 1/6/1960, m. Leona Duke, b. 9/5/1887, d. 10/14/1963. Their child: Wilma Grace Cherry.
- iii. William Tanner Cherry, b. 6/20/1880, d. 12/17/1952, m. Lou Lyon. Issue: Harvey, Dorothy, William Pirkle, Perren Allen, and William Tanner Cherry Jr.
- iv. Fanny Cherry, b. 8/23/1882, m. Sam Cameron Martin. Issue: Louis Cameron and Stella Martin.
- v. Sarah Cherry, b. 11/26/1884, m. Charlie Rogers. No issue.
- vi. Louis Mansel Cherry, b. 2/28/1887, d. 3/15/1965, m. Arsena Winburn. Chn: Louis Mansel Jr. and James Wiley Cherry.

    vii.   Allen Turner Cherry, b. 4/29/1889, d. 1965, m. Grace Bailey. No issue.

    viii.   Mattie Susan Cherry, b. 3/13/1892, m. Ray Crawford. No issue.

9. Mary Eliza Cherry, b. 9/1/1850, d. 4/5/1895, m. 2/2/1875 in Haywood Co., Tenn., Josephus S. Jones, b. 4/15/1851, d. 4/27/1892. Issue:

    i.   Annie Etta Jones, b. 12/14/1875, d. 6/2/1898, m. 5/3/1893 in Haywood Co., Walter Neely, b. 9/9/1870, d. 5/10/1953. Issue: Mary Leonora Neely (Bollinger) and Irma Etta Neely (Walton).

    ii.   Charles Jones, b. 1877, d. in childhood.

    ii.   Sula Jones, b. 1880, d. in childhood.

    iv.   Ruth Myrtle Jones, b. 2/27/1882, d. 9/13/1918, m. 7/17/1904 in Madison Co., Tenn., William Walter Holmes, b. 9/1/1877, d. 4/23/1962. Issue: Mary Olivia Holmes and William Walter Holmes Jr.

    v.   Joseph Jones, b. 7/19/1884, d. 1/12/1906.

    vi.   Lillian Jones, b. 5/29/1887, d. 6/12/1902.

    vii.   Samuel Jones, b. 7/15/1889, d. 1/27/1923, m. 1/15/1916 in Madison Co., Carolyn Allison, b. 6/12/1892, d. 10/27/1961. Issue: Samuel Harold and Joseph Harville Jones.

    viii.   Inez Jones, b. 9/24/1892, d. 6/18/1951, m. 9/3/1914 in Madison Co., James L. Woodward, b. 9/21/1889. Issue: Ruth Elizabeth Woodward (Barentine), Thelma Grace Woodward (Pfeiffer), and James Harold Woodward.

10. Wiley P. Cherry, youngest child of Wiley and Julia Cherry, was b. 12/6/1852, twelve days after his father's death. He removed to Texas when a young man, and there is no record of him, nor of his family.

REFS: <u>Minute Bk. E, p. 256</u>, Haywood Co. Court House, Brownsville, Tenn., 12/6/1852. "---------- to minor children of Wiley P. Cherry."

    <u>Minute Bk. F, p. 58</u>. "W. Cherry, deceased, Julia E. Cherry, widow."

    <u>Minute Bk. F. p. 375</u>, "Oliver Alexander, Adm. of Wiley Cherry Estate."

Census Records for Haywood Co., Tenn., 1860 and 1870.
Madison Co. Court House, Jackson, Tenn., Bk. 3, p. 100, marriage of Ruth M. Jones to Walter Holmes 7/17/1904.

****

Data contributed by: Mary Olivia Holmes
231 Jackson Street
Jackson, Tenn.

Note: For Wynn-Wynns lineage, see "Historical Southern Families", Volume II, page 267.

BOAT(W)RIGHT FAMILY OF VIRGINIA

A genealogy can be, and often is, a cold recital of names, dates, and statistics. Very few of our ancestors left so detailed a record of their lives that we are able to know them as they were. Therefore, we must depend upon official documents to tell us what little we know about them.

It is the hope of the compiler that this genealogy will help the descendants to know something about their forebears and the part they played in developing America.

The data which follows represents many hours of time and labor over a period of years. Information has been received through correspondence from interested members of the family; from the Virginia State Library, Richmond, Virginia; the Kansas City Library, Kansas City, Missouri; the Tulsa City Library, Tulsa, Oklahoma; the Missouri Historical Society Library, Columbia, Missouri; and from Professional Genealogists. In 1928 a Mr. Z.S. Farland, of Richmond, Virginia, was employed by Mr. R.G. Boatright, Cushing, Oklahoma, and in 1962 Mr. Charles Hughes Hamlin, Richmond, Va., was employed by the Compiler.

This assembly of events would not have been possible without the assistance of interested relatives, and I want to express my gratitude to all of them, but there are a few who are outstanding in their interest whom I must name.

My thanks go to my Mother, Grace Caroline Woods Miller; my Aunt Fannie May Woods Flint; Mr. R. G. Boatright, Mr. John Taylor Boatright, Mrs. Edna Boatright Lee, Mrs. Margaret Frances McMillen Winegardner, Mr. Earl Cleo Boatright, Lt. Col. William Erasmus Boatright (Retired), Mrs. William Leonard Fleming, Mrs. Carl Zimmerman, and a special thank you to my immediate family for all their encouragement and help.

                    Lorene Miller Wallace
                    Bartlesville, Oaklahoma
                    January 31, 1966

THE BOAT(W)RIGHT FAMILY OF VIRGINIA

The name "Boatwright" is of English origin and was probably derived from a trade or craft, eg., a boat builder. Several different spellings of the name have been found, which are: Botwright, Bootwright, Baughtwright, Boatwright, and Boatright. The early family records show the name spelled Boatwright, which was the "Old English" spelling. The later generations omitted the letter "W" and used the shorter spelling, Boatright. However, even in the earlier generations the name was spelled "Boatright", which would suggest it was spelled phonetically.

The first of the name Boatwright may be found in "The History of Corpus Christi in the University of Cambridge" by Robert Masters, pages 42-48, inclusive. This book is in the Public Library of Boston, Massachusetts. Considerable space is devoted to John Botwright, D. D., who was Master of Corpus Christi from 1443 until his death in 1474. In Chapter VII, Page 43, reference is made to John Botwright who in 1443 was unanimously chosen as "Master of the College upon the Feast of St. Mark the Evangelist", after having been "Proctor" of the University with Master, John Wolpit. John Botwright had a fellowship at the University before the year 1430, and he probably resigned upon being presented to the Rectory of Swaffham Market in Norfolk (the place of his birth in 1400) by his Patron the Duke of Bedford. About the year 1447, he was made Chaplin to Henry VI who subsequently presented him to a Canonry in the Church of Clonfort in Ireland.

The Coat-of-Arms appears on Page 43 of the above mentioned book, and a description thereof showing colors, etc., may be found on Page 77 in another book in the same library titled, "Proceedings of the Cambridge Antiquarian Society." This Coat-of-Arms was probably granted John Botwright, D.D. about 1443 by King Henry VI. John Botwright was an intimate friend of the King who gave him rich gifts and all the revenue of the tin and lead mines of Devon and Cornwall.

The first Boatwright names found in America are taken from the following:

"Early Virginia Immigrants" 1623-1666 by Greer.
    Boatwright, John, 1654, by Humphry Dennis, Gloucester Co.

"Virginia Magazine of History," Volume 31, Page 215.
    Virginia Quit Rent Rolls, 1704 - New Kent County Rent Roll, a rent roll of the lands held of her Majestie in the Parish of St. Peters, and St. Pauls, Anno 1704: Baughtwright (Boatwright), Jno., 250 acres.

"Annals of Henrico Parish Diocese of Virginia" by Burton: "When in 1634, the Colony was divided into 8 shires, after the English fashion, the bounds of Henrico were made to include the present Chesterfield and Powhatan Counties, on the south of the river, and Goochland on the north" ... Page 31 - January ye 1st, 1735-36 Processioned the following lines between John Stweed and William Finney etc. . . . . Thomas Bootwright Not, he being absent.

"Southside Virginia Families" by Boddie, Volume II, Page 53 - Thos. Boatright:
On May 2, 1751, John Branch of Edgecombe sold to Wm. Hendly for Ł 16 - 250 acres part of a tract granted Edward Poor for 500 acres August 14, 1740, it being the land on which Thomas Boatright did live. (Book 4, P. 900). This was signed John (B) Branch.

From Mr. Z.S. Farland's notes (1928):
"The first 'Boatwright' name we have been able to find in America appears to be Thomas Boatwright."
"The first of the name in Virginia was Thomas Boatwright who patented 322 acres of land in Henrico County, Va., June 20, 1733. His descendants settled in Henrico, Hanover, Cumberland and Prince Edward Counties."
"Revolutionary soldier, John Boatwright, died in Prince Edward County. He enlisted from Cumberland County under Captain Crad (or Brad) Haskins in the winter of 1780-81. Daniel and Micajah Boatwright were also in the Revolutionary War."
"I have examined the Henrico County records and find that Thomas Boatwright who patented the 322 acres of land in 1733, on May 3, 1736, makes a deed to William Safoon for this same land. The name then disappears from Henrico County records. Thomas evidently moved to Hanover County where I find from the Government Census that James, John, Benjamin and Daniel Boatwright were residing in 1782. Unfortunately, the Hanover County early records have been destroyed by fire so that I cannot connect your Benjamin with 'Thomas the Emigrant', although I am satisfied that he (Benjamin) was either a son or grandson. I had hoped to find the Will of Thomas in the Henrico County records, but he had only lived in that County three years."

The above is given for future reference. It is possible that the Boatwrights of Virginia were descendants of any of the above listed names. However, no proof has been established at this time.

JAMES BOATWRIGHT
(ca 1745/50-1815)

James Boatwright, the known progenitor of the family in Virginia, has been found in Cumberland County in 1782. (This information was taken from the Personal Property & Land Taxes for Cumberland County, Virginia as compiled by Mr. Charles Hughes Hamlin, Professional Genealogist, P.O. Box 9246, Richmond, Virginia.) It is very likely that he had resided in this County for some years previous to this time.

Although no record has survived to establish the date of birth or the age of James Boatwright, it is estimated that he was born about 1745/50, since Benjamin, his first child, was born 1769. From his Will he died in the year 1815. By estimating his date of birth his death would then be placed between the age of 70 and 75. This age is not unusual as in the years to follow many Boatwrights lived to see their 70th, 80th, and 90th birthdays, and one, Mary Elizabeth Scaff Boatright Polk, lived to celebrate her 103rd birthday. She was born April 11, 1862 and died May 18, 1965 at Mt. San Rafeal Hospital, Trinidad, Colorado.

The tradition handed down from the Benjamin Boatwright branch of the family is that Benjamin was born September 8, 1769, near Richmond.

Henrico County was the original county formed in 1654, and present day Richmond is located in this county. Goochland County was formed from Henrico in 1728 and Cumberland County was formed from Goochland in the year 1749, therefore, the birthplace of Benjamin and the residence of James, could have been in that part of Henrico County which was made into Cumberland County in 1749. According to the Personal Property & Land Tax records, the Public Service Claims of 1782, and also the 1790 Census of Virginia, many Boatwright families were living in Cumberland County.

On file with the Public Service Claims, 1782, Virginia State Library, Richmond, Virginia the following Boatwright names are listed:

BOATWRIGHT, Benjamin   Cumberland County
               Benoni   "   "
               Daniel   "   "
               JAMES   "   "
               Jesse   "   "
               John   "   "
               Mary   "   "
               William   "   "
               Daniel   Fluvanna County

Any proven descendant of the above is eligible for membership in the Daughters of the American Revolution or Sons of the American Revolution by reason of their ancestor "furnishing supplies and/or services" and as a "proven patriot."

The Public Service Claim for James is as follows:
PUBLIC SERVICE CLAIMS, CUMBERLAND CO. CERTIFICATES 65-2764 - Cumberland August 1, 1784

The Commonwealth of Virginia is indebted to James Boatright for the delivery of thirty-one, and three quarters pounds of Bacon to be discharged at Twenty Dollars pr pound.

Ben Wilson, D.C.

The family line of James Boatright, through his son, Benjamin; through Benjamin's son, William VanRanselear; through William VanRanselear's son, Jacob Gates; through Jacob Gates' daughter, Mary Paralee; through Mary Paralee's daughter, Grace Caroline Woods; through Grace Caroline's daughter, Mary Loren Miller; and through Mary Loren's daughter, Mary Jean Wallace, has been established with the Daughters of the American Revolution. This DAR Number is 517322, and was accepted by the National Organization June 9, 1966.

From a Bible record which belongs to the Chesley Hood family. (This Bible was in the possession of James C. Boatright, great-grandson of Chesley Hood, until his death. William Freeman Boatright, the youngest brother of James C., is trying to locate the Bible.) James married Elizabeth Kidd and they had the following children.

Benjamine	born	Sept. 8, 1769
Samuel		Apr. 17, 1771
Jessee		Aug. 30, 1772
Elizabeth		Nov. 7, 1773
Martha		Nov. 9, 1775
David (Daniel ?)		Apr. 13, 1777

Since Benjamine was born September, 1769, James, no doubt, married Elizabeth sometime in the year 1768. Nothing has ever been found on the Kidd family. Sometime between April, 1777 and 1779 Elizabeth died and James married her sister, Mary Kidd, and continued the family:

Sally	June 11, 1779
John	Oct. 1, 1780
James	Jan. 4, 1782
Nancy	Apr. 5, 1783

```
William              May 29, 1784
Drury                June 11, 1785
Susan                Jan. 22, 1787
Mary                 Mar. 27, 1788
Judith               Oct. 27, 1789
Drucillah            Apr. 27, 1791
Leonard              Apr. 3, 1793
John                 Aug. 22, 1795
Chesley Hood         Nov. 25, 1797
```

In later generations several members of the Boatwright families were Baptist Ministers, including Chesley Hood, ("History of Arkansas Baptist" found in the Little Rock Public Library, 700 Louisiana Street, Little Rock, Arkansas, lists: C. H. Boatright, Huntsville, under the heading Missionary Baptist Preachers -- 1855.) youngest son of James. Therefore, this must have been the religion of James Boatwright and his family.

James Boatwright made his Will the 10th day of Jan. in the year 1814.

"In the name of God amen, knowing that it is appointed for all men once to die, I James Boatright of Cumberland County and State of Virginia being in my right mind and of disposing memory, do make this my last will and testament (viz):

1st.   I give to my son Leonard Boatright my island on James River known by the name of Daniels Iland (or Dansils Ilana?) as also my Punch Creek tract of land by him paying in two years after my death two hundred dollars to my estate to him and his heirs forever.

2dly.   I give to my son John Boatright my tract of land in the County of Fluvanna, which I purchased of Matthew Wills containing one hundred and twenty four acres be the same more or less, by him paying fifty dollars in two years to my estate after my death to him and his heirs forever.

3rdly.   I give to my son Chestly Boatright my tract of land on which I live of one hundred and nineteen acres be the same more or less as also my still and still vessels privisor that the said Chestly Boatright lets my daughter Drucilla Boatright remain in the mantion house on said plantation with him after my death and boarding free until she marrys to him and his heirs forever.

4thly. I give to each of my children as they may need that have not received heretofore one bed and furniture.

5thly. I give to my son Drury Boatright ten dollars in addition to what I have deed him Proviso he obliges himself to give free liberty or use of the spring called Drummons.

6thly. I give the balance of all my estate not heretofore mentioned, or willed, to be equally divided among my sons Samuel Boatright, James Boatright, <u>Benj'n.</u> Boatright, Daniel Boatright and William Boatright and my daughters Ann Steger, Judith Martin, Drucilla Boatright, Patsy Boatright and Polly Boatright, giving to my son Samuel Boatright my negro Tarlton at valuation, giving to my son James Boatright my negro George at valuation, giving to my daughter Ann Steger my negro Sally at valuation, giving to my son William Boatright my negro Nelson at valuation, giving to my daughter Judith Martin my negro Julia at valuation and giving to my daughter Drucilla Boatright my negroe Cloe at valuation each of them paying the overplus should there be any at the division, and lastly I do hereby constitute and appoint my sons <u>Benjamin,</u> Samuel, Leonard and Chestly Boatright Executors of this my last will and testament hereby revoking all other or former wills or testaments by me heretofore made

In witness whereof I have hereunto set my hand and affixed my hand and affixed my seal this 10th day of January in the year one thousand eight hundred and fourteen 1814.

Signed sealed, published and declared

                    his
           James X Boatright
                   mark

as and for the last will and Testament of the above named James Boatright in presence of us.

D. Shield
Wm. Montague
Abraham Daniel
Cumberland August Court 1815."

189

    This last will and testament of James Boatright deceased was exhibited in Court and proved by D. Shields William Montague and Abraham Daniel the witnesses thereto and ordered to be recorded, and on the motion of Samuel Boatright one of the Executors therein named who made oath according to law certificate is granted him for obtaining a probat thereof in due form on giving security, whereupon he with David Shields Abraham Daniel and John Martin his securities entered into bond according to law and liberty is reserved to the other Executors to join in probat when they may think proper.
                Test:
                     John W. Cormack, Jr. D. C.
A Copy --
    Teste:
        R. H. Blanton Clerk.
(Seal) Circuit Court of Cumberland County
        Will Book 5 - Page 86

    Mary, the wife of James, apparently died before 1815 as she is not mentioned in the Will. Of the children of this family a record has been found for only Benjamin and Chesley Hood.

BENJAMIN BOATWRIGHT
(1769-1816)

    Benjamin Boatwright, son of James and Elizabeth (Kidd) Boatwright, was born September 8, 1769, near Richmond. (This information was received from Mr. R. G. Boatright, Cushing, Oklahoma. Mr. Boatright became interested in the family history in 1928, a date early enough that there were some members of the family living who possessed some knowledge of the earlier generations. He received some of his data from William Taylor Boatright (1847-1933), son of William Van and Sallie Wadkins (Gates) Boatright; a great deal from Catherine Elizabeth (1878), the daughter of Jesse Stinson Boatright; and some from William Louis (1876-1938), son of James Blackburn Boatright.) From the Bible record showing the birth of Benjamin his name appears as Benjamine. Apparently, as he grew older he decided to drop the e as his name has appeared in the records as

Benjamin and Ben.

The first record found for Benjamin was in the year 1788 in Cumberland County, Virginia. James, the father of Benjamin, reports his son as a "Tithe." According to the law, when a son reached the age of 16, he was to be reported to the Court, and each year thereafter until he reached the age of 21, after which time, he would report himself. According to the law, Benjamin should have been reported in the year 1785. It is, however, well known that in quite a few cases, the father did not report his son when he became age 16 until he was reminded by the Clerk or Court to do so. Between the years 1788-1791 James reports Benjamin as a tithe.

After 1791, age 21, Benjamin does not report himself, therefore, he must have left Cumberland County or may have been working on a plantation and thus would not be required to report himself on a Tax List as his employer would have to do this and to pay, or be responsible for the tax.

The first appearance of the name Benjamin Boatwright in Powhatan County, Virginia is found on the Powhatan Personal Property Tax List in the year 1796. The County Land Tax Records of Powhatan were also examined from 1782 thru 1799 and no one of the name Boatwright reports himself as owning any land which proves that Benjamin was probably working for someone else.

Benjamin married Elizabeth Blackburn, April 19, 1797, in Powhatan County, Virginia. This marriage license is on record at the Virginia State Library in the Powhatan County Marriage Register, 1777-1853, Page 34:

>1797 Apr. 18 Benjamin Boatwright Elizabeth Blackburn
>James Blackburn, father of Buckingham County
>Witnesses: John Radford, Judith Blackburn.

Benjamin and Elizabeth settled in Powhatan County, Virginia, where they purchased land, a plantation of 190 and 3/4 acres, lying on both sides of the main Buckingham Road. (The Indenture made between James Blackburn Boatright and Mary P., his wife, and Elizabeth

Boatwright, (see later,) locates the plantation that Benjamin lived at the time of his death.) Also living in this county was William Blackburn, an uncle of Elizabeth. During the years 1809-1816 numerous deeds may be found in the Virginia State Library involving Blackburn and Boatwright, such as:

Powhatan County, Deed Book 4, 1809-1814

    Reel 2, p. 106 Deed of five acres from William Blackburn to Benjamin Boatright - recorded December 20, 1809.

    Ibid. p. 445-447 Deed of 100 acres from William Blackburn to Benjamin Boatright - recorded October 23, 1812.

Powhatan County, Deed Book 5, 1814-1816

    Reel 3, p. 95-97 Deed of one half acre from William Blackburn to Benjamin Boatright recorded August 17, 1814.

On file at General Services Administration, National Archives and Records Service, Washington, D.C., 20408, are the following records for the War of 1812:

    Benjm Boatright
        priv. Capt. Hudson M. Wingfield's Co. of Infantry, 4 Reg't Virginia Mil.

        WAR OF 1812
        COMPANY MUSTER ROLL
    for Mar. 16 to Apl. 11, 1814
    Roll dated Norfolk, Va.
                Apl. 11, 1814
    Date of appointment
    or enlistment Mar. 16, 1814
    To what time engaged
    or enlisted Apl. 11, 1814
    Present or absent   Present
    Distance from place
    of discharge to regimental
    rendezvous 160 miles
                    Metcalf
       (569)   copyist

Also on file with the General Services Administration is another record for Benjamin Boatright, Pvt. of a Company of Militia under command of Capt. Jesse Woodson of the 1 Reg't. stationed at Camp Holly Springs, War of 1812, dated October 1 to November 30, 1814 at which time Benjamin substituted for Richard Boatright. And another for Benj Boatwright in the Company of Capt. John Pollock's Co. of Light Infantry, 1 Battalion, 7 Regiment Virginia Militia, War of 1812, dated Dec. 28, 1814 to Feby. 21, 1815, Camp Carters at which time Benjamin substituted for Shad^h Alvis, Senr.

It is not known if these records are for the Benjamin Boatwright of Powhatan County or not. William E. Boatright of Caboole, Missouri is preparing the Boatwright Family History for the family of John Boatwright, born in Amherst County, Virginia in 1764, and married Elizabeth Frances Tinsley November 24, 1785, in Powhatan County, Virginia. (The record for this marriage is found in the Powhatan County, Virginia Marriages, from the notes of Charles Hughes Hamlin.) John and Elizabeth Frances had a son Littleberry Boatwright born October 12, 1794, and another son, Richard, date of birth unknown. Littleberry Boatwright and Richard Boatwright are listed in the 1820 Census Record for Powhatan County. It is possible that there was some relationship between them and Benjamin. As to the Shad^h Alvis nothing has been found, a search of the Census records may show that he also lived in Powhatan County.

The children of Benjamin and Elizabeth were:

Martha Gill	b. Mar. 2, 1798	d.	Nov. 25, 1881
Mira B.	b. Nov. 2, 1799	d.	Sept. 17, 1800
James Blackburn	b. May 26, 1801	d.	
William V.	b. Oct. 19, 1803	d.	Apr. 28, 1867
Eliza (Elizabeth)	b. June 18, 1806	d.	1840
Alexander Allen	b. Jan. 3, 1808	d.	Jan. 21, 1885
Infant	b. Jan. 3, 1811	d.	infancy
Rhoda Ann	b. May 20, 1812	d.	May 31, 1895
Lucy	b. Aug. 11, 1814	d.	
Benjamin Daniel	b. Dec. 11, 1816	d.	1889

Benjamin died June 13, 1816, at the age of 47 years, which, no doubt, was an untimely death. Elizabeth was expecting a child in December of that year. Benjamin had not made a Will, therefore, on July 17, 1816, Elizabeth went to court with her uncle, William Blackburn and George Mosely (his identity or relationship is unknown)

and was appointed administratrix of the estate of Benjamin Boatwright. The bond, Inventory, and Appraisement of the Estate are as follows:
Powhatan County, Will Book 5, 1815-1819
106 - Elizabeth Boatwright's Bond as admix. of Benjamin Boatwright:
Know all men by these presents, that we Elizabeth Boatwright, George Moseley, and Wm. Blackburn, are held and firmly bound unto Thomas Miller, John H. Steger, Jesse Hughes, and Littleberry H. Mosby, Gentlemen, Justices of the County of Powhatan, now sitting, in the just and full sum of Five thousand Dollars; to the payment whereof, well and truly to be made to the said Justices, or their successors, we bind ourselves, and each of us, our, and each of our heirs, executors, and administrators, jointly and severally, firmly by these presents; Sealed with our seals and dated this 17th day of July 1816, in the 41st year of the Commonwealth.

The condition of the above obligation is such, that if the said, Elizabeth Boatwright administratrix of the goods, chattels, and credits of Benjamin Boatwright, deceased, do make a true and perfect inventory of all and singular the goods, chattels, and credits of the said deceased, which have; or shall come to the hands, possession or knowledge of her, the said administratrix, or into the hands or possession of any other person or persons for her, and the same so made do exhibit into the said County Court of Powhatan, when she shall be thereto required by the said court; and such goods, chattels, and credits do well and truly administer according to law; and further do make a just and true account of her actings and doings therein, rest of the said goods, chattels, and credits, which shall be found remaining upon the account of the said administratrix, the same being first examined and allowed by the Justices of the said Court, for the time being, shall deliver and pay unto such persons respectively, as are entitled to the same by law; and if it shall hereafter appear, that any last will and testament was made by the deceased, and the same be proved in Court, and the executor obtain a certificate of the probate thereof, and the said Elizabeth Boatwright do in such case, being required, render and deliver up her letters of administration, then the above obligation to be void, else to remain in full force.

Signed, sealed and acknow-) Elizabeth Boatwright(seal)
ledged in presence of Pow-) George Moseley   (seal)
hatan County Court   )   his
and ordered to be recorded) Wm. X Blackburn (seal)
                                mark

(Examined) Teste, Wm. S. Dance, C.

Powhatan County Will Book 5, 1815-1819

122

Benjamin Boatwright's Appraisement: An Inventory and appraisement of the estate of a personal kind belonging to Benjamin Boatwright decd. Lately of Powhatan County: to wit;

1 Negro man Nelson	$ 550.00
1 D . . . . Len	500.00
1 Negro Woman Grace	300.00
1 Negro child Archer	200.00
1 D . . . . Daniel	150.00
1 D . . . . George	100.00
1 Grey Mare	50.00
1 Sorrel horse	30.00
1 Dark mare	40.00
14 old sheep	35.00
7 Lambs	12.25
1 Yoke of oxen & ox cart	65.00
8 head of cattle	89.00
35 head of hogs	85.00
6 Beds and furniture belonging to the same	210.00
1 mahogany writing desk	15.00
1 walnut table	4.00
3 Common pine Tables	3.00
9 Split bottom Chairs	4.50
2 Painted Chests	4.00
1 Case and 4 Bottles	5.00
1 Trunk	2.00
1 Press and table furniture therein	10.00
Carried over	$ _____
Brought over	$

123 Sundry Tubs, potts, pails, etc. being the Kitchen furniture	$ 12.00
2 Casks of Whiskey containing each about 33 gallons	46.20
Sundry old plows and Collars	3.30
6 Pole axes and 1 large board Az	5.00
1 Still and Tub and sundry Barrels and mauby stands	49.00
1 hand Saw, drawing knife, sundry chisels and auger, and two hammers and 3 gimblets and a flat iron	1.50
Sundry pair of traces and hames and other plowing gear	3.50
2 Grubbing hoes, 1 Spade and 6 hilling and weeding hoes	5.00
2 Blades and Cradles	1.50
Sundry old books	1.50
Saddle and bridle	5.00
2 meal bags and a small trunk	1.75
41 lb. of bar iron	2.50
2 Shovels	.75
2 Candle Sticks and 1 lantern	1.25
Sundry pieces of old iron	2.50
4 Slays and harness	2.50
1 Gun	3.00
1 Flax wheel and 2 Cotton D . and 3 pair of cards	6.50
1 Meal chest	.50
3 Jugs and two bottles	1.00
1 Side Saddle	.25
1 Frow, 2 pair of wedges, and 1 slate	2.34
3 Stands of bees	1.00
3 butter pots and 4 bells	2.00
2 Reep hooks	.02

124   Powhatan County, Sot.

    In obedience to an order of the worshipful the Court of Powhatan County, we, the undersigned, being first sworn, have viewed and appraised the personal estate of Benjamin Boatwright decd. and find it to consist of the articles above specifyed, and of the value above stated. Given under our hands this 16th day of August in the year 1816. --

Peter Dupery
John Maxey Iun
Joseph B. Davis

At a Court of monthly sessions holden for the county of Powhatan on the 21st day of August 1816. This appraisement of the personal estate of Benjamin Boatwright deceased was presented in Court and was by the Court ordered to be recorded.

(Examined)   Teste, Wm. S. Dance C.

The 1820 Census of Powhatan County shows Elizabeth Boatwright head of the house, as Benjamin died in 1816. Also listed in this Census of 1820 is William Blackburn, uncle of Elizabeth, and Drury Boatwright. Referring to the Will of James Boatwright, there was a son, Drury, so this could have been Benjamin's brother.

CHESLEY HOOD BOATWRIGHT
(1797-1867)

Chesley Hood Boatwright, youngest son of James and Mary (Kidd) Boatwright, was born November 25, 1797 in Virginia.

Chesley Hood married Louisa Taylor, daughter of Hugh Owens and Elizabeth "Betsy" (Cannon) Taylor.

Chesley was sent from Virginia as a missionary of the Baptist Church to Tennessee and Arkansas. He also did some missionary work with the Indians of Oklahoma.

The book, "History of Arkansas Baptist," lists:

    C. H. Boatright, Huntsville - Missionary Baptist Preacher - 1855.

Chesley and Louisa had the following children:

Mary Elizabeth born	Mar. 22, 1819
James Hughes	Feb. 21, 1821
Cynthia Emily	May 17, 1823
Harvy Woodson	Nov. 2, 1825
Rachel Louisa	Feb. 23, 1828
Rietta Jehoshabeth	Feb. 26, 1832
Chesley Taylor	June 13, 1834
Martha E. G.	Sept. 8, 1836
Nancy Kesia	Feb. 21, 1839
Edna Ann	June 11, 1841
Eliza Virginia	Nov. 5, 1843

Chesley Hood died in Madison County, Arkansas, date unknown.

The Bible which contains the births of the children of James Boatwright is in the family of James Hughes Boatright, second child of Chesley Hood. James Hughes is the grandfather of William Freeman Boatright, Route 1, Elkins, Arkansas 72727, from whom the record was received for this Chapter.

ELIZABETH BLACKBURN BOATWRIGHT
(1779-1862)

Elizabeth Blackburn Boatwright, daughter of James and Rhoda (Baugh) Blackburn, was born July 1, 1779. There is a picture of Elizabeth, the original of which is in the possession of Margaret Frances McMillon Winegardner. Margaret Frances is a great-granddaughter of Elizabeth. On the back of this picture it reads:
"Elizabeth Blackburn born July 1, 1779
Cumberland City, Virginia."

There is no Cumberland City listed in the present day Virginia; however, there is a Cumberland County and is near to the Buckingham County line.

James and Rhoda Blackburn lived in Buckingham County, Virginia. According to the Personal Property Tax List of this County, James died in 1786, when Elizabeth was seven years old. Family records which have been passed down through years indicate that Elizabeth had a half-sister by the name of Polly Carter. (Correspondence from Mr. R. G. Boatright.) Perhaps James did have an early death and his widow, Rhoda, remarried. No proof has ever been found to substantiate this, however.

The parents of James Blackburn have never been found. Rhoda was the daughter of Abraham and Judith (Colman) Baugh ("A History of the Pioneer Families of Missouri" by Wm. S. Bryan and Robert Rose, published 1876.) who lived in Powhatan County, Virginia. No further record has been found for Rhoda, after James' death.

Elizabeth resided in Powhatan County until 1821, when she moved to Kentucky and settled in Paint Lick,

Garrard County, which is very close to the Madison County line. Members of this family lived in both Garrard and Madison Counties, therefore, records have been found in the two counties. By 1820 there were Blackburns and Baughs listed in Garrard and Madison Counties Census records, no doubt, members of Elizabeth's family, which was the reason she, too, decided to move to this state.

It is thought that she took all of her children with her except Martha Gill, who had married James Kelly, Aug. 27, 1818, in Powhatan County, Virginia. Whether Martha Gill went with her mother at the time of the move in 1821 is not known, but she is buried in the same cemetery as Elizabeth. Her tombstone reads:

    Martha Kelley
    Born March 2, 1798
    Died Nov. 25, 1881

After the death of Benjamin, Elizabeth appeared in Court July 17, 1816 with her uncle, William Blackburn and George Moseley, and was made administrator of the Estate of her late husband. Apparently, before the estate was settled Elizabeth took her family and furniture and moved to Kentucky. A copy of a Complaint made by William Blackburn is as follows:

> To the Honorable Judge of the Garrard Circuit Court in Chancery sitting the orator, William Blackburn, complaining, showeth unto your honor that Benjamin Boatright, late of Powhatan County, Virginia departed this life intestate on the ____ day of June, 1816 in said County of Powhatan, and on the 17 day of July 1816, Elizabeth Boatright, his widow, who is made defendant hereto qualified as his administratrix in the County Court of said County and then and there entered into an Administration Bond with George Mosely and your orator, as her securities in the penalty of 5,000 Dollars a copy of which bond for greater certainty is here exhibited marked A. The personal estate constituting appoints and then have aforesaid addition was appraised to 2,674.60 Dollars as will appear by reference to a certified copy of said appraisement here exhibited and marked B. Decedent at his death left the following children, the following

199

heirs to wit: Martha, James, <u>William</u>, Eliza, Allen, Rhodeanne, Lucy, and Benjamin Boatright. The last five of whom are infants. About three years ago said Administrator with the said children who are also made defendants removed to Garrard County, in Kentucky, without having returned any Inventory of said estate, or have made any settlement thereof with the County Court of Powhatan, that he knows of and bringing with her all or most of the said estate or its proceeds, she had made no allotment for distribution of said estate among said children, but is managing and disposing of the same, as if it were her own.

Your orator is apprehensive that said estate may be wasted or illegally and improvidently managed to his eventual injury as security as aforesaid. By removal to Kentucky said Elizabeth has become unexcessible by the County Court of Powhatan. In this perdictment your orator does not only endanger of ultimate liability and loss as security but is removeless except in your Court of Chancery.

In tender consideration whereof and as he is remideless at law, he prays interposition of your Honor he prays that defendant may be compelled to answer this bill. He prays that you will restrain by interposition from sellers or otherwise, putting out of her hands said property or any part thereof until this bill be heard and disposed of he prays that on the final hearing your Honor will make said injuction perpetual or take said estate out of the possession of said Administrator unless you will indemnify your orator aforesaid any liability as security as aforesaid, that you will compel said heirs to make distribution among themselves of the said estate liable to such distribution or waive any claim hereafter on your orator as security as aforesaid. And that you will grant such other and faithful relief as may be just and proper.

       William Blackburn
       G. Robertson, as Council

STATE OF KENTUCKY
COUNTY OF GARRARD SCT
 I, William R. Layton, Clerk of the Garrard County

do hereby certify that the foregoing is a true and correct copy as presented to me, as found in Box 17, Bundle 68, Suit 522, Circuit Clerk's Office.

This 13 day of November 1965

Attest William R. Layton, Clerk G. C. C.

by Doris King, D. C.

It is fortunate that the above is on record as the names of all the children of Benjamin and Elizabeth are recorded.

It is likely that Elizabeth did not understand the law as an Indenture made August 13, 1824, between James Blackburn Boatright and Mary P. his wife, of Madison Co. and Elizabeth Boatright of Garrard Co. shows James Boatright deeding his 1/8th part of the estate back to Elizabeth. No deeds or Indentures have been found where the other seven children deeded their part back to their mother. The Indenture:

THIS INDENTURE made this 13th day of August One thousand eight hundred and twenty four; Between James B. Boatright and Mary P. his wife (heirs and legatees of Benjamin Boatright, dec'd,) of the County of Madison and State of Kentucky of the one part and Elizabeth Boatright of the county of Garrard and state aforesaid:

Witnesseth that the said James B. Boatright and Mary P. his wife for the consideration of One hundred dollars (Specie) doth acknowledge that they have granted, sold, allied, enfeaffed and confirmed, and by these presents the said James B. Boatright and Mary P. his wife for themselves and their heirs do freely clearly and absolutely grant, sell, alien, enfeaff and confirm unto the said Elizabeth Boatright and unto her heirs and assigns forever all my interest (it being the eighth part) in a tract or parcel of land containing One hundred and ninety and three fourth acres, situated, lying, and being in the County of Powhatan state of Virginia and lying on both sides of the Buckingham Road, it being the land and plantation whereon Benjamin Boatright deceast lived on his death, with all wood and water courses thereunto belonging or in any wise appertaining to the same with the reversions, remainders, rents, issues, and profits, of all and singular the land and premises and of every part and parcel thereof unto her the said Elizabeth and unto her heirs and assigns forever: To have and to hold all my interest aforesaid in the land aforesaid, and all and every part, rights, members, and appurtenances unto the said Elizabeth Boatright and unto her heirs and assigns forever; and the said James B. Boatright and Mary P. his wife for themselves and their heirs do freely and clearly give up all rights, titles, claims or demands, whatsoever they have, unto the said land and premises before mentioned with all their rights, member and apurtenances unto the said Elizabeth Boatright and her heirs and assigns forever, and the said James B. Boatright and Mary P. his wife, for themselves, and their heirs do and shall and will warrant and defend the title of the aforesaid land and premises, and will forever warrant and defend, the same against themselves, their heirs, executors and all and every other person or persons whatsoever unto the said Elizabeth Boatright her heirs and assigns forever.

In Witness whereof we have hereunto set our hands and affixed our seals the day and year above written.

                                 James B. Boatwright (SEAL)
Signed, sealed, and acknowledged) her
in Presents of us.)   Mary X P. Boatwright (SEAL)

STATE OF KENTUCKY, MADISON COUNTY C CT

   I, David Frame Clerk of the County for the County aforesaid do hereby certify that this Deed of Coveyance from James B. Boatright and Mary his wife to Elizabeth Boatright was this the 10th day of September 1824 produced to me in my office and acknowledged by the said James B. Boatright and Mary his wife to be their act and deed for the purposes therein mentioned; And having first explained the contents of the said deed to her the said Mary Boatright and having privately examined her separate and apart from her husband as the law directs she freely and voluntarily relinquished all her right and title to the premises hereby conveyed. In Testimony whereof I hereunto set my hand and affix my seal at

Office this 10th day of September 1824.
(SEAL) David Frame
STATE OF KENTUCKY, MADISON COUNTY (C CT)
I Joseph Miller presiding Justice of the Peace for the County aforesaid do hereby certify that David Frame whose name is affixed or signed to the foregoing certificate is and was Clerk at the time of said signature of the Court for the County of Madison and that due faith and credit is and ought to be given to all his official acts as such and that the seal thereto affixed is the seal of said Court. Given under my hand and seal Sept. 13th, 1824.
Joseph Miller
(SEAL)

VIRGINIA to-wit:
At a Court of Quarterly Session holden for the County of Powhatan in the state aforesaid in the 18th day of November 1824 This Indenture of bargain and sale, which, has been duly acknowledged in Kentucky by James R. Boatwright and Mary his wife, parties thereto to be their act and deed, and certified was presented in this Court and ordered to be recorded.
Teste: Wm. Dance C
A Copy
Teste: Wm. E. Maxey, Jr. Clerk
Deed Book #9, Page 62
July 25, 1961

Elizabeth, who was a widow at the age of 37, reared her family until they were married and able to take their place in the world. On September 11, 1862 Elizabeth died at Paint Lick, Garrard County, Kentucky, and is buried in the Boatright Burial Ground, which in August of 1963, was located on what was known as the George Todd Farm, about one mile up Paint Creek from a Mr. Ralston's home. Her tombstone reads as follows:

Elizabeth Boatwright
wife of
Benj Boatwright
Born July 1, 1779
Died Sept. 11, 1862

THE CHILDREN OF BENJAMIN BOATWRIGHT

MARTHA GILL BOATWRIGHT
(1798-1881)

Martha Gill Boatwright, daughter of Benjamin and Elizabeth (Blackburn) Boatwright was born in Powhatan County, Virginia, March 2, 1798. She was married August 27, 1818, to James Kelly as shown by the following record:
"Powhatan County, Virginia - Marriages"
August 27, 1818 - Martha G. Boatwright (daughter of Benjamin Boatright, deceased) to James Kelly - James B. Boatwright, Security."
Whether Martha Gill went with her mother at the time of the move to Kentucky is not known but she is buried in the same cemetery as Elizabeth, her tombstone reads:
Martha Kelley
Born March 2, 1798
Died Nov. 25, 1881

JAMES BLACKBURN BOATWRIGHT
(1801-)

James Blackburn Boatwright, the eldest son of Benjamin and Elizabeth (Blackburn) Boatwright was born in Powhatan County, Virginia May 26, 1810. James married Mary P. Elam October 17, 1821, in Kentucky.

The only other record which has been found for James is the 1830 Census record for Graves County, Kentucky where he is listed with his brother, William.

All trace of James from 1830, has been lost. Tradition in the family has been that he, too, moved to Northwest Missouri and settled near St. Joseph, Buchanan County, Missouri, but nothing has been found to prove this.

There is no record as to the date or place of the death of James or his wife, Mary P.

WILLIAM VAN RANSELEAR BOATWRIGHT
(1803-1867)

William Van Ranselear Boatwright, (The middle name

of William was received from Margaret Frances McMillen Winegardner who is a grand-daughter of William.) Son of Benjamin and Elizabeth (Blackburn) Boatwright was born Oct. 19, 1803, (The date of William's birth was first received from Mr. R. G. Boatright. Later the Bible page was received from Margaret Frances McMillen Winegardner.) in Powhatan County, Virginia on the Plantation where his father died, June 13, 1816. William, apparently, dropped the Ranselear in his middle name as the records have been found William V., William Van, but the most common has been William Von, no doubt, the Van was mistaken for Von. A few records have been found William B., (William's marriage record has been found William B., also the death certificate of Jacob Gates Boatright, lists his father, William B.) which must have been mistaken in sound.

William went with his mother and family to Kentucky where he met and married Sally Wadkins Gates. Their marriage record is on file in Garrard County and is as follows:

Garrard County Kentucky Marriages
W. B. Boatwright to Sally Gates, bondsman, Jacob Gates - March 3, 1825
Note: This record showed B and not V - could have been mistaken in sound.

GATES

Sallie Wadkins, the daughter of Jacob G. and Susanna (Gates) Gates, was born June 29, 1806, in Virginia. (All Census records which have been checked have shown that Sallie was born in Virginia. An obituary for Sallie has been found and this, too, states she was born in Virginia.) The records for Sallie's name have been found Sally, however, the one found most often has been Sallie.

This Gates family lived in Chesterfield County, Virginia. The earliest record which has been found is for a Rebeccah Gates, whose Will is recorded in Chesterfield County, Will Book #1, Page 286, dated November 23, 1757. No record has been found for the husband of Rebeccah. In her Will she mentions the following child-

ren:
      Sons: William; James
      Daughters: Margaret Nunnery; Frances Hatcher;
                       Martha; and Jane Robertson

William Gates, son of Rebeccah Gates, married Susannah (_____) Gates. They lived in Chesterfield County, Virginia. Their children were:
      Sons: William; Edward; James
      Daughters: Mary; Elizabeth; Lucy

William died December 28, 1751. His Will is dated March ye 13th 1750-51, and is found in Will Book 1, Page 31 and 32, the inventory of his estate is found in Will Book 1, Page 105 and 106. Sussannah followed William, her husband, in death as William named his wife, Susannah Gates and his son, Edward, Executors of his Will.

Edward Gates, son of William and Susannah (_____) Gates, was born in Chesterfield County, Virginia, November 6, 1727. This birth is found in the Bristol Parish Vestry Book and Register, 1720-89, Page 307:
      Edward son of Wm and Susannah Gates Born 6th
      Novm' 1727.

Edward Gates married a girl by the name of Rebecca _____. They lived in Virginia for awhile but then moved on to Garrard County, Kentucky. Edward left a Will dated April 19, 1807. His Will was probated in Garrard County, February, 1819, and may be found in Will Book "D", Page 567, of the records of Garrard County. In his Will he names the following heirs, to wit:
        "To my son William Gates,   10 shillings,
        To my daughter Lucy Moore,   10 shillings,
        To the heirs of James Gates,   10 shillings,
        To my son Jacob Gates and the heirs of Eppes Gates, dec., all my real and personal estate to be divided equally between my said son and the the heirs above, except a negro man named Archer, which I give and bequeath to my said son Jacob."
      Executors: Jacob Gates and Martin Daniels.

James Gates, son of William and Susannah (_____) Gates, was born September 11, 1741. James had three marriages. His first wife was Priscilla Jackson and their children were:

Elizabeth	b. Oct. 22, 1762
Alexander	b. Nov. 3, 1765
Priscilla	b. Nov. 19, 1768

Priscilla died December 1, 1768. James' second wife was Sarah Bailey. They were married November 11, 1773 and their children were:

Phebe	b. Oct. 7, 1774
William	b. May 11, 1778
Salley	b. May 13, 1780
Susannah	b. Sept. 13, 1782
Nancy	b. Jan. 21, 1784
Martha	b. Sept. 20, 1786
James R.	b. Feb. 19, 1789

Sarah Bailey Gates died May 1, 1794. James' third wife was Obediance Binns, a widow, they were married Jan. 24, 1796. Obediance had two children by her former marriage, Daniel Binns and Townes Binns. James and Obediance had no children.

The record for the above births was obtained from a photocopy of a Bible record which has been presented to the Virginia State Library by Mr. Thurlow Gates Gregory. Mr. Gregory is a descendant of James R. Gates.

James Gates' Will is found in Chesterfield County, Virginia, Will Book #9, Page 337, dated February 16, 1820, and probated April 9, 1821.

Jacob G. Gates, son of Edward and Rebecca (_____) Gates, was born July 22, 1777. He married Susannah Gates, his first cousin. Susannah was born September 13, 1782, in Chesterfield County, Virginia, and was the daughter of James and Sarah (Bailey) Gates. Edward and James were brothers.

The following records have been found for the marriage of Jacob and Susannah:
Chesterfield County Court House Marriage Records 1771-1783, part 2, Page 391:
1800 March --- Jacob Gatts to Susannah Gatts
Minister, Charles Forsee.
Marriages of Chesterfield County Virginia 1771-1815 Compiled and Published by Catherine L. Knorr: Page 56:

14 March 1800 -- Jacob Gatts and Susannah Gatts - married by Rev. Charles Forsee, Minister Skinquarter Baptist Church.

Jacob and his family moved to Garrard County, Kentucky sometime after the birth of their daughter, Sallie Wadkins, 1806, as all records for the birth of Sallie state she was born in Virginia. Also in the Chesterfield Court House records there is the following:

Deed Book #17, Page 586, Jacob and Susannah, his wife, sold a small parcel of land to Benjamin Wilkinson, 7 1/6 acres for sixty pounds, July 9, 1807. James Gates was a witness to the transaction.

The Gates and Boatwright families were friends in Garrard County, Kentucky and may well have known each other while still in Virginia, since they resided in the same section of the state. On November 29, 1828, Jacob G. Gates was appointed guardian for the five younger children of Elizabeth (Blackburn) Boatwright. (Received in a letter from Mr. R. G. Boatright.)

Records have been found which show that Jacob Gates had some knowledge of the law or that he had a Power of Attorney. The following is quoted:

Deed Book 28, Page 489, Chesterfield County, Va.

Know all men by these present that I, John Elam, and I, Harriett Elam, of the County of Weakley in the state of Tennessee, do appoint Jacob Gates of the same county and state as our lawful attorney to settle our business in Chesterfield County, October 23, 1831.

From the above it would appear that Jacob and Susannah left Kentucky and moved to Tennessee. No record has been found as to the place or date of Jacob's death. The place of Susannah's death is not known but her date of death was July 14, 1841.

William V. Boatwright was a farmer and miller. (From the Biography of William Taylor Boatright as Published in 1891, from "Portrait & Biographical Album" containing the biographies of a large number of pioneer settlers in Sumner County, Kansas, copyrighted by Chapman Brothers in 1885 and published in 1891.)

William and Sallie remained in Garrard County, Kentucky until October, 1828, (From the Obituary of Sallie Gates, from the Darlington Record, September 13, 1885.) at which time they moved on west with the pioneers and settled in Graves County, Kentucky.

By 1830 William and Sallie were settled in Graves County as shown by the Census record for that county. Also listed was William's brother James Blackburn Boatwright.

BOATWRIGHT, WILLIAM		BOATWRIGHT, JAMES B.	
Males	Females	Males	Females
2 under 5	2 under 5	1 under 5	2 under 5
1 20-30	1 20-30	1 5-10	1 20-30
		1 30-40	

James left Graves County before 1850, however, William remained until 1851. The 1850 Census record shows:

Dist 1 Page 434   #141   born
W. V. Boatwright   47 m farmer   Va.
S.   "   44 f   Va.
S.   "   22 f   Ky.
E.   "   21 f   Ky.
J.   "   19 m   Ky.
B.   "   17 m   Ky.
J.   "   15 m   Ky.
Francis   "   12 m   Ky.
Joseph   "   7 m   Ky.
W.   "   4 m   Ky.
P. Gates   65 (?)   Va.
E. Gates   30 f   Va.

Who P. Gates and E. Gates were is not known, but Sallie had a sister named Phoebe G. Gates and one named Eliza Ann Gates.

Before William and Sallie left Kentucky all of their children had been born, they were:

Susan Frances   b. Aug. 18, 1826; d. Nov. 12, 1921
Elizabeth Jane b. Feb. 19, 1828; d. Dec. 25, 1906
Rebecca G.   b. Jan. 5, 1830; d. Jan. 5, 1830
Jesse Stinson   b. Dec. 11, 1830; d. Nov. 9, 1905
Benjamin Allen b. Mar. 11, 1833; d. Jan. 18, 1853
Jacob Gates   b. Sept. 5, 1835; d. Aug. 26, 1923

Francis
  Alexander   b. Jan. 17, 1838; d. Dec. 27, 1918
  Joseph Marion   b. Feb. 18, 1841; d. Killed at Per-
                       ryville, Ky., while in Confeder-
                       ate Army, 1865
  Mary Ann Eliza   b. Jan. 20, 1844; d. Nov. 5, 1920
  William Taylor   b. Jan. 5, 1847; d. Dec. 22, 1933
  James
    Blackburn   b. Oct. 19, 1850; d. Dec. 31, 1931

William and his family left Kentucky in 1851, (From the Obituary of Sallie Wadkins Gates, and from the Biography of William Taylor Boatright as published in 1891.) crossed the Mississippi River and traveled on to Northwest Missouri settling in Platte County. Here they remained for about eighteen months, removing then to Gentry County, Missouri. (Ibid.)

With them on this trip was a colored woman who had been a slave for the Boatwright family, and had helped to raise William. Her name was Mariah, but she was called Aunt Rier by everyone. Aunt Rier went with them not as a slave but as a trusted member of the household. During the Civil War she kept William's money and hid it in a secret hiding place. He did not know where the money was, but when he needed any he went to her for it. That way he could tell the marauders that he did not keep any money. William built a small house in his backyard for Aunt Rier and she lived and died there. She is buried in the Boatwright Cemetery in Darlington, Missouri. (Information furnished by Margaret Frances McMillen Winegardner, and Mary Elizabeth Scaff Boatright Polk.)

In 1894 John Sloan, the husband of Elizabeth Boatright, completed the job of tearing down and sawing into stove wood an old log house. This building was the first meeting house West of the Grand River in Gentry County and was used by the Primitive Baptist Congregation when the country was first settled. It is believed to be the original home built by the William Van and Sallie Wadkins (Gates) Boatwright family when they settled in the county, as it was built on a section of their homestead. (Ibid.)

Susan Boatright, oldest daughter of William and Sallie, was the first woman school teacher in Gentry County. She taught a subscription school in a log house. (Ibid.)

Four of William and Sallie's sons fought in the Civil War; Jacob Gates and William Taylor on the Union side and Francis Alexander and Joseph Marion on the Confederate side. The family being from Virginia and Kentucky, they might well be divided in their feelings and beliefs during this crisis.

William died April 28, 1867 and is buried in the Boatwright Cemetery in Darlington, which is located on property now owned by Elza Christian. This property was originally the homestead of William and Sallie.

Sallie survived her husband for a period of eighteen years, remaining a widow. She died in Gentry County, Missouri, September 13, 1885 and is buried beside her husband in the Boatwright Cemetery. After the death of William, Sallie lived with her daughter, Mary Ann Eliza.

Unfortunately, the Court House in Gentry County burned March 6, 1885, therefore, no record of a Will has been preserved.

ELIZA (ELIZABETH) BOATWRIGHT
(1806-1840)

Eliza (or Elizabeth) Boatwright, daughter of Benjamin and Elizabeth (Blackburn) Boatwright, was born June 18, 1806 in Powhatan County, Virginia. She was married August 14, 1828, to William Foley. She died October 22, 1840. No further record for her or her family.

ALEXANDER ALLEN BOATWRIGHT
(1808-1885)

Alexander Allen Boatwright, son of Benjamin and Elizabeth (Blackburn) Boatwright, was born January 3, 1808 in Powhatan County, Virginia. He was married to Martha Elizabeth Joplin who was born January 6, 1811, and died January 25, 1840, at Paint Lick, Kentucky. They had one child:

    Eliza Ann   b. Dec. 25, 1839; d. Apr. 17, 1920

Alexander Allen lived on Walnut-Meadow Creek just above the junction of Meadow Creek and Paint Lick Creek, near Paint Lick, Kentucky. He was Baptist Minister. Alexander Allen died January 21, 1885, and is buried in the same cemetery as his mother, Elizabeth.

RHODA ANN BOATWRIGHT
(1812-1895)

Rhoda Ann Boatwright, daughter of Benjamin and Elizabeth (Blackburn) Boatwright, was born May 20, 1812, in Powhatan County, Virginia. She was married to the Rev. James Wesley Foley April 15, 1828. The Rev. Foley was a Baptist Minister and by 1850 he and his family were located in Platte County, Missouri. He was born June 7, 1807 in Virginia. Rhoda Ann and James had the following children:

        Benjamin   b.   1829
        Martha Jane   b. Apr. 17,   1835
        Mary
          Elizabeth   b. about   1843
        Nathan   b. about   1844
        James Riley   b. May 25,   1845
        Zachary Tay-
          lor   b. Dec. 13,   1848
        Andrew
          Baker   b. Apr. 22,   1853
        Nannie Belle   b. Sept. 7,   1856
        Elizabeth A.
        Jonathan W.

Rhoda Ann died May 31, 1895 and is buried in Mt. Bethel Cemetery, 8 miles N.W. of Weston, Platte County, Missouri. James Foley died September 17, 1866, and is buried by the side of his wife.

LUCY BOATWRIGHT
(1814-   )

Lucy Boatwright, daughter of Benjamin and Elizabeth (Blackburn) Boatwright was born August 11, 1814, in Powhatan County, Virginia. She was married April 6,

1837, to Isaac Cox.

Family tradition is that Lucy and her husband, Isaac, went to Northwest Missouri at the same time her brothers and sister did, but no record has been found for her.

BENJAMIN DANIEL BOATWRIGHT
(1816-1889)

Benjamin Daniel Boatwright, son of Benjamin and Elizabeth (Blackburn) Boatwright was born December 11, 1816, in Powhatan County, Virginia, six months after the death of his father. He was married December 12, 1839, to Julia Ann Paterson who was born March 15, 1815. Julia Ann was the daughter of John Patterson and Rhoda Blackburn. Rhoda Blackburn was a sister of Elizabeth Blackburn Boatwright (1779-1862).

Benjamin Daniel Boatwright and his wife, Julia Ann Patterson, were cousins. They had two children:

Sallie Ann   b. Oct. 13, 1840; d. July 9, 1869
John Waller   b. Apr. 3, 1843; d. Jan 8, 1913

Benjamin Daniel was a Master Mason and was Secretary of Masonic Lodge No. 183 of Kirksville, Kentucky, from 1849 to 1878. His home was located about two or three miles Northeast of Paint Lick, Kentucky, on the Paint Lick Berea Highway.

Benjamin Daniel died at Paint Lick, Kentucky, about 1889. Julia Ann died April 4, 1844.

THE CHILDREN OF WILLIAM VAN BOATWRIGHT

SUSAN FRANCES BOATRIGHT
(1826-1921)

Susan Frances, daughter of William V. and Sallie Wadkins (Gates) Boatright, was born August 18, 1826. Susan Frances was married February 18, 1858, to George Fox Scaff; (born September 13, 1826.) They had the following children:

Lucy Ann   b. Oct. 6, 1859; d. early 1940's
Sallie Jane   b. Feb. 25, 1861; d. Feb. 2, 1956
*Mary Elizabeth   b. Apr. 11, 1862; d. May 18, 1965

Susan Frances Paralee
        b. Sept 29, 1866; d. Sept. 10, 1886

*Mary Elizabeth Polk lived to be 103 years old.

Susan Frances died January 25, 1921, in Darlington, Missouri and is buried in the Boatright Cemetery. George Fox Scaff died November 12, 1912, and is buried by the side of his wife.

ELIZABETH JANE BOATRIGHT
(1828-1906)

Elizabeth Jane, daughter of William V. and Sallie Wadkins (Gates) Boatright, was born February 19, 1828. She married John Sloan who was born in the year 1832. They had the following children:

Sally Ann	b. July 19,	1859; d. Mar. 3,	1938
Josephine	b.	1861; d.	1938
Clarissa (or Kate)	b.	1863; d. Feb. 17,	1938
Addie	b. Oct.	1867; d. Apr. 20,	1901
Jennie	b.	d. when young	

Elizabeth Jane died December 25, 1906 in Darlington, and her husband, John, died January 31, 1908. They are buried in the Gribble Cemetery in Darlington, Missouri.

JESSE STINSON BOATRIGHT
(1830-1905)

Jesse Stinson Boatright, son of William V. and Sallie Wadkins (Gates) Boatright was born December 11, 1830. He married Mary Evaline (Molly) Miller October 22, 1852, they had the following children:

Martha Ann	b. Oct. 4, 1853; d.
Susan Alice	b. Mar. 8, 1855; d.
Mary Ellen	b. Aug. 25, 1856; d.
William Newton	b. Oct. 7, 1857; d.
Theodocia	b. Nov. 21, 1859; d.
Ada	b. Mar. 21, 1861; d.
Isabelle (Belle)	b. Feb. 1, 1863; d.
John Lee	b. May 26, 1865; d.

George W.	b. Feb. 20, 1867; d.
Julia M.	b. Aug. 30, 1869; d.
Evaline	b. Feb. 5, 1872; d.
Jesse L.	b. July 21, 1874; d.
James R.	b. Apr. 21, 1876; d.
Catherine Elizabeth	b. Apr. 27, 1878; d.
Eudora Pearl	b. May 25, 1880; d. 1964
Myrtle	b. Jan. 6, 1883

Jesse Stinson and Mary Evaline had sixteen children, all of whom lived to be married except John Lee who died in his teens.

Jesse Stinson and his family left Platte County, Missouri about 1857, and went to Arkansas. About 1862, he moved to Texas, however, he returned to Van Buren, Arkansas about 1866. Later he moved to Wagoner, then Indian Territory, Oklahoma.

Jesse taught school in his younger years, was also a merchant and an insurance salesman. In the 1890's he was secretary of the Watt's Association. It was here that he spent considerable time and money, as well as others of the family, in trying to prove the family had some Cherokee Indian blood which came through the Blackburn family of Virginia. However, being unable to establish proof, he was unable to be enrolled on the rolls of the Five Civilized Tribes which was then being revised.

It was at Wagoner, Oklahoma that Jesse died November 9, 1905, and where he is buried. His wife, Mary Evaline, also died at Wagoner but the date of her death is unknown.

BENJAMIN ALLEN BOATRIGHT
(1833-1853)

Benjamin Allen Boatright, son of William Van and Sallie Wadkins (Gates) Boatright was born March 11, 1833. He married Mary Blaylock in 1851, and they had one child:

Arminta Paralee   b. Oct. 18, 1852; d.

Benjamin Allen was killed January 18, 1853, when some logs which he was helping to move fell on him. He is buried in Darlington, Missouri.

215

In 1856, Benjamin's wife, Mary, married Samuel Sloan, a brother of John Sloan, husband of Elizabeth Jane Boatright. Samuel died in 1887, from this time on Mary, the widow of Samuel, made her home with her children until her death April 4, 1907.

JACOB GATES BOATRIGHT
(1835-1923)

Jacob Gates Boatright, son of William V. and Sallie Wadkins (Gates) Boatwright was born in Graves County, Kentucky September 5, 1835.

Jacob went with his family to Northwest Missouri in 1851, where he grew to manhood. Jacob stood 5 feet 9 1/2 inches tall, was light complexed, with blue eyes and light colored hair. (The Civil War Record for Jacob gave his description.) His occupation was a farmer, but he also did some ministering for the Primitive Baptist Church. Sinch the home of his father and mother was used as a meeting place for this church, this, no doubt, had some influence on his life.

On October 3, 1854, Jacob Gates married Clarisa Caroline Cook at Bedford, Taylor County, Iowa. Clarisa Caroline was the daughter of Nazareth and Celia (Dinkens) Cook. (The parents for Clarisa Caroline Cook were obtained from a death certificate for Thomas J. Cook, brother of Clarisa, who lived in Bedford, Taylor County, Iowa.) Nazareth and Celia were both born in North Carolina and migrated to Henry County, Tennessee where Clarisa Caroline was born January 8, 1837. As to what happened to Nazareth and Celia nothing has ever been found, nor is there any indication that they went with their children to Northwest Missouri and then to Bedford, Iowa.

Jacob Gates was somewhat of a rover. He was restless and wanted to be always on the move. Sometime between 1854 and 1860 Jacob and Caroline (as Jacob called her) made a trip to Texas. The exact place in Texas is not known. Mary Paralee Boatright Woods told her children that she was born in Dallas, Texas, however, her obituary states she was born near Union Star, De Kalb County, Missouri. Her daughter, Mary Belle

Gunter, was the informant. Mary Paralee was born September 26, 1856; perhaps she was born in Missouri before the trip was made to Texas. Louisa Jane, their second daughter, was born March 16, 1858 in Texas. The 1860 Census record shows her birthplace as Texas and when she celebrated her 95th birthday, the newspaper article gave her birthplace as Dennison County, Texas.

In the present day Texas there is no Dennison County listed but there is a Denton County. From the 1850 Census records for Denton County, Texas there was an Amasa Baugh, age 62, born in Kentucky, mother and father born in Virginia. This Baugh family had a child born in Texas in the year 1857. There surely was some relationship between this Baugh family and Jacob and perhaps that was the reason for the long trip. (See Baugh lineage in this Volume.)

By 1860 Jacob and Caroline were back in Gentry County, Missouri as they appear in 1860 Census record:

1860 CENSUS OF GENTRY CO., MO.
Township 62   Page 62   20   June

	Age		Born
399/296			
Jacob Boatright	26	farmer	Ky.
Caroline	22		Tenn.
Louisa	2		Texas

In 1860 Jacob and Caroline had been married six years. During this time they had had three children, but only one, Louisa, shows on the Census record. Thomas A. was born August 12, 1855, and died October 14, 1855, but Mary Paralee does not show as being in the household of Jacob and Caroline. Grace Caroline Woods Miller and her sister Fannie May Woods Flint recalled that their mother, Mary Paralee, lived most of her childhood with another family. Neither could remember the name of the family or if they were related.

On October 6, 1863, Jacob enlisted for service in the Civil War at Albany, Gentry County, Missouri. He served in the 12th Cavalry Volunteer Regiment as a Private in Company G, under Captain Kerrigan. He was mustered into service on February 21, 1864 and was discharged July 1, 1865. On September 6, 1910, Jacob applied for a pension, Certificate No. 664262, which he received until his death.

For a number of years the family lived in Albany and Pickering, Missouri. The family also lived in Iowa for a time but the location is not known. (The places of residence were obtained from the Civil War Record.) During the year 1887 Jacob and Caroline moved to Southern Missouri, were located for awhile in Barry County, Missouri and later moved to Joplin, Jasper County, Missouri. This location is where Caroline died January 3, 1907. She was a person who had enjoyed good health during her life, but the winter of 1907 she became ill with pneumonia and in a few days passed away. There was a death notice in the newspaper which is on file in the Missouri Historical Society Library at Columbia, Missouri which reads:

"Clarisa Boatright, age 70, died January 3, 1907. She was buried at Pickering, Missouri."

Jacob and Caroline had the following children:
Thomas Allen, b. 8/12/1855; d. 10/14/1855;
Mary Paralee, b. 9/26/1856; d. 10/11/1929;
m. Andrew Jackson Woods;
Louisa Jane, b. 3/16/1858; d. 1/3/1958; m.
William A. Shelman;
Sarah Frances, b. 1/15/1861; d. 4/9/1861;
Laura Ellen, b. 1/14/1862; d. 8/31/1953; m.
Charley Shelman;
Alice Von, b. 2/16/1864; d. 8/9/1956; m.
Joseph C. Deem;
Martha Belle, b. 5/22/1866; d. 10/?/1881;
James Albert, b. 8/12/1867; d. 7/1/1910; m.
Mary Elizabeth Scaff;
Emma Arene, b. 2/7/1869; d. 3/3/1960; m.
Samuel Brown;
William Nelson, b. 2/9/1871; d. 3/29/1930; m.
(1) Sadie Jane Pistole; (2) Sylvia M. Kunkle;
Francis Marion, b. 7/31/1873; d. 11/17/1878;
Flora Anne, b. 6/3/1875; d. 11/?/1955; m.
Charlie LaTurner;
Minnie Catharyn, b. 7/2/1877; living; m.
Perry Owens;

Adina (Ada) Ethel, b. 8/11/1880; d. 1/3/1953; m. James Arthur Burgess.

Louisa Jane (1858-1958) died a short time before her 100th birthday. Of the above children very little is known except for Mary Paralee.

On January 11, 1908, Jacob married for the second time. He married Mary Jane Mustain Duff, the widow of James H. Duff who was also in the Civil War, Co. I, 133 Illinois Inft. James died March 22, 1903. Mary Jane was the daughter of William and Anna Mustain and was born Jan. 29, 1857, at Springfield, Green County, Missouri. She died February 25, 1927, at Joplin, Missouri.

Jacob died August 26, 1923 at Joplin, Missouri and is buried by the side of his first wife, Caroline, at Pickering, Nodaway County, Missouri.

FRANCIS ALEXANDER BOATRIGHT
(1838-1918)

Francis Alexander Boatright, son of William Van and Sallie Wadkins (Gates) Boatright was born January 17, 1838. He married Esther Amanda Kittrell August 22, 1861. They had the following children:

Eliza Jane   b. July 6, 1862; d. June 3, 1864
Charles
  Henry   b. May 23, 1864; d. June 24, 1865
John James   b. Sept. 6, 1866; d. May 10, 1950
Sally Adaline b. Nov. 11, 1868; d. Oct. 1, 1872

Francis Alexander fought in the Civil War for the Confederate side. His wife, Esther Amanda, died March 11, 1869; she is buried in the Gill Cemetery about 3 miles east of Van Buren, Arkansas.

On August 22, 1869, Francis Alexander married Elizabeth Ann Frances Dannells Jolley who was a widow of Thomas B. Jolley. They had the following children:

William Vaugh   b. Dec. 2, 1870; d. Jan. 18, 1872
Franklin Bowden   b. Dec. 10, 1873; d. Oct. 19, 1935
Albert Bunyan   b. Jan. 30, 1877; d. Mar. 28, 1906
Joseph Benjamin   b. Nov. 6, 1879; d. July 11, 1937
Edna Elizabeth   b. Oct. 17, 1883; d. Sept.   1964

James Blackburn b. Nov. 22, 1885; d. Jan. 12, 1933
Frances Alexander died December 27, 1918 in Weleetka, Oklahoma and Elizabeth Ann Frances died January 24, 1932 in Wagoner, Oklahoma. Both are buried in Gill Cemetery, Van Buren, Arkansas.

JOSEPH MARION BOATRIGHT
(1841-1865)

Joseph Marion Boatright, son of William Van and Sallie Wadkins (Gates) Boatright was born February 18, 1841. He married Sarah Davidson; they had only one child:
J. E. Boatright b. Sept. 10, 1863; d.

Joseph enlisted in the Civil War on the Confederate side at DesArc, Arkansas, September 3, 1861. Joseph was a Private in Company B of the 10th Arkansas Infantry. The 10th Ark. served in Missouri, Kentucky, at Shiloh, was captured at Vicksburg, participated in Prince's Missouri Expedition after exchange. It was in this service that Joseph was killed at Perryville, Kentucky in 1865.

Sarah (Davidson) Boatright was born in Tennessee and came to Andrew County, Missouri with her parents. She lived on the farm which she and Joseph settled on after their marriage until her death in December 1900 at the age of 63.

MARY ANN ELIZA BOATRIGHT
(1844-1920)

Mary Ann Eliza Boatright, daughter of William Van and Sallie Wadkins (Gates) Boatright was born January 20, 1844. She married George Buton Thomas McMillen in Gentry County, Missouri, June 12, 1863. George Burton was born June, 1838. They had the following children:

Permelia Ann   b. May 31, 1865; d. Sept. 13, 1938
William Johnatan b. Feb. 11, 1867; d. July 22, 1952
Alfradine Buanna b. July 11, 1868; d. June 16, 1952
Lugema Jane   b. Mar. 1, 1870; d.
James M.   b. Aug. 10, 1871; d. Dec. 20, 1871

Delsa May b. Mar. 1, 1874; d. Feb. 15,1915
Limon Van
  Ranselear b. July 28, 1876; d. Dec. 14,1877
Sara A. b. Mar. 30, 1878; d. Aug. 30,1879
Margaret Frances
  b. Dec. 20, 1880; d.
Mary Ann Eliza died November 5, 1920 and her husband, George Burton, March 31, 1921. They are buried in the Gribble Cemetery, Darlington, Missouri.

Margaret Frances, the youngest of this family, is living in St. Joseph, Missouri (1966). She has been very helpful in supplying information for the William Van Boatright family.

WILLIAM TAYLOR BOATRIGHT
(1847-1933)

William Taylor Boatright, son of William Van and Sallie Wadkins (Gates) Boatright was born January 5, 1847. He married Sarah Ellen Burger January 3, 1869. Sarah Ellen was born February 27, 1851, at Pulaski County, Kentucky. They had the following children:

Levi Jackson b. Oct. 16, 1869; d. Nov. 1, 1949
Laura Adaline b. Mar. 10, 1871; d. Nov. 14, 1950
Elizabeth b. Dec. 26, 1872; d. Jan. 16, 1873
James Franklin b. Oct. 7, 1874; d. Sept. 24, 1953
Orilla Josephine b. Nov. 14, 1878; d. Aug. 7, 1895
Jesse Oriville b. Nov. 25, 1881; d. July 13, 1960
Charles William b. Dec. 24, 1884; d. Dec. 29, 1947
Viola May b. Nov. 12, 1887; d. June 8, 1912
John Taylor b. Jan. 5, 1891; d.

When William Taylor was only seventeen years old he enlisted his services for the Civil War. He was with Company D, Forty Third Missouri Infantry, which operated mostly in the state of Missouri. During the Price raid William was captured, October 15, 1864, at Glasgow, Missouri, but was soon paroled and sent to Benton Barracks, near St. Louis. He was mustered out June 30, 1865.

In 1884 William and his family traveled to Sumner County, Kansas by covered wagon where he purchased a farm and remained until his death, December 22,1933.

His wife, Sarah Ellen died January 28, 1929.
In 1928, Mr. R. G. Boatright, Cushing, Oklahoma became interested in the Boatright Family History and began to keep a record. It was from William Taylor that he received a great deal of information.
John Taylor Boatright, youngest son of William Taylor is living in Wichita, Kansas (1966). He, too, has been very helpful in passing on facts about the family.

JAMES BLACKBURN BOATRIGHT
(1850-1931)

James Blackburn Boatright, youngest son of William Van and Sallie Wadkins (Gates) Boatright, was born October 19, 1850, just prior to when the family left Graves Co., Kentucky and made the trip to Northwest Missouri.
James Blackburn grew to manhood in Darlington, Missouri and married Hattie Adaline Christian. Hattie Adaline was born December 18, 1856, and died December 18, 1886. She was a sister to Lenox K. Christian who married Sally Ann Sloan, daughter of Elizabeth Jane Boatright and John Sloan.
James Blackburn Boatright was a harness maker and a farmer.
James Blackburn and Hattie Adaline had the following children:

> William Louis   b. June 14, 1876; d. Nov. 25, 1938
> Sophrona Viola   b. Aug. 26, 1878; d. Aug. 5, 1879
> Jesse Janetty   b. Mar. 31, 1880; d. Nov. 6, 1880
> Harvey Ezra   b. Mar. 8, 1882; d. Sept. 7, 1954

Hattie Adaline died December 18, 1886, and in December, 1892, James Blackburn married Mary Emma Cogdill Wright, the widow of William Wright. Mary Emma was born November 13, 1857 in California and died July 15, 1913, in Colorado. James Blackburn and Mary Emma had the following children:

> James Nealy   b. Sept. 24, 1893; d.
> Earl Cleo   b. Apr. 18, 1895; d.
> Clarence Harold   b. Mar. 20, 1897; d. July 12, 1952
> Paul Thomas   b. Jan. 3, 1899; d. Jan. 19, 1899
> Otis Francis   b. Oct. 4, 1901; d.

James Blackburn and his family moved to Colorado Springs, Colorado, where he remained until his death Jan. 1, 1932. He is buried in Darlington, Missouri.

William Louis, oldest son of James Blackburn Boatright, was a prominent figure in Republican circles of the state of Colorado, having served as Attorney General of Colorado from 1925 to 1929.

MARY PARALEE BOATRIGHT
(1856-1929)

Mary Paralee Boatright, daughter of Jacob Gates and Clarisa Caroline (Cook) Boatright was born September 26, 1856. (Date of Mary Paralee's birth was given on her death certificate, also the Civil War Record for Jacob Gates gave the date of birth for all his children.) The exact place of her birth has not been determined, whether it was Missouri or Texas.

On September 26, 1877, her birthday, Mary Paralee married Andrew Jackson Woods. Their marriage is on file in Maryville the county seat for Nodaway County. It is as follows:

State of Missouri)
County of Nodaway)
   This is to certify that on the 26th day of September A.D., 1877, Mr. Andrew J. Woods and Miss Mary P. Boatright were by me united in marriage according to the Laws of God, and of the State of Missouri at Nodaway County, Missouri.
        Thornton Fakes
        M. G.
Filed for record January 16th 1878
   Recorder

Andrew Jackson Woods was born in Belmont County, Ohio, July 25, 1845. He was the son of Conard Woods, (Andrew Jackson Woods has been found in the household of Conard Woods in the 1850 Census record for Belmont County, Ohio. Also he was named in the Will of Conard Woods. Grace Caroline Woods Miller remembered her grandfather as she was seven years old when he died.) born in Pennsylvania, March 4, 1800, and Ann Eliza Trigg, born Belmont County, Ohio August 7, 1820. They were married in Belmont County in 1841, record of which is in the Belmont County Court House, St. Clairsville, Ohio in book 5, page 258.

In 1858 Conard and Ann Eliza brought their family to Northwest Missouri and settled 2 1/2 miles Northeast of Clyde, where they lived until their deaths. Conard died April 3, 1892, and was at the time of his death 92 years and 1 month. The oldest man in Jefferson township, if not in the county. (From the obituary of Conard Woods as found in the Maryville Daily Democrat, Tuesday April 5, 1892.) A year later, Ann Eliza followed her husband in death, March 27, 1893, in the 73rd year of her life. (From the obituary of Ann Eliza as found in the Maryville Republican, 1893.) They are buried in the Sweet Home Cemetery which is located 2 miles north of Sweet Home; 2 or 3 miles east of Ravenwood, Missouri.

Mary Paralee and Andrew lived in Nodaway County for awhile and then moved to Stanberry, Gentry County, Missouri. Andrew was a Blacksmith by trade and had a shop in Stanberry.

Mary Paralee was a Baptist, as were her father and grandfather. She, with her husband and family, belonged to the Stanberry Baptist Church and was a member for 42 years. They had the following children:

Ralph Conard, b. July 2, 1878; d. about 1945; buried
L.A., Calif.
Minnie Ann, b. Oct. 18, 1879; d. Apr. 6, 1952;
buried Kansas City, Kansas.
Thomas Jacob, b. Nov. 13, 1880; d. Jan., 1952;
buried St. Joseph, Mo.
Edwin Lewis, b. Oct. 9, 1882; d. Dec. 8, 1958;
buried Stanberry, Mo.
Dana Amos Evert, b. Feb. 2, 1884; d. 1935; buried
Stanberry, Mo.
<u>Grace Caroline,</u> b. Dec. 11, 1885; lives in Kansas
City, Kansas.
Martha, b., d., in infancy; buried Stanberry, Mo.
Mary Bell, b. July 25, 1890; lives Montana.
Kittie Alice, b. June 16, 1892; buried Stanberry, Mo.
Fannie May, b. Dec. 15, 1893; lives Kansas City,
Kan.
William Francis, b. Aug. 11, 1895; lives L.A.,Calif.

Fred, b. , d in infancy; buried Stanberry, Mo.
Angie Emmalee, b. Oct. 24, 1900; lives L. A. ,Calif.
    Ralph Conard m. Maud Booker
    Minnie Ann m. James Frier
    Thomas Jacob m. Allie Conner
    Edwin Lewis never married
    Dana Amos Evert m. Ida Humphrey
    <u>Grace Caroline</u> m. Roy Ozias Miller
    Martha, died in infancy
    Mary Bell m. (1) Bill Garver, (2) Charlie
        Matteson (killed on railroad), (3) Tom
        Gunter
    Kittie Alice m. Orville Goodwine
    Fannie May m. Leroy Carl Flint
    William Francis m. Orda Vance
    Fred died in infancy
    Angie Emmalee m. Henry Janto (changed spel-
        ling of name from Jameto)

  After the Woods children were grown, but still living at home, the family moved to St. Joseph, Missouri where the older children obtained employment to help with the living expenses.

  One by one the young people were married and left home, and it was then that Mary Paralee and Andrew moved back to Stanberry and located on a farm about five miles north of the town. Here they lived until their deaths. Andrew died February 6, 1924, in Stanberry and Mary Paralee, October 11, 1929, at the home of her daughter, Mary Bell Gunter, St. Joseph, Buchanan County, Missouri. They are buried at the High Ridge Cemetery, Stanberry, Missouri.

GRACE CAROLINE WOODS
(1885-   )

  Grace Caroline, daughter of Mary Paralee (Boatright) and Andrew Jackson Woods, married Roy Ozias Miller June 17, 1912 in Gentry County, Missouri. Roy Ozias was the son of John Wesley Miller and Emma Ozias.

  Emma Ozias was the daughter of Thomas Ozias, born Feb. 21, 1814, and died December 31, 1893, who married April 3, 1853, Martha A. (Millie) Walton, born January 10, 1835 and died July 22, 1883. Thomas and Martha went to Buchanan County, Iowa from Ohio. (From the "History of the Osio, Osius, Ozias Families" compiled by Albert Lawrence Rohrer, 1943.) This Ozias family line is on record with the Daughters of the American Revolution for John Ozias (Osier), North Carolina. The National DAR No. 483890 is active and is held by Mary Lorene Miller Wallace.

John Wesley Miller was born March 9, 1853 and died January 18, 1933. John Wesley was the son of Ephriam Miller and Rebecca Wilson, they were married in Wayne County, Ohio and migrated to Buchanan County, Iowa in 1850, where they died and are buried in the Wilson Cemetery. Ephraim Miller was the son of Jacob Miller and Catherine Gumm who went from Cumberland County, Pennsylvania to Wayne County, Ohio about 1828. (From the obituary of Rebecca Wilson Miller, 1899, and Ephraim Miller, 1906. Also death certificate of John Wesley Miller and the death certificate of Mary Marinda Baker, sister of Ephraim Miller and mentioned in his obituary as Mrs. J. L. Baker, La Porte City, Iowa.)

Grace Caroline and Roy Ozias Miller had the following children:

Willa Mae, b. Sept. 24, 1913 at Stanberry, Mo.
Mary Lorene, b. Apr. 16, 1917 at Stanberry, Mo.
Emma Louise, b. Oct. 5, 1918 at Elk Springs, Mo.

Roy Ozias died October 22, 1955, at McDonald County Missouri, he is buried at Carthage, Missouri. John Wesley and Emma Ozias are also buried here.

WILLA MAE MILLER
(1913-   )

Willa Mae Miller, daughter of Grace Caroline (Woods) and Roy Ozias Miller was born September 24, 1913. She married Jack Emmett Bridges July 26, 1931. Jack Emmett died November 11, 1939. They had one child:

Susan Lynne, b. May 12, 1939 at Kansas City, Mo.

Willa Mae married William Leonard Fleming September 27, 1947, at Kansas City, Kansas. William

Leonard was born February 9, 1903. They had the following children:
> Mary Alice, b. Feb. 6, 1949 at Kansas City, Kan.
> Brent Leonard, b. Nov. 4, 1953 at Kansas City.

MARY LORENE MILLER
(1917-   )

Mary Lorene Miller, daughter of Grace Caroline (Woods) and Roy Ozias Miller was born April 16, 1917. She married Robert Cavett Wallace on April 15, 1945 at the Washington Avenue Methodist Church, Kansas City, Kansas by the Rev. Eugene Frank. Robert Cavett, born April 11, 1914, is the son of R. Boyd Wallace and Cleo Fern Nelson.

Mary Lorene and Robert Cavett Wallace had the following children:
> Mary Jean, b. July 16, 1946 at Kansas City, Kansas
> Patricia Louise, b. Jan. 21, 1951 at Bartlesville, Oklahoma.

EMMA LOUISE MILLER
(1918-   )

Emma Louise Miller, daughter of Grace Caroline (Woods) and Roy Ozias Miller was born October 5, 1918. She married Carl Herman Zimmerman April 11, 1943 in Kansas City, Mo. They had the following children:
> Janet Lorene, b. Nov. 24, 1945 at Kansas City, Kan.
> Larry Allen, b. Oct. 9, 1948 at Kansas City, Kan.

FANNIE MAY WOODS
(1893-   )

Fannie May Woods, the daughter of Mary Paralee (Boatright) and Andrew Jackson Woods was born December 15, 1893. She married Leroy Carl Flint August 20, 1927, at St. Joseph, Missouri.

Leroy Carl was born November 6, 1892 at Schell City, Missouri, he was the son of John Thomas Flint and Mary Ellen Hornbuckle. John Thomas and Mary

Ellen were married at Prairie City, Bates County, Missouri.

Fannie and Leroy had one child:
Ila Jean, b. Apr. 7, 1930 at Kansas City, Kan.

ILA JEAN FLINT
(1930-   )

Ila Jean Flint, daughter of Fannie May (Woods) and Leroy Carl Flint, was born April 7, 1930. She married Buddy Jack Carlyle and they have the following children:
Steven Bruce, b. Sept. 26, 1955 at Kansas City, Kan.
Donald Brent, b. Aug. 15, 1957 at Kansas City, Kan.

Compiled by: Lorene Miller Wallace
1808 College View Drive
Bartlesville, Oklahoma.

VIRGINIA COUNTY FORMATION

Henrico
1654

Goochland   Chesterfield
1728   1749

Albemarle   Cumberland
1744   1749

                                   Powhatan
                                   1777

Amherst   Buckingham   Fluvanna
1761   1761   1777

Nelson   Appomattox
1808   1845

Dale Parish was formed 1735

****

THE BAUGH FAMILY OF VIRGINIA

The Baugh family originated in Gloucestershire, England. The Coat-of-Arms: Gules, a fesse vaire between three mullets argent. Crest: Out of a Ducal coronet, or, a talbot segreant sable.

These were the arms as borne and used by the emigrant William Baugh, "Gentleman Justice" of Henrico, who was the founder of this family in Virginia. Granted 11 November, 1574. (Visitation of Gloucestershire, p. 11.)

The further identity of William Baugh is attested in an account of a legal controversy, June 5, 1639, Car. 1. Subject: Richard Kimble of London, merchant tailor, William Baugh, late of London, now gone into Virginia. He was born circa 1610, "Gentleman Justice" of Henrico 1656, died 1687.

William Baugh (in Virginia 1639 & c.), late of London. (Probably William Baugh, who was b. in 1610, and was J.P. for Henrico Co., 1656, & c.) V.M., XIX, 193. (From "Some Emigrants to Virginia", by W.G. Stanard, p. 11.)

The Henrico records, Vol. I, p. 265, mentions a court being held at Fort Henry, Jan. 15, 1656. William Baugh is mentioned as being present as a Justice. Ft. Henry was located where the mansion of "Montview" in Petersburg, Va., now stands.

In April 1681, William Baugh, Sr., Gent., deeded to his grand-daughter, Priscilla Baugh, wife of William Farrar, a tract of land which he had previously deeded to a grandson, William Baugh.

William Baugh and Robert Pitt jointly patented 1800 acres in the Isle of Wight. He, Col. Pitt, and John Bridger patented 3000 acres in Isle of Wight Co. Abell Gower, a large proprietor of Henrico, married Mrs. Jane Baugh, widow of William Baugh who was her second husband. Her maiden name was not known. Gowere d. in 1689. (W. & M. Q., Vol. 24)

The facts about William Baugh are quoted as a ref.

WILLIAM BAUGH
(ca 1610-1687)

William Baugh patented 577 acres in Henrico County, Virginia (now Chesterfield) January 16, 1668. This is the first ancestor to whom later generations can be traced.

In 1656 William was one of His Majesty's Justices in Henrico County. There is much to be found about him in the counties of Henrico and Chesterfield. His Will is on file in the year 1687, and mentions his sons: John, William, and JAMES; daughters: Priscilla and Mary; also a grandson, John. Apparently, another son, Thomas, died prior to the writing of the Will, 1687.

William Baugh was born in England about 1610, he died in Henrico County, Virginia April 1, 1687. William was married in England first to (name unknown) and second to Elizabeth Paker als Sharp. There is also indication that he was married for the third time. Perhaps his third wife was Jane, who was the widow of William Baugh and married Abell Gower (Gowere) as found in the W. & M. Q. Vol. 24. However, she is not mentioned in the Will of William Baugh.

The children of William were:
    William, b. ca. 1638, d. ____ ; m. _____
    John, b. ca. 1642; d. _____ ; m. Margaret ___
    Thomas, b. ____ ; d. prior 1687; m. _____
    JAMES, b. ca. 1655; d. about 1722; m. _____
    Mary, b. ____ ; d. ____ : m. _____ Howlet
    Priscilla, b. _____ ; d. _____ ; m. _____ .

THE CHILDREN OF WILLIAM BAUGH

Of the children of William Baugh, nothing is known about William (ca 1638).

John Baugh (ca 1642) left a Will which is on file in Wills 1725-38 for Henrico County. In this he names his wife, Margaret; sons: John, Henry; and daughters: Hanna, Ann, Martha, Sarah, and Mary wife of Henry Walters.

Thomas left no children.
Nothing is known about Mary or Priscilla.

231

JAMES BAUGH
(ca 1655-ca 1722)

James Baugh, the fourth son of William Baugh, was born ca 1655 and died ca 1722. The known children of James are:

    THOMAS, b. ca 1690; d. ca 1762; m. Sarah Ashbrook.
    William, b. ca. 1693; d. ca 1753; m. _____.
    Sarah, b. _____; d. _____; m. _____ Stuart.

THE CHILDREN OF JAMES BAUGH

THOMAS BAUGH
(ca 1690-ca 1762)

Chesterfield County, Virginia, Will Book 1, page 333 lists:
    WILL OF THOMAS BAUGH, DALE PARISH, dated September 20, 1751.

There is no date of probate given for this Will but as it follows a Will of John Baugh, inventory and appraisal dated March 30, 1762, Thomas, no doubt, also died in 1762. The Will is as follows:

    In the name God Amen. I Thomas Baugh of Dale Parish in the County of Chesterfield being of perfect mind and memory do make my last Will and Testament in manner following

First   I commend my soul into the Hands of Almighty God hoping to receive free pardon and forgiveness of all my sins and my Body I commit to the earth to be decently entered at the descretion of my Executor hereafter named as for what Estate it hath pleased Almighty God to bestow upon me I bequeath in manner following

First my will is that my Debts and Legacies hereafter given and my funeral charges be first paid by my Executor out of my Estate and that my Estate shall not be appraised.

Secondly I give to my son, Joseph Baugh one shilling Sterling

Thirdly I give to my son Thomas Baugh one shilling

Sterling

Item   I give to my son <u>Abraham Baugh</u> one shilling Sterling

Item   I Will to my Daughter Martha Russell one shilling Sterling

Item   I give to my Daughter Judith Farguson one shilling Sterling

Item   I give to my Daughter Sarah Ashbrook one shilling Sterling

Item   I Will to my Daughter Jane Baugh one shilling Sterling

Item   I give and Bequeath to my son James Baugh my part of the fishing place at <u>Cobbs</u> known by the name of Baughs to him the said James and his heirs forever. I also give to my son James the land I live on to him the said James and his heirs forever. I likewise give to my son James Baugh my land known by the name of France containing one Hundred Acres to him the said James and his heirs forever --

Item   I give and bequeath to my son James all the rest of my Estate both real and personal to him the said James and his heirs forever. I do also ordain constitute and appoint my son James Baugh sole Executor of this my last Will and Testament. Witness my hand and Seal this Twentieth day of September in the year of our Lord Christ one thousand seven Hundred and fifty one.

                          Thomas Baugh (Seal)

Signed and Sealed)
in the presence of)
Edward Wilkinson
John Turner
Levi Baugh (?)

Sarah, the wife of Thomas, was not mentioned in his Will.

The children of Thomas and Sarah were:

Joseph, b. _____; d. about 1777, m. Rachel ____; d. 1787.

Thomas, b. _____; d. _____; m. _____.

<u>ABRAHAM</u>, b. _____; d. 1797; m. Judith Colman

James, b. _____; d. 1778; m. _____.

Martha, b. _____; d. _____; m. _____ Russell.

Judith, b. ____; d. _____; m. _____ Ferguson.
Jane, b. _____; d. _____; m. _____.
Sarah, b. _____; d. _____; m. _____.

WILLIAM BAUGH
(ca 1693-ca 1753)

 William Baugh, the son of James and brother of Thomas, left a very important Will which proves that William and Thomas were brothers.
 Chesterfield County, Virginia, Will Book 1, page 134.
 Will of William Baugh of Dale Parish, dated January 15, 1753, no date of probate is given but an Inventory and Appraisal of his Estate is dated September 1, 1753; legatees:

sons:	John, Frederick, William
daughters:	Agnes Baugh, Sarah Walthall
sister:	Sarah Stuart
BROTHER:	<u>THOMAS BAUGH</u>
Executor:	my son, William
Witnesses:	Peter Baugh, John Osborne, William Bass

 In this same Will book, page 332 dated March 30, 1762, Inventory and appraisal of the Estate of John Baugh, deceased. This appraisal includes names of 19 slaves, 14 cattle, 24 sheep, 30 hogs, etc. Total 1219 pds 11 shillings 10 pence.
 This John Baugh was a very wealthy man and is, no doubt, the son of William (ca 1693).

SARAH BAUGH
( )

 Nothing is known about Sarah except that she is mentioned in the Will of her brother, William (ca 1693), and that she married someone by the name of Stuart.

THE CHILDREN OF THOMAS BAUGH

 Of the children of Thomas and Sarah (Ashbrook) Baugh nothing is known about Thomas, James, Martha,

Judith, Jane, and Sarah.

JOSEPH BAUGH
(-ca 1777)

Joseph Baugh, son of Thomas and Sarah (Ashbrook) Baugh and brother of ABRAHAM BAUGH, lived at the time of his death in that part of Cumberland County, Virginia that was made into Powhatan County in 1777. His Will is on file in Powhatan County and is found in Will Book 1, (1777-1795) page 4.

Will of Joseph Baugh of Southam Parish in the County of Cumberland, dated June 5, 1776, Probated December 18, 1777.

To my wife, Rachel Baugh, the tract of land I now live on for her natural life and after her death to MY BROTHER, ABRAHAM BAUGH, also to my wife, eleven negroes (named) etc.

To Thomas Baugh, son of my brother ABRAHAM BAUGH, of the County and Parish aforesaid, one negro man named Ned, etc.

To my Brother, James Baugh of Dale Parish in the County of Chesterfield one negro girl named Rose, etc.

To my brother, ABRAHAM BAUGH, the remainder of my negroes, etc.

I also leave Henry More and his wife, (?) More the use of my adjacent plantation they now live on during their natural lives providing they continue to live there and not move and to pay the usual rent, after their decease I give and devise (?) to Thomas Baugh, son of ABRAHAM BAUGH, etc.

To Israel Winfrey one acre of land adjoining his mill.

To Phebe Rusil (Russell) daughter of my sister, Martha Rusil (Russell)

Executor: ABRAHAM BAUGH and Charles Hatcher
Witnesses: Charles Hatcher, Seth Hatcher, and Gideon Hatcher.

In the Archives of the Virginia State Library at Richmond, Virginia under the Public Service Claims, 1782, for Powhatan County, Virginia appears "Joseph

Baugh, Estate of Rachel Baugh." These are the original claims for material, supplies or services furnished the Continental Army in the Revolutionary War by the individuals. Proved descendants are eligible for membership in the Daughters of the American Revolution or the Sons of the American Revolution by reason of their ancestor's "furnishing supplies and/or services" and as a proven patriot.

From the Will of Joseph, it is assumed that Joseph and Rachel had no children.

ABRAHAM BAUGH
(- 1797)

Abraham Baugh, son of Thomas and Sarah (Ashbrook) Baugh, died in Powhatan County, Virginia in the year 1797. His Will was probated in this county, August 16, 1797. The date of his birth is not known. Abraham lived in that part of Cumberland County that was made into Powhatan County, 1777.

From the book "Names of Residents of Cumberland County Prior to the Establishment of the Republic in 1789" Compiled by Garland Evans Hopkins and Joseph W. Bland --- Cumberland County, Virginia lists Abraham Baugh.

From "A History of the Pioneer Families of Missouri" Compiled by Wm. S. Bryan and Robert Rose, 1876, pages 131-132, the following reference is quoted:

BAUGH --The Baughs were doubtless of German descent; but there is no authentic record of the origin of the family, beyond the fact that three brothers of that name settled near Jamestown, Va., at an early date. Abram, a son of one of these brothers, married Judith Colman, of Powhatan county, and by her he had---Joseph, Thomas M., Edsa, William, Alexander, Abram, Jesse, Mary, Judith, and RHODA. Joseph married Nancy Gentry, and settled in Madison county, Ky., in 1781; and in 1816 he removed to St. Charles, county, Mo. He served five years in the Revolutionary War. His children were -- William, Benjamin, Judith, Alsey, Nancy, Mary, Patsey, and Lucinda. William married Susan Carter,

of Kentucky, and settled in St. Charles county, Mo.,
but removed from there to Montgomery county in
1832. His first wife died, and he was married the
second time to Mrs. Nancy V. Haslip, whose maiden name was Chambers.

Where the German descent was obtained is not known but from the facts which have been established it is more likely this is in error and the Baughs were of English descent.

From this book we have found that the wife of Abraham was Judith Colman, also Abraham's Will gives his wife as Judith. Whether Judith's last name was spelled Colman or Coleman is not known. Coleman was a family name which was in this country at an early date, from Westmoreland County Wills, a William Coleman's Will is found dated April 12, 1665. From all the early records checked the name was spelled Coleman. There were no Colmans (or Colemans) listed in Powhatan County, Virginia in the 1790 Census, however, Cumberland County listed the following Colemans:

    COLEMAN Patience
                     Gulleelmeis
                     Parmenus
                     William
                     Daniel
                     Thomas
                     Elizabeth

A check was made with the Probate Clerk of Cumberland County to determine if any of these people listed might have left a Will naming Judith (Coleman) Baugh as a daughter, there was none. Nothing has been found about Judith's family to date.

The children of Abraham and Judith were:
    Joseph, b. 1758; d. after 1843; m. Nancy Gentry.
    William, b. 9/17/1765; d. 4/12/1841; m. Elizabeth Ashbrook.
    <u>ABRAHAM,</u> b. 8/7/1773; d. 1833; m. Martha Johnson (See later).
    Thomas M., b. ____; d. ____; m. Elizabeth Johnson.
    Amasa, b. ____; d. ____; m. Patience Cheatham.
    Elsa, b. ____; d. ____; m. _____.

Alexander, b. _____ ; d. _____ ; m. _____ .
Jesse, b. _____ ; d. _____ ; m. _____ .
Mary, b. _____ ; d. _____ ; m. James Routten.
Judith, b. _____ ; d. ___ ; m. Daniel Johnson.
RHODA, b. ___ ; d. ___ ; m. James Blackburn before 7/1/1779.

The following marriage records are on file in the Powhatan County Marriage Records:

Aug. 16, 1785 James Routon and Mary Baugh, Sur. Amasa Baugh, Powhatan County Marriage Register, p. 8.

Apr. 18, 1793 Daniel Johnson and Judith Baugh dau. of Abraham Baugh, Sr. Sur. Alexander Baugh, Powhatan County Marriage Register, p. 24.

Dec. 21, 1793 Abraham Baugh and Martha Johnson dau. of Wm. Johnson. Sur. Abraham Baugh, Jr., Thomas Baugh of Chesterfield Co., Powhatan Marriage Register, p. 26.

Feb. 17, 1794 Thomas Baugh and Elizabeth Johnson, dau. of Wm. Johnson who consents. Sur. Abraham Baugh, Jr., Thomas Baugh of Chesterfield County, Powhatan County Marriage Register, p. 26.

Chesterfield County, Va. Marriages, by Knorr, page 9, Apr. 15, 1784 Amasa Baugh to Patience Cheatham.

Chesterfield County Marriage Bonds 1771-1815
Amasa Baugh and Patience
Married by Rev. William Hickman Minister of Skinquarter Baptist Church, Ministers' return, p. 369.

Madison County Kentucky Marriage Records
Mar. 3, 1796 Joseph Baugh to Nancy Gentry - bond Martin Green.

The above marriage records have been found for the children of Abraham and Judith. A search for the record of Rhoda and James Blackburn has been made but nothing has been found. Since Elizabeth (Blackburn) Boatwright, daughter of Rhoda (Baugh) and James Blackburn was born July 1, 1779, and from the marriage records above, it would seem that Rhoda was one of the oldest children of the family.

On file at the Virginia State Library, Richmond, Virginia under the Public Service Claims of Powhatan County is the following:

PUBLIC SERVICE CLAIMS POWHATAN COUNTY,
COURT BOOKLET 64-2426

1781   ABRAHAM BAUGH
May 5   For 50 lbs Fodder
Oct. 11   V.. 475 lbs grass beef

This claim proves that Abraham aided in the cause of the Revolutionary War and his proven descendants are eligible for the Daughters of the American Revolution or Sons of the American Revolution.

The Will of Abraham is on file in Powhatan County, dated October 23, 1794, probated August 16, 1797, and is as follows:

LAST WILL AND TESTAMENT
of
ABRAHAM BAUGH

In the Name of God amen, I Abraham Baugh of the County of Powhatan being well in health and in perfect mind and memory praised be God, do make and ordain this my last Will and Testament in manner and form following. I lend my well beloved wife Judith Baugh the use of my land and plantation that I now live on also three Negroes called Frank, Nance, and Lewis during her natural life, and then to descend to my two sons William Baugh and Abraham Baugh as I shall hereafter mention I also lend my well beloved wife Judith Baugh all my stock of horses, Cattle, sheep and hogs household and kitchen furniture plantation utensils all except such part as I shall hereafter give away and at her death to descend to my son Abraham Baugh to him his heirs and assigns forever. I give and bequeath to my son Thomas Baugh one Cow and calf one feather bed and furniture to him his heirs and assigns forever. I give and bequeath to my son Joseph Baugh one negroe boy cald Ned one Cow and Calf to him his heirs and assigns forever. I give and bequeath to my son Amasa Baugh one negroe called Jacob to him his heirs and assigns forever. I give and bequeath to my son Alexander Baugh one negroe called Pompey to him his heirs and assigns forever. I give and bequeath to my son Abraham Baugh one negroe called Stephen and Sorrel Mare one Cow and Calf and after the death of my said wife I also give and bequeath to my said son Abraham Baugh the land and plantation whereon I now live with all the rest of my estate both real and personal I have lent my said wife to him his heirs and assigns forever I give and bequeath unto my son William Baugh all the rest of my Land on the East side of Abraham Baughs line including a small field and Loghouse and also Shop. Beginning at Swift Creek on a small branch up the branch to large gulley up the gulley to the road and so on agreeable to the last survey to him his heirs and assigns forever.

 I give and bequeath to my daughter <u>RHODA BLACKBOURN</u> Two negroes called Saru and Olive to her heirs and assigns forever. I give and bequeath to my daughter Mary Routten two negroes called Tobb and Rose during her natural life they and their increase to be equally divided between three heirs of her body lawfully begotten to them their heirs and assigns forever.

 I give and bequeath to my daughter Judith Johnson Two negroes called Sall and Luce during her natural life. Then they and their increase to be equally divided between the heirs of her body lawfully begotten to them their heirs and assigns forever.

 Lastly I appoint and ordain my said Wife Judith Baugh and my Son Abraham Baugh to be my hole and Sole Executors of this my last Will and Testament I desire my estate may not be appraised In Witness whereof I have hereunto set my hand and affix my seal this twenty third day of October one Thousand seven hundred and ninety four.

Signed Seal and acknowledged   Abraham Baugh
In presents of us   (SEAL)
A Haskins
   his
Philip   X Hambleton
   mark
Pendexter Noell

At a Court held for Powhatan County the sixteenth day of August 1797. The last Will and Testament of Abraham Baugh deceased was proved by the oath of Poindexter Noell and Aaron Haskins two of the witnesses thereto and it is ordered to be recorded and on the motion of Abraham Baugh the executor therein named who made oath thereto and together with Henry W. Watkins John Cheatwood and Benajah Watkins his securities entered into and acknowledged their bond in the penalty of Seven thousand dollars conditioned as the law directs, certificate is granted him for obtaining a probate in due form and libertyes reserved for Judith Baugh the executrix named in the said Will to join in the probate when she shall think fit.

                       A. C. Crump   C T Court

A copy
Deed Book #2, page #368
July 25, 1961   Teste: (s) Wm. E. Maxey, Jr.
                                 Wm. E. Maxey, Jr., Clerk

The descendannts of Abraham Baugh settled in Virginia while others moved on West with the early Pioneers. Abraham settled in Garrard County, Kentucky; Joseph, Madison County, Kentucky and later St. Charles County, Missouri; William, Madison County, Kentucky but later moved farther south into Laurel County, Kentucky. From Kentucky the families branched out into Texas, Missouri and, no doubt, many other states.

THE CHILDREN OF ABRAHAM BAUGH, SR.

RHODA BAUGH
(   )

Rhoda Baugh, daughter of Abraham and Judith (Coleman) Baugh, date of birth and death unknown, married James Blackburn.

James Blackburn lived in Buckingham County, Virginia. From the Personal Property & Land Tax List it is found that for the years 1782 to 1785, Mary Blackburn and James Blackburn are the only individuals of the surname "Blackburn" who own land in Buckingham

County. As to whom Mary was, is not known, unless she could have been the mother of James, and a widow.

In the year 1786, James Blackburn died and from then on the same 200 acres of land he had reported was reported by James Blackburn, Jr. In the year 1787, this land was reported by James Blackburn, Jr. and Samuel Routon, therefore, it is assumed that James Blackburn, Jr. was under the age of 21, and that Samuel Routon was the overseer. For the year 1789 James appears for the first time in his own right, thus he is age 21 and he must have been born 1768 or 1769.

It is of interest to note that August 16, 1785, Mary Baugh, sister of Rhoda (Baugh) Blackburn, married James Routon (see previously), and Samuel Routon was overseer for the land of Rhoda (Baugh) Blackburn and her son, James, after the death of the husband and father.

James Blackburn, Jr. apparently sold this land by 1802, as his name no longer appears on the tax list after this date.

It has been found that James had a brother by the name of William who lived in Powhatan County, Virginia. This William was helpful to his niece, Elizabeth (Blackburn) Boatwright at the time of her husband's death in 1816.

What happened to Rhoda, after the death of her husband, James, is not known. If she did remarry, it was after her father, Abraham Baugh, wrote his Will as she is named Rhoda Blackbourn.

The known children of Rhoda and James are as follows:

        James, Jr., b. 1768 or 1769, d. _____.
        Elizabeth, b. 7/1/1779, d. 9/11/1862.
        Rhoda, b. ____; d. _____.

Nothing is known about James Blackburn, Jr. other than he is listed in the Tax Lists for Buckingham County, Virginia, but disappears after 1802.

Rhoda Blackburn, daughter of Rhoda (Baugh) and James Blackburn, married John Patterson. On March 15, 1815, they were residing in Madison County, Kentucky, and to them was born a daughter whose name was Julia Ann Patterson. This Julia Ann married

Benjamin Daniel Boatwright, the youngest son of Elizabeth (Blackburn) and Benjamin Boatwright. (See Boatwright lineage.)

ABRAHAM BAUGH, JR.
(1773-1833)

Abraham Baugh, Jr., son of Abraham and Judith (Coleman) Baugh was born August 7, 1773, in that part of Cumberland County, Virginia that was made into Powhatan County in 1777. Abraham married Martha Johnson, born October 3, 1773, who was the daughter of William and Polly Johnson.

From a Bible record published in 1740, and in the possession of Pearl Baugh Dannel, the children of Abraham, Jr. and Martha were copied, and are as follows:

    William Johnson, b. 9/20/1794, d. _____.
    Jesse Gill, b. 10/3/1796, d. _____.
    <u>ELISHA P.</u>, b. 7/7/1798, d. 11/1/1867. (See later)
    Rowena, b. 8/7/1799, d. _____.
    Caelia, b. 5/10/1801, d. 7/13/1801.
    Twins, b. 8/7/1803, d. 1803.
    Abraham G., b. 10/15/1805, d. _____.
    A son, b. 1806, d. 1806.
    Darias, b. 12/3/1809, d. _____.
    Marcellus, b. 2/4/1812, d. _____.
    Martha Ann, b. 8/27/1814, d. _____.

From the Will of his father, Abraham received some land in Powhatan County, Virginia; however, he must have disposed of this land as he moved on to Garrard County, Kentucky.

Abraham's wife, Martha, died before 1827, as in the year 1827 Abraham married Elizabeth Brown in Garrard County. Abraham died sometime between June 1833, and December 1933. His Will written June 25, 1833, was produced in Court December 1833. It is as follows: (W. Bk. G, p. 44, Garrard Co., Ky., Records)

    In the name of God amen, I, Abram Baugh of Garrard County, State of Kentucky, being in low state of helth but of sound mind and memory blesed

by God do make and ordain this my last Will and
Testament as followeth: First: I give and bequeath
to beloved wife Betsy Baugh all the property she had
when we were married also one gray horse and sor-
rell filla, two plougs and one pear of gears one cow
and calf and one sow and pigs chois, 6 chois head of
hogs, six head of sheep also the stock of fowls, also
1 large Pron Kettle, 1 ten gallon kettle, and 1 small
iron kettle, 1 oven, 1 shovel and five dogs, 1 pole
ox, wieding hoes, chois, 1 iron wedge my cubbard
furniture and all the ware thereunto belonging, 1
look glass 1 table and all the chairs and the loom.

    Item 2nd. My well beloved Betsy Baugh the use
of one negro girl, Caleo Mariah, during her life,
and at her death to sold with her increase if any to
the highest and best bid in one record of twelve
months, and third part of her amount of said sail I
give and bequeath unto my said wife to do of as she
may think proper also I lend her my negro man
named Lewis during her life and at her death to be
free to act and to do for himself. The other two
thirds of the aforesaid Sail I desire to be qually divided between Martha Ellis, late Martha Baugh and
Amos A. Baugh to them their heirs and assigns forever. I also give my son Amos A. Baugh my Flax
Hackle and 1 ten gallon kettle to be kept by his step
mother till he arrives to the age of 21 years old also
my home and shiving tools whenever he is old enough
to use them. I also give my son Amos A. Baugh one
bay mare with colt and it is my desire that he is to
stay with his step mother and go to school and that
she board and clothe him while going to school and
for him to aid and assist at all times when not at
school and at the end of the year to be put to any good
trade he may choose to go to (a shoemaker excepted)
and when he leaves his step mother to go to his trade
the mare or the colt which ever they may think most
advantageous to be sold for his benefit and the other
to be kept by her for him till he gets his trade or
becomes of age.

    Then I give and bequeath to my son Elisha P.
Baugh my watch to him and his heirs and assigns

forever.

I third I give and bequeath to my son <u>DARIUS BAUGH,</u> Rifle gun and all that to belonging to go with her to him his heirs and assigns forever.

Item. To each of my children not before mentioned (to-wit) William J. Baugh, Jesse J. Baugh, Rowena Levridge, Abraham G. Baugh and Marcellus Baugh one dollar each for ever and their heirs.

Lastly I appoint Garland Brank, James Patterson my hole and sole Executors of this my last Will and testament hereby involving all wills by me made and that these executors sell all the balance of my Estate not herein specially given away and after paying all expenses the balance to be applied to the schooling Amos and his benefit in testimony whereof I have hereunto set my hand and seal this 25th day of June 1833.

 Signed, sealed and acknowledged in the presence of us.

 Interlined before assigned.

     Abraham Baugh (SEAL)

STATE OF KENTUCKY
GARRARD COUNTY SCT.

 I, James H. Letcher Clerk of the County in and for the County aforesaid certify that the foregoing will of Abraham Baugh was produced to Court Dec. 1833 and ordered to be recorded and the same is now done accordingly.

     Attest James H. Letcher

STATE OF KENTUCKY
COUNTY OF GARRARD SCT.

 I, William R. Layton, Clerk of the Garrard County Court do hereby certify that the foregoing is a true and correct copy as found in my office in Will Book G, page 44.

 This 25 day of March 1964.

 Attest William R. Layton, Clerk G. C. C.

  By Doris King, D. C.

ELISHA P. BAUGH
(1798-1867)

Elisha P. Baugh, Sr., was b. 7/7/1798 in Virginia and d. 11/1/1867 in Nacogdoches County, Texas. He m. Sarah C. Green 9/5/1822 in Madison County, Alabama; they are buried in Stone Cemetery, near Nacogdoches on Highway 21.

Children:
1. Elizabeth G. Baugh, b. 7/24/1823, m. 2/4/1842 John B. Chilcoat.
2. Sophronia E. Baugh, b. 2/12/1826, d. 4/19/1861, m. James Scogin 12/15/1859. One child: Sarah G. Scogin.
3. John A. Baugh, b. 11/30/1828, d. 8/7/1865, m. Mrs. Nancy T. (Richmond) Brazelton. Children: Mattie and Sophronia Baugh.
4. James D. Baugh, b. 2/28/1833, d. 10/4/1900, m. Almira Roberts 11/24/1859. They left Nacogdoches Co., and removed to Comanche Co. before his mother died in 1882. Later they moved into Washington State, where James d. in 1900. Their children: James, Alice, Sarah, Joseph, Jasper, Bertha, Melissa, Ada, and Clarence Baugh.
5. Joseph M. Baugh, b. 11/25/1835, d.s.p. 11/2/1858.
6. Michael Van Buren Baugh, b. 7/28/1838, d. 6/14/1928, m. Mrs. Nancy Scogin in Rusk Co., Texas, 7/26/1865.
   Children:
   (1) John Young Baugh, b. 7/24/1866, d. 5/31/1931, m. Hortensia Pool 12/6/1888.
       Children:
       a. John Edward Baugh, m. Addie Schultz.
       b. Robert Quincy Baugh, d.s.p.
       c. Lottie Baugh, m. Ollie Hall.
       d. Charles Oscar Baugh, m. Cora Elizabeth Drury 7/1/1917, d. 2/14/1956, buried in Oak Grove Cemetery, Nacogdoches. Their dau., Maxine Baugh, b. 11/1/1920, m. Archie T. Erwin, 12/2/1942. They have Sandra Erwin, b. 9/23/1943 who m. Jim Laney; one son, Terry Erwin Laney.

e. Abe Boston Baugh, m. Dullie Mae Pinkston.
f. Orpha Baugh, m. Elvin Straham. Their son Lamar m. Virginia Stephenson.
(2) Hollis Baugh, b. 4/1/1876, d. 6/17/1959, m. Mary Christopher 12/17/1897. Children:
   a. Archie Lee Baugh, b. 11/16/1899, d. 4/24/1925, m. Nellie Christian 11/30/1919. Children:
      (i) Lillian Marie Baugh, b. 1/21/1921, m. John Campbell Webb 3/5/1943. They have Katherine, John, and Peggy Webb.
      (ii) Hazel Kathleen Baugh, b. 2/1/1924, d. in infancy.
   b. Minnie Mae Baugh, b. 4/21/1900, m. Lewis Carlin 5/22/1937. No issue.
   c. Aaron Benton Baugh, b. 11/16/1901, m. Malie Daniels 7/30/1936. Children:
      (i) Hollis Alford Baugh, b. 9/8/1937, m. Peggy Ward 6/25/1961.
      (ii) Mary Elizabeth Baugh, b. 12/12/1938, m. Don E. Brown 5/13/1958.
      (iii) John Lindley Baugh, b. 6/28/1940, m. Iva Carpenter 6/1/1961.
      (iv) Benton Frederick Baugh, b. 10/30/1942, m. Paula Bailey 8/24/1963.
      (v) Nancy Sue Baugh, b. 8/17/1944, m. Robert Stevens 7/5/1963.
      (vi) Kathy Ann Baugh, b. 6/17/1947.
   d. John Riley Baugh, b. 11/3/1903, m. Rochelle Winford 7/6/1940. They have Dennis Baugh, b. 12/6/1942, and Janet Baugh, b. 7/25/1949.
   e. Rosie Velma Baugh, b. 1/5/1908, d. 12/30/1956, m. Frederick Herrin.
   f. Alice Virginia Baugh, b. 9/25/1914, m. Price Coleman.
7. Martha Jane Baugh, b. 1/2/1841, m. John W. Johnson 1/3/1867. She is buried in Stone Cemetery, Nacogdoches, Texas. Children:
(1) Sarah Elizabeth Johnson, b. 12/7/1868, d. 9/4/1899, m. E. M. Stone.

    (2) William Palmer Johnson, b. 4/26/1871, d. in infancy.
    (3) Martha Wilson Johnson, b. 7/29/1875, m. J. A. Christopher.
    (4) Charlie Preston Johnson, b. 7/10/1880, d. young.
8. Elisha Poke Baugh, Jr., b. 11/30/1843, m. Susan Scogin 5/3/1866. Children:
    (1) Sarah Mary Baugh, b. 2/27/1867, d. young.
    (2) Caley Baugh, b. 4/24/1868, d. 8/18/1904, m. John Jones 7/22/1883.
    (3) Sophronia Baugh, b. 5/12/1870, d. 2/18/1910, m. J. M. Rogers 4/1/1886.
    (4) Dora I. Baugh, b. 5/19/1872, m. William N. Parrish 11/28/1889.
    (5) Theodocia Baugh, b. 3/4/1874, m. Jim Miller.
    (6) James Baugh, b. 2/16/1876, d. 11/1/1947.
9. Sarah Clementine Baugh, b. 8/27/1849, d. 1885, m. Thomas Alvin Rodgers 4/5/1875. Children:
    (1) Jesse Rodgers, b. 10/9/1876, d. 6/19/1956, m. Alpha Beatrice Floyd 1/20/1915.
    (2) Paralee Rodgers, b. 3/28/1879, d. 5/20/1936.
    (3) Samuel Rodgers, b. 10/15/1880, d. 12/14/1947, m. Lizzie Wisener 10/29/1901.
    (4) John Rodgers, m. Mary Ophelia Mills.
    (5) Joseph Madson Rodgers, b. 6/14/1884, d. 11/11/1952, m. Priscilla Agnes Drury 7/24/1907. He is buried in Sunset Memorial Cemetery, Nacogdoches. Child:
        a. Marvis Jeannette Rodgers, b. 6/21/1908, m. Charlie Mack Bailey, Sr., 6/21/1925. Children:
            (i) Marvis Jeannette Bailey, b. 5/7/1926, m. 5/30/1946, Alton Porter. They have Judith Ann Porter, b. 8/28/1947, m. Charles Daniel Dempsey 9/25/1965; and Charlie Mack Bailey Porter, b. 7/11/1949.
            (ii) Charlie Mack Bailey, Jr., b. 9/23/1927.

(The lineage of ELISHA P. BAUGH was compiled by Jeannette B. Porter, of Nacogdoches, Texas.)

DARIUS BAUGH
(1809 -   )

Darius Baugh, son of Abraham and Martha (Johnson) Baugh was born December 3, 1809, in Kentucky. Darius married Sarah Triplett who was also born in Kentucky. The known child of Darius and Sarah was:
    Roena, b. Dec. 12, 1829, d. Jan. 28, 1915.
Roena Baugh married Perry Louis Stalcup. Roena and Perry had one child:
    John Ode, b. Nov. 15, 1876, d. Apr. 12, 1950.
John Ode Stalcup married Nevada Frances Williams. They had one child:
    Frances Nevada, b. May 21, 1899, d. (?)
At the time of birth of Frances Nevada her mother, Nevada Frances, died, May 21, 1899.

John Ode left home at this time and went to California where he died, April 12, 1950. He left his daughter in the care of his parents, Roena (Baugh) and Perry Louis Stalcup. The grandparents became the guardian of Frances Nevada Stalcup.

John Ode Stalcup had a second marriage to Lucy L. Brown.

Frances Nevada Stalcup married George W. Cain, Nov. 17, 1916. George W. Cain was born September 8, 1892. Frances Nevada and George W. had the following children:
    George Cain, b. Oct. 6, 1917.
    William Lewis Cain, b. June 22, 1919.

****

PROOF FOR THE BAUGH FAMILY HISTORY

Information for the generations of:
    William Baugh   (ca 1610-1687)
    James Baugh   (ca 1655- ca 1722)
was furnished by Mrs. Jeannette Porter, 1512 North St., Nacogdoches, Texas 75961. Mrs. Porter wrote to the Compiler stating she was in the process of filing the Baugh material in the Colonial Dames of the XVII Century. To date it is not known if this

line has been established with this organization.

Proof for the generations of:
    Thomas Baugh   (ca 1690-ca 1762)
    Abraham Baugh, Sr.   (-1797)
    Rhoda (Baugh) Blackburn (   )
    Elizabeth (Blackburn)   (1779-1862)
      Boatwright
was furnished by Mr. Charles Hughes Hamlin, Richmond, Virginia.

Proof for the generations of:
    Darius Baugh   (1809 -   )
    Roena (Baugh) Stalcup (1839 -1915)
    John Ode Stalcup   (1876 -1950)
    Frances Nevada   (1899 -   )
      Stalcup
    William Lewis Cain   (1919 -   )
was furnished by William Lewis Cain who lives in Bartlesville, Oklahoma.

                          ****

Compiled by: Lorene Miller Wallace
                 1808 College View Drive
                 Bartlesville, Oklahoma

GRUBB, BEESON, BOREN, BOWLES
AND RELATED FAMILIES
of
ENGLAND, PENNSYLVANIA AND NORTH CAROLINA

The Grubbs belong to an old English family, the name appearing in the records of Kent, Cornwall, Hertfordshire and other counties in the thirteenth century. (D.A.R. Magazine, Vol. IV, number 1, p. 38. Jan. 1921).

Henry Grubbe was a member of Parliament for Devizes, Wiltshire, in 1571. He died in 1581. He married Joan Radcliffe, and their son Thomas Grubbe was born at Eastwell Potterne, Devizes, Wilts., and died 2/2/1617. The name of Thomas's wife is not known. His son was the Rev. Thomas Grubbe Jr., Rector at Cranfield, Bedfordshire, who graduated M.A. from Oxford University. His son was John Grubb, 1610-1667, a Royalist who supported the Church of England. After the death of Charles 1, he settled in Cornwall and married Helen Vivian. Their son was John Grubb Jr., b. 4/20/1652 in Cornwall, died 3/10/1798 at Marcus Hook, Pennsylvania.

John Grubb Jr. was the progenitor of this family in America. He arrived in the ship "Kent" in 1677, at Burlington, West Jersey, and received 340 acres of land on Chester Creek. "Grubb's Landing", Brandywine Hundred, Delaware, was known as early as 1682. He was a member of the Colonial Assembly of Pa. for New Castle County in 1692, 1698, and 1700; Colonial Justice in 1693; and a member of the Provincial Council for New Castle Co. (now Delaware) in 1700. John Grubb married Frances Vane at Chester Co., Pa., and they had nine children, including dau. Charity.

Charity Grubb was b. 9/29/1687 at Grubb's Landing, near Wilmington, Del., and died 11/22/1761 in Randolph Co., N.C. She was buried at Center Quaker Church, Guilford Co., N.C. Charity married 10/24/1706 in Chester Co., Pa., Richard Beeson, who was b. October 1684 in Chester Co., died 1/1/1777 in Randolph Co. (Ref: Hinshaw's ENCYCLOPEDIA OF AMERICAN QUAKER GENEALOGY, Vol. 1, p. 649.) Richard Beeson was a son of Edward Beeson, the Quaker immigrant to Chester County,

Pennsylvania, born 1652 in Lancaster, England, died 20 August 1712 in Chester County, Pennsylvania,married (1) Rachel Pennington, daughter of Isaac and Mary Proude Pennington, (2) Elizabeth _____, mother of Richard Beeson and other children. Edward Beeson, the immigrant, was a son of Thomas Beeson and wife, Anne.

Benjamin Beeson, son of Richard and Charity (Grubb) Beeson, was b. 1/14/1714 at Chester Co., Pa., and 6/14/1794 in Guilford Co., N.C. He married Elizabeth (Hunter?) in 1738 at Hopewell Monthly Meeting, northern Virginia. Their daughter Jane was born 3/22/1760 in Guilford Co., and d. 1/9/1792. Jane Beeson married 1/28/1778, John Bond, who was b. 5/30/1755, d. 1795, in Guilford Co. Their children were:
1. Martha Bond, b. 8/19/1778, of whom nothing is known.
2. Joseph Bond, b. 2/29/1780, d. Feb. 1853, m. Abigail Hinds 1797.
3. Benjamin Bond, b. 10/19/1781, married out of Meeting.
4. Joel Bond, b. 1/18/1784, m. Jane Hinds.
5. Isaac Bond, b. 12/27/1785, m. Anna Holmes.
6. Elizabeth Bond, b. 12/18/1787.
7. William Bond, b. 12/5/1789.
8. Jane Bond, b. 1/7/1792, of whom later.

(Ref: BOND GENEALOGY, by Samuel Bond Garrett, pp. 21-23.)

Jane Bond, daughter of John and Jane (Beeson) Bond, born in Randolph Co. and died there in 1883. She married 12/13/1809 Samuel Lineberry, son of Jacob and Mary (Youngblood) Lineberry. Jacob was a Revolutionary soldier, Randolph Co., son of Jacob Lineberry Sr., (Leinberger, Lienbarger, Lineburger, etc.) who because of religious persecution emigrated from the Harz mountain area of Brunswick in north-west Germany, and settled near the Chatham County line, in what is now Randolph Co., N.C. His wife was Catherine _____. Samuel Lineberry was born 5/7/1789 and died in 1874 in Randolph Co. He and his wife Jane (Bond) had daughter Edith Lineberry, b. 3/5/1813, d. 12/24/1877 in Randolph Co. She married in Aug. 1829 Reuben Smith, who was b. 4/2/1810, d. 4/22/1877. (Ref: Bible records, and Gray's Chapel

Methodist Church Records; Randolph Co. Marriage Bonds, Asheboro, N.C.)

Archibald Murphey Smith, son of Reuben Smith and Edith (Lineberry) Smith, was born 9/26/1848 and d. 5/10/1905 in Randolph Co. He married Emily Foust 10/27/1870, who was b. 10/10/1839, d. 5/8/1903. (Ref: Foust-Smith family Bible, owned by Paul Foust of Asheboro, N.C.) Their daughter Ida Irene Smith was born 2/23/1878 at Gray's Chapel, N.C., and died 12/2/1959 at Greensboro, N.C. She married at Gray's Chapel, 12/24/1899, George Denny Pugh, who was born 11/6/1874, and died 4/5/1936. (Tombstone Records in Cool Springs Church Cemetery, Randolph Co.) Their daughter Maxine Pugh married 1/19/1954 at Palm Beach, Florida, James Gwaltney Westwarren MacLamroc. They have two sons: Alan Gwaltney Westwarren MacLamroc, born 12/26/1954, and Brian Gwaltney Westwarren MacLamroc, born 2/24/1956.

****

WILL of RICHARD BEESON of Randolph Co., N.C., proved 1782. (W.Bk. 1, p. 58).

WHEREAS I, Richard Beeson of Deep River in Guilford Co. (it became Randolph Co. in 1779) North Carolina, being far advanced in years and knowing the uncertainty of life and certainty of death, do therefore think fit to make this my last will and testament in manner and form as follows: first I recommend my soul unto the Lord and my body to the earth to be buried in a Christian-like manner at the discretion of my executors hereafter to be named - and as touching such worldly substance wherewithal it hath pleased the Lord to bless me in this life, I dispose thereof in the following manner and form:
1st: I order that all my just debts and funeral charges be paid by my executors hereafter to be named.
2nd: I give to my grandson Stephenias Haworth 200 acres of land I now live on including all improvements, to him and his heirs and assigns and no more.
3rd: I give to my two sons Benjamin Beeson and Isaac Beeson, and to their heirs and assigns, the remaining part of the said tract of land to each an equal part and to Benjamin to have the east and Isaac to have the west end.
4th: I give to my son Benjamin, two feather beds and

all the furniture belonging thereunto. I give to my son
Isaac the feather bed I now lie upon and all the furniture
thereunto belonging.

5th: It is my will that the remaining part of my movable estate shall be equally divided amongst all my children (then living) to wit: Benjamin, Isaac, Phoebe and Charity, in the best and most suitable manner it can be done by my executors.

6th: And further I do give to all or any of my issue that doth or may lay claim hereafter to any right of kinship, to each and severally one shilling sterling and no more, to be paid by my executors hereafter to be named.

7th: I ordain, constitute and appoint my two sons, Benjamin and Isaac, whole and sole executors of this my last will and testament, hereby utterly disallowing and revoking and making void all other and former wills, testaments and legacies by me made, ratifying and confirming this and no other to by my last will and testament.

In witness whereof I have hereunto set my hand and affixed my seal this 29th day of the month called March in the year 1775.

RICHARD BEESON (Seal)

Signed, sealed, pronounced to be the said Richard Beeson's last will and testament in the presence of

    Jeremiah Reynolds
    Joseph Lamb
    John Beeson, Jr.

****

WILL OF JOHN GRUBB (1652-1708):

I, John Grubb, of the County of Chester in the Province of Pennsylvania, tanner, being at present weak in body, but of sound and perfect mind and memory, do make this my last will and testament in manner following, that is to say:

First, my will is that all my just debts and funeral charges be paid and discharged.

Also, I give unto my daughter Charity, the wife of

Richard Beeson, the sum of five pounds.

Also, I give unto my daughter Phoebe Grubb, the sum of fifteen pounds to be paid her when she attains the age of eighteen years or is married, whichever shall first happen.

Also, I give unto my dear wife Frances Grubb, one third part of all my personal estate and her choice of one of the best cows upon my plantation besides.

And also all of the rest and residue of my estate, both real and personal, of whatsoever I give, devise and bequeath unto my sons Emanuel, John, Joseph, Henry, Samuel, Nathaniel, and Peter, to be equally divided between them, share and share alike, and to their heirs and assigns forever as tenants in common and not as joint tenants.

And lastly, I make and ordain my said son John, and my said wife Frances, Executors of this my last will and testament.

In witness whereof I have hereunto set my hand and seal the twelfth day of the month called February in the sixth year of the reign of Queen Anne over Great Britain, anno Domini 1707/8.

John Grubb (seal).

Signed, sealed, published and declared by the above named John Grubb to be his last will and testament in the presence of

Thomas Pryor
Thomas Harding
Richard Heath
John Redman

Richard and Charity Beeson were both ministers of the Society of Friends. One of their sons was Benjamin Beeson, as previously shown; another son was Isaac Beeson, who m. Phoebe Stroud. Isaac and Phoebe (Stroud) Beeson were the parents of Benjamin Beeson II, who married Rachael Harold. Their daughter Phoebe m. Elijah Boren (of whom later) who, with his brothers Jeremiah and Hezekiah Boren, migrated south from Nantucket Island, Mass., about 1775. They (or their father) came from England to Nantucket. Elijah Boren remained in the Quaker settlement in and around New Garden, now Guilford College, near Greensboro, North Carolina, and his brothers, who have numerous descendants, went further south into South Carolina, and later to Crab Orchard, Kentucky.

ELIJAH BOREN died in Henry Co., Indiana, in 1853. He married (1) Phoebe Beeson, who d. Feb. 16, 1816. Their children were: John, Basil, Benjamin (of whom later), Pleasant, Elizabeth, Mary and Rachael. Elijah Boren m. (2) Nancy Knight, by whom he had two daughters, Rhoda and Nancy.

BENJAMIN BOREN was born in Guilford Co., N.C., Nov. 22, 1798, and died in Indiana in 1874. He married Eunice Knight, who was b. April 23, 1800; they removed to Indiana in 1836. Children:

1. Jesse Franklin Boren, b. June 27, 1821.
2. Addison P. Boren, b. August 30, 1822-23, d. Jan. 27, 1897 (of whom later).
3. William U. Boren, b. Sept. 7, 1824.
4. Cyrus H. Boren, b. Jan. 13, 1826.
5. Emily Weeks Boren, b. Aug. 17, 1828.
6. Lucinda Copeland Boren, b. April 28, 1830.
7. Elijah Boren ll, b. Sept. 5, 1833.
8. Jabez Boren, b. Oct. 16, 1835.
9. Benjamin Boren Jr. and
10. Richard Boren, twins, b. June 16, 1838.
11. Prudence Boren, b. July 4, 1840
12. Pleasant Boren, b. Sept. 28, 1842.

ADDISON P. BOREN remained in Guilford Co., North Carolina. He married Oct. 7, 1852, Mary Jane Smith of Rockingham Co., N.C., born Aug. 2, 1832, d. 1915, dau. of Clement Smith (b. Aug. 1, 1798 in Rockingham Co., d. Aug. 10, 1866 in Guilford Co.) and of his wife Nancy Simpson (b. April 9, 1809 in Caswell Co., N.C., d. Sept. 7, 1845 in Rockingham Co.); they were married in 1828. Clement Smith was the son of Samuel Smith, Revolutionary soldier, born Nov. 16, 1758, in Rockingham Co. (then Rowan Co.), died May 6, 1839 in Rockingham Co., married Martha Nance, April 3, 1783, (she was b. 1765, d. 1853). Samuel Smith was a son of John Smith who was awarded a tract of land in N.C. in 1755 by the British Government for his bravery in the Indian War.

ADDISON P. BOREN and his wife Mary Jane Smith

had issue:
1. Josie Boren, b. July 25, 1853, m. John W. Cook.
2. Adna Boren, b. June 1, 1855, d. Nov. 7, 1899, m. Henry C. Edwards.
3. C. C. Boren, b. April 30, 1857.
4. William Clement Boren, b. March 9, 1859, m. Annie Dundas, May 13, 1884. Children:
    (1) Clara Boren, m. Wilson L. Peebles. No children.
    (2) Mamie Boren, m. Joseph Spence. No children.
    (3) Chase Boren, m. Donald M. Stafford. Their dau. Sarah died young.
    (4) William Clement Boren Jr., m. Ruth Adams. Their son:
        i. William C. Boren 3rd. m. Doris Hanes. Children: William C. Boren 4th, and Hanes Boren.
    (5) Louise Boren, m. John William Andrews. Their son:
        i. J. William Andrews Jr.
    (6) Eva Boren, m. Roy C. Millikan. They have several children.
    (7) Sarah Boren, m. T. Helm Jones. Two children.
    (8) Cam Boren, m. Hoyt W. Boone. One son, one daughter.
5. Charles Phillips Boren, b. Jan. 15, 1861, d. Oct. 26, 1919, m. July 19, 1888, Etta Amelia Taylor, who was b. Jan. 15, 1868, d. May 30, 1947. Children:
    (1) Maude Boren, m. J.A. Jones.
    (2) Kemp Boren, m. Patricia Jones.
    (3) Helen Boren, m. (1) Charles W. Cloninger and (2) Mose Kiser.
    (4) Grace Boren, m. Joseph M. Hunt Jr.
    (5) Elizabeth Boren.
6. Richard Benjamin Boren, b. Sept. 25, 1863, d. May 21, 1936, m. (2) Aug. 12, 1894 Ida Norman. Children:
    (1) Norman A. Boren, m. Estelle Petrea.
    (2) Richard P. Boren Jr., m. Nell Reich.
    (3) Mary Boren, m. George C. Hampton.
7. Mollie Lucas Boren, b. Dec. 3, 1866, m. April 25, 1888, the Rev. James Archibald Bowles. Children:
    (1) James Archie Bowles Jr., m. (1) Virginia W. Brown and (2) Madeline Hyams. No children.

(2) Hargrove Bowles, m. Kelly Bess Mooneyham. Children:
    i. John Bowles of Los Angeles, Calif., m. Norma Landwehr.
    ii. Hargrove Bowles Jr., m. Jessamine Boyce.
    iii. James Archie Bowles 3rd., m. Margaret Barker.
    iv. Richard Kelly Bowles, m. Louise Horner, dau. of William E. Horner of Sanford, N.C.
(3) Mary Lucas Bowles, m. Clarence A. McDaniel. They have Clarence A. McDaniel Jr.
(4) Eva Cook Bowles, m. Cameron LeRoy Jenkins. They have one child, Mollie Gayle Jenkins who m. R. Marshall Clegg.
(5) David Addison Bowles, m. Margaret Helms. One child, Margaret, who m. Raymond Parker.
(6) Joseph Cates Bowles, m. (1) Gladys Gunn and (2) Agnes Urquart.
(7) Wade Anderson Bowles, m. Lottie Newman. Children:
    i. Nancy Ellen Bowles, m. Robert Conrad.
    ii. Mary Frances Bowles, m. Ralph Stockton Jr., of Winston-Salem, N.C.
    iii. Elizabeth Anne Bowles, m. Stuart Miller.
    iv. Wade A. Bowles Jr., m. Barbara Flynn.
(8) Annie Maie Bowles, m. Thomas E. Hanner. One child, Annie Lou Hanner, who m. T. E. Floore.
(9) The Rev. Dr. Charles Phillips Bowles, m. Mary Wooters. Children:
    i. Charles P. Bowles Jr., m. Anne Marie White.
    ii. The Rev. Joseph Cates Bowles II.
    iii. Mary Lynne Bowles, m. Dr. James Arlyn Rogerson (Ph. D.)

8. Gurney Simpson Boren, b. Oct. 1869, m. March 1898 Martha Jane Cook. Children:
(1) G. Simpson Boren, Jr., m. Mollie Matheson.
(2) Allan Cook Boren, m. Elizabeth Fair of Louisville, Miss. Several chn.
(3) Marian Boren, m. (1) Dr. Allan Banner and (2) J. Gray Hicks.

9. Cecil Addison Boren, b. Oct. 13, 1872, m. June 23,

1898 Ada McMichael. Children:
(1) Orton A. Boren, m. Madeline Call. Children:
  i. Clarence Boren (dau.) who m. William S. Jones of Greensboro, North Carolina.
  ii. Salley C. Boren, m. Dr. Alexander F. Goley of Burlington, N. C.
  iii. Madeline Boren, m. Thomas E. Chandler of High Point, N. C.
(2) Cecil A. Boren Jr., m. (2) Nanalyn Fuller.
(3) Ralph Boren, d. s. p.
(4) Benjamin M. Boren, m. Frances Wheeler.
(5) John B. Boren, m. Margie Perry.
(6) Della Boren, m. Reuben B. Arthur.
(7) Kathleen Boren, m. Paul Martin.

****

RELATED FAMILIES OF PITCHER, LANCASTER, DOUGLAS, GEORGE, JORDAN, BOOTH and JACKSON of MARYLAND, NORTH CAROLINA, TENNESSEE, KENTUCKY and VIRGINIA

PITCHER

THOMAS PITCHER, born 1615 in England, came to America in the "Plain Joan", attesting to conformity to the Church of England. He settled in Northampton Co., Virginia, in 1635. There is a generation missing here. Next we have Thomas Pitcher, grandson of Thomas the immigrant, shown in Northampton D. Bk. 3, Va., 1734. By deduction, his son was William Pitcher, who fought in the Revolution with the Va. Infantry. His name appears in the Army Register, "but did not receive bounty land."(Va. in the Revolution, p. 627; Va. Revn. War Records, p. 209.)

WILLIAM PITCHER was in Duchess Co., N.Y., after the Revolution, (N.Y. Census, 1790), but evidently returned to Virginia, as there is a record of the sale of land to him in Washington Co., May 9, 1792: "50 acres on the waters of the North Fork of Holston, and on both sides of the East Fork of Battle Creek."

HENRY PITCHER, son of William, is shown in the census of Columbia Co., N.Y., 1790. The name of his wife is not known. He had a son Thomas (2nd. Census of Ky.) who m. in Madison Co., Ky., May 8, 1803, Polly Douglas, of whom later. (Burns' Madison Co., Ky., Marriage Records, p. 87.)

WILLIAM DOUGLAS PITCHER, son of Thomas and Polly (Douglas) Pitcher, (Boone Co. Census, Ky., 1840) died in Boone Co. before 1854. He m. Sarah Booth Lancaster, who was b. in Green Co., Ky. Madison and Greene Counties were formerly part of Lincoln Co.

ISABEL LANCASTER PITCHER, dau. of William and Sarah (Lancaster) Pitcher, b. July 22, 1838 at Walton, Boone Co., Ky., married at Ludlow, Kenton Co. in 1854

Dexter Davis Hardy, inventor and Civil War volunteer, from Cincinnati, Ohio, but was b. in Providence, Rhode Island, Dec. 8, 1833. Isabel died Dec. 26, 1914 in Chicago and is buried in Rosehill Cemetery there. Isabel and Dexter Hardy had twelve children, of whom eight lived to maturity.

Other daughters of William and Sarah (Lancaster) Pitcher were Ann, Lucinda, Matilda and Catherine.

Mrs. Warren Harrington Morse of Phoenix, Arizona, who contributed the data for this chapter, is a granddaughter of Isabel Lancaster Pitcher.

LANCASTER

Tradition states that three Lancaster brothers, John, Benjamin, and Joseph, came to America from England ca. 1634. They purchased all of Cobb's Neck, in Maryland, a Cape extending into Chesapeake Bay between Baltimore and Annapolis. They imported square brick from England to build their home, a portion of which may still be seen, called "Rock Hall". It is thought that Benjamin, born ca. 1610, married in Maryland after 1635, was the progenitor of this line, because of the given names of the next generation. Henry Lancaster (second generation) named one son Benjamin, but he named no son John or Joseph.

HENRY LANCASTER, by deduction the son of Benjamin the immigrant, was a planter. His will, dated May 9, 1717, and recorded in Cecil Co., Md., leaves his entire estate equally to his children: Benjamin, George, Philip, Elinor, Catherine, and William.

WILLIAM LANCASTER, b. in Maryland, d. in Surry Co., Va., 1740. The name of his wife is not known. He had a son, HENRY LANCASTER, listed as a taxpayer in Pasquotank Co., North Carolina, 1795. He is thought to have married a daughter of William Mallory of Elizabeth City, N.C., as the name Mallory is given to one of his grandchildren, and the two families lived near each other.

HENRY LANCASTER, son of Henry, was b. 1749. He served in the Cavalry in the Revn. War. Most of his life was spent in Edgecombe Co., and he enlisted there in 1778, serving 20 months, in the Battles of Briar Creek (under Gen. Ashe), Eaton and Guilford. He served under

Capt. Edward Clinch as First Sergt., and under Col. Thomas Eaton; in 1779 he served for three months under Capt. James Wilson, scouring the country in search of Tories and outlaws. In the Roster of N. C. soldiers in the Revolution, he is listed as #885, Sergt. in Militia, Edgecombe Co.

Henry Lancaster m. Susan Swann in Edgecombe Co. and had issue: Henry, Elizabeth, Susan, Sarah, Milly, Mallory, and Nancy Lancaster.

HENRY LANCASTER, born Jan. 1, 1773 in Edgecombe Co., N. C., married there in 1795 Hannah Booth. He migrated to Greene Co., Ky., (Greene Co. Census, 1800) and enlisted in the Ky. Mounted Volunteer Division under Capt. Joseph B. Lancaster. He also served under Capt. James Robinson in a Detached Militia. (Records in Military Dept. Office of Adj. Gen. at Frankfort, Ky.) Children: James Mallory, William, Hickerson, Polly, Joseph, Elizabeth, Lucy, Sarah, Robert Jackson, and Malinda.

SARAH BOOTH LANCASTER was born in Greene Co., Ky., Aug. 22, 1812, and m. ca. 1830 William D. Pitcher. They removed to Boone Co., Ky., before 1838.

(Refs: "Adventurers of Purse and Person", pp. 270-271; "Memoirs and Records, Eastern N. C." p. 92.)

DOUGLAS (DOUGLASS)

The first of this line in America was EDWARD DOUGLASS, who arrived before 1643. He paid for his own passage and for the passages of several other immigrants, for which he received land grants in Northampton Co., Virginia, where he established Douglass Plantation. He also patented 1,100 acres in Accomack Co., Va. He died before 1644, leaving his estate to his son Edward.

EDWARD DOUGLAS, Jr., was born in Northampton Co. and m. Isabella _____. He was Capt. of Magotha Bay, and became a Lt. Colonel. He was appointed to Command Districts at a Court May 10, 1651. He was a lawyer, and in 1656 was named as overseer for the Dale Estate. Dame Elizabeth Dale, his cousin, assigned 2,000 acres to him in her will made in England. Colonel Littleton, Edmund Scarborough, and Col. Obedience Robins were his neighbours. Edward Douglas raised cattle rather than tobacco. He had 3,700 acres in Northampton Co. and additional acreage in Accomack Co. He was overseer for the estate of Mrs. Anne Littleton when she was the widow of Col. Nathaniel Littleton in 1656. Anne Littleton's son, Col. Edward Littleton, married Edward Douglas's daughter Sarah in 1658. Sarah died soon after marriage. Edward Douglas made his will 1657 at the home of a friend, Edmund Bowman, where he became ill, leaving the bulk of his estate to his son Edward[3] Douglas. The widow of Edward[2] Douglas married the Rev. Thomas Teackle. (See Teackle and Littleton lineage, The Upshur Family, H.S.F., Vol. X.)

EDWARD[3] DOUGLAS inherited the Douglas Plantation, which passed to his sister Elizabeth, (wife of John Willett) when he died. It has not been established that James Douglas of Eastern Virginia was son of this Edward, nor has it been proven that Edward[4] Douglas, born 1713 in Fauquier Co., Va., was a son of James.

EDWARD[4] DOUGLAS married Sarah George, b. 1726 (of whom later). After his marriage and before the Revolution he migrated to Warrenton, N.C. He lived in Chatham Co. during the Revolution and served as Colonel. (Wilford-Williford Family, p. 396.) He later moved to Sumner Co., Tenn., where he was one of the first two lawyers. He was elected to the N.C. Convention in 1788, and was a member of the First Constitutional Convention of Tenn. in 1796. He died Jan. 2, 1797 and is buried with his wife at Cage's Bend, Sumner Co., Tenn. Edward and his wife had issue:
1. John Douglas, b. 1741, killed by Indians.
2. Edward Douglas, b. 1745, m. Elizabeth Howard. Served in the Revn.
3. William Douglas, of whom later.
4. Elmore Douglas, b. 1753, m. Betsy Blackmore.
5. Elizabeth Douglas, b. 1754, m. Major Wm. Cage.
6. Ezekiel Douglas, m. Mary Gibson.
7. Sally Douglas, m. Thomas Blackmore.
8. Reuben Douglas, m. Elizabeth Edwards.
9. James Douglas, b. 1763, m. Catherine Collier.
(Bible Records; Marriage Bonds, Acklen, p. 166).

WILLIAM DOUGLAS, born 1742, m. Peggy Stroud

in Orange Co., Virginia. He was #72, Corporal in the
Revn. War, and received 1,000 acres in 1783 for 84
months' service as Captain. (Roster of American Soldiers
in the Revolution.) With his family, he removed to Washington Co., Va. His brother John, killed by Indians, was
probably buried in Washington Co., as his estate was
settled there by his father. The Douglas family then migrated to Davidson Co., Tennessee, and later held land
in Sumner Co. (Tennessee Cousins, by Ray, p. 657:"The
Douglas family came originally from Eastern Virginia.")
In 1800 William Douglas was in Madison Co., Ky.,
where his daughter Polly married. His will was probated
in Sumner Co. in 1814. His children were: John, Elizabeth, Jesse, Sally, Polly, James and Alfred. Polly married Thomas Pitcher, of whom previously. (Ref: Virginia's
Eastern Shore, Whitelaw, p. 98.)

****

GEORGE

1. HENRY GEORGE, b. in England, came to America in
"Assurance", a ship carrying 221 passengers of distinguished families. The George family was armigerous. Henry George had sons, Robert and John.
2. JOHN GEORGE, b. 1610, m. Jane_____. He was a Colonel, and a member of the House of Burgesses in Isle of
Wight Co., Va., 1653. In 1668 he had 200 acres surveyed
in Maryland, called "Fareall". His son
3. ROBERT GEORGE, who d. in Middlesex Co., Va. in
1734, m._____Elmore(?). He had lived in Kent Co., Md.,
1732. He had children: Richard, Susanna, Catherine and John.
4. JOHN GEORGE, b. 1704, d. 1784, m. (1) Mary Jordan.
They had children: Reuben, John, James, Ann, Elizabeth,
Mary, and Sarah. John George m. (2) Ursula Dudley, dau of
Ursula Beverly and grand-daughter of Ursula Byrd, of
Westover Estate in Va.
5. SARAH GEORGE, b. 1726 in Caroline Co., Va., m. 1740
Colonel Edward Douglas. They removed to Chatham Co.,
N.C. and from there to Davidson Co., Tenn. Their children:
John, Elizabeth, Elmore, Ezekiel, Sarah, Edward, Reuben,
James, and William. Edward Douglas Sr. was b. in Fauquier
Co., Va., in 1713. He was a Colonel in the Revolution, from
Chatham, N.C. Later, he was one of the first two lawyers in

Davidson Co., where the Capitol now is. He was elected to the N. C. Convention from Tenn. in 1788, and was a member of the Constitutional Convention. He owned many parcels of land in Tenn. by grant and by purchase. All his sons served in the Rev. War. Edward and his wife Sarah (George) Douglas are buried at Cage's Bend in Sumner Co., Tenn. Their wills are recorded there.

6. WILLIAM DOUGLAS, b. N. C. 1742, m. Peggy Stroud in N. C. Their children: John, Elizabeth, Jesse, Sarah, James, Alfred and Polly. William Douglas served in the Rev. War as Captain from N. C. He removed to Tenn. with his parents and his will is recorded in Sumner Co.

7. POLLY DOUGLAS m. Thomas Pitcher in Madison Co. Ky., 5/8/1803. Their son

8. WILLIAM DOUGLAS PITCHER, d. before 1854 in Boone Co., Ky., m. Sarah Lancaster of Greene Co., who was b. 8/22/1812. Their children: Ann, Lucinda, Matilda, Catherine and Isabel.

9. ISABEL LANCASTER PITCHER was b. 7/22/1838 at Walton, Boone Co., Ky., m. 1854 at Ludlow, Kenton Co., Dexter Davis Hardy of Cincinnati, Ohio, who was b. in Providence, R. I. Isabel d. in Chicago, Illinois, 12/26/1914, and is buried there in Rosehill Cemetery. Dexter Hardy was a volunteer in the Civil War, and was an inventor. Their daughter Martha Waite Hardy married Hermie Van Higgins.

Refs: "Cavaliers & Pioneers" by Nugent: pp. 93, 127-130.
"Hist. Caroline Co., Va." by Wingfield.
"17th Century Isle of Wight Co." by Boddie.
"Old King William Co.", p. 33, by Clarke.
"Tennessee Cousins" by Ray.
"Roster of N. C. Soldiers". D. A. R. Records.

****

JORDAN

1. SAMUEL JORDAN was born in England and came to America in the "Sea Venture" in 1609, being wrecked on an island in the Bermudas. Also in the same ship were John Rolfe and other adventurers, including many wealthy noblemen and London merchants. Samuel spent a year on the island where he was wrecked, and then went to Jamestown. He was granted 450 acres of land in his own right by the Governor and Capt. General of Va., and 250 acres more for transporting his five servants (John Davis, Thomas Matterly, Alice Wade, Robert Marshall, and

Thomas Studd) from England in 1620. Samuel's estate was known as "Jordan's Journey", situated across from Berkeley. He was a young widower when he arrived in America, having left three sons, Thomas, Samuel, and Robert, in England. He m. (2) in Va. Cicely Reynolds, by whom he had three daughters. After Samuel's death in 1623, a muster of the inhabitants of "Jordan's Journey" was taken, listing Cicely Jordan with three daus., ten servants named, coats of mail, five houses, and two boats.

SAMUEL JORDAN was a Member of the First Assembly at Jamestown in 1619, and was listed as "Gentleman Planter" at Charles City. He was a member of a committee to review the first four books into which the Great Charter of Va. was divided. Samuel Jordan Jr. settled in Surry Co., and Robert was killed by Indians. The other son:

2. THOMAS JORDAN, b. in England in 1600, came to America in the ship "Diana" in 1623. He was a Burgess from Isle of Wight Co., Va., 1629-1632. Received a land grant 1635. He m. Lucy Corker, dau of Capt. William Corker of Surry Co., Va., and his wife Lucy(White) Corker. William Corker was a Burgess at James City 1641, 1655-56, and Capt. of Militia. His father was Capt. John Corker, known to have been in Jamestown 1637; he was patented 6 acres on James Island near Goose Hill; Burgess 1633-45, and Clerk; patented 1,150 acres in Surry Co., on the south side of James River, another patent in 1640; died at James City. The will of William Corker is recorded in Surry Co. 9/4/1677. Son of Thomas Jordan and wife Lucy:

3. THOMAS JORDAN, b. 1634 in Isle of Wight Co., Va., m. Margaret Brasseur, b. 1642, dau of Robert Brasseur of Va. and Md., where he is reported to have given the land on which the Capitol of Md. was built. They had a son:

4. JOSHUA JORDAN, b. 1681, m. Elizabeth Sanbourne, dau. of Daniel and Sarah Sanbourne. Their daughter:

5. MARY (or Millicent) JORDAN, m. John George in 1724. (See GEORGE lineage previously.)

Refs: "Adventurers of Purse and Person", Jester & Hiden.
"17th Century Isle of Wight Co.", Boddie.
"Cavaliers & Pioneers", Nugent.
"Hist. of Perquimmins Co., N.C." p. 366.
"Sidelights of Md. History", Vol. 2, p. 285.

****

BOOTH

1. THOMAS BOOTH, b. 1663 in Lancashire Co., England, d. 1736 in Gloucester Co., Va., m. 1701 Mary Cooke, dau of Mordecai Cooke. Thomas Booth was a direct descendant of Magna Charter Barons in England. He amassed a large fortune in America through merchandising; he was Justice of the Peace; also agent, factor, and attorney for Robert Bristow, a London merchant. Children of Thomas and Mary (Cooke) Booth were: Dr. George Booth, planter, merchant and ship-owner; William Booth, who went west; Capt. John Booth, Master Mariner; Mordecai Booth, who received part of his father's land in Gloucester Co.; and Thomas Booth.

2. THOMAS BOOTH, b. 1702 in Gloucester Co., m. (1) _____ White of Tyndal's Point, no issue; He removed to Hanover Co., Va., and m. (2) Anne Buckner (3) Susanna Thornton, and (4) Lucy Cooke, his second cousin (see lineage later). Thomas Booth was elected to Petsworth Vestry. When he d. in 1756 he left to his son Thomas "half of the tract purchased of the Hon. William Byrd, Esq., whereon I now live.... to be divided by a line from the bottom of Crump's Neck to the main road.... he to have the upper part including the buildings."

3. THOMAS BOOTH, b. 1741 in Hanover Co., Va., d. Edgecombe Co., N.C.; will recorded there 5/17/1777. He m. Hannah Jackson of Pasquotank and Bertie Co., N.C. Their chn. were James, Benjamin, Robert, John, Dorcas, and Hannah. JAMES BOOTH had 200 acres in Ky., where he served as a Rev. soldier.

4. HANNAH BOOTH, dau of Thomas Booth, m. 1796 Henry Lancaster of Edgecombe Co., N.C., later of Greene Co., Ky. Their chn. were James, Hickerson, Polly, Joseph, Lucy, Elizabeth, Robert (who m. Mary Taylor,

niece of President Zachary Taylor), Malinda, and Sarah Lancaster. Henry Lancaster was in the Ky. Mounted Volunteer Infantry, War of 1812; his father, Henry Lancaster Sr., served in the Rev. War, First Sergt., Cavalry.

Refs: Wurt's "Magna Charta", Vol. 3, p. 447.
"Va. Magazine", Vol. 60, p. 189.
N. C. Wills, Edgecombe Co., 1777.
Family Bible Records.
"Descendants of Mordecai Cooke & Thomas Booth", by Stubbs.

****

JACKSON

1. SAMUEL JACKSON was b. in England, and m. Anne Clarke, grand-daughter of Sir John Clarke and Elizabeth Steed of Hautsham in England. Samuel died at his estate "Abergaveney" in Maryland in 1688. He was in Isle of Wight Co., Va., in 1639, with a patent of 200 acres. In 1640 he had 700 acres on the lower Bay, on the west side there. In 1661 he had 1200 acres of fertile land in Somerset Co., Md., and he purchased a tract in Mecklenburg Co., N. C., where President Andrew Jackson's father settled. In 1668 Samuel received a grant from Calvert. He was a man of education, and prominent in financial matters. In 1669 he and his son were associated with the defense of the Province. His son Jonathan inherited his estate, together with 100 acres on the south side of the Quantico. "Danbury", an estate of 300 acres in Somerset Co., Md., was surveyed for Samuel in 1672. Children of Samuel Jackson were: Samuel Jr., Daniel, Susan, Mary, Elizabeth, and Jonathan.

2. JONATHAN JACKSON purchased Warwick and Warrington in Somerset Co., Md. His will at Annapolis was dated 8/22/1739. Children: Joshua, Samuel, Thomas, Daniel, and Isaac.

3. DANIEL JACKSON m. Ann (Davis?). He migrated to Pasquotank Co., N. C., where he died. Will dated 2/14/1734-35. He was a member of Capt. Scott Day's Company of Militia 1748. Children: Daniel, Samuel, Davis, Ruth, Ann, and Elizabeth. Daniel Jackson left his

plantation to his son Davis.

4. SAMUEL JACKSON was an executor of his father's estate. He was of Edenton, Chowan Co., N.C., and Bertie Co. (parent Co. of Edgecombe). Listed in the House of Burgesses. He m. Mary _____. Made his will in Pasquotank, where he d. 3/20/1750. He left land described in his will to his son Mathias, and his plantation to his son Absolom; he mentions daughters Mary and Hannah.

5. HANNAH JACKSON, m. Thomas Booth of Edgecombe Co., N.C. She was not mentioned in her husband's will so probably died before 1777. Her daughter Hannah Booth was probably reared by her brother James, who was listed in the same place in 1785, that is, in Bracken Co., Ky. (See Booth lineage).

Refs: "Sidelights of Md. History", Vol. 2, pp. 76, 322, 365.
"N.C. Hist. and Gen. Reg.", Vol. 1, p. 328.
"Journal of the House of Burgesses".
"Cavaliers & Pioneers", p. 115, by Nugent.
"Abstracts of N.C. Wills", pp 180-181, by Grimes.
Family Bible Records

****

SIR WILLIAM BARNE, a member of the Virginia Company, m. Ann Sandys, a sister of Sir Edwin Sandys, who helped to establish representative Government in America. Their daughter Lady Anne Barne m. Sir William Lovelace, also a member of the Va. Company. Their dau. Ann Lovelace m. the Rev. John Gorsuch, and their dau was

1. ANN GORSUCH, who came to America after the death of her first husband in England, and was in Gloucester Co., Va., 1651. There she m. (2) Capt. Thomas Todd. Their son:

2. THOMAS TODD, Capt., m. Elizabeth, dau of Col. William Bernard, a descendant of Magna Carta Barons. Their dau

3. ANN TODD m. John Cooke. Their dau

4. LUCY COOKE m. Thomas Booth as his 4th wife. (see Booth lineage).

Refs: "Adventurers of Purse and Person", pp. 83, 93, 213, 226.

****

Data contributed by: Mrs. Warren Harrington
                       Morse
                       3107 W. McLellan Blvd.
                       Phoenix, Arizona.

BREED (BREDE) OF SOUTH CAROLINA OF GEORGIA

JOHN BREED, son of William Breed and Frances Brantly (H.S.F., Vol. X, p. 138) was born in Warren County, Georgia, about 1800. He died ca. 1868 in Griffin, Ga. John and two of his brothers, Phillip Brantly Breed and Captain Nathan Breed obtained land grants in Henry County, Ga., which later became Spaulding County. The 1860 census record of Spaulding Co. shows him to have been a prosperous farmer, owning slaves. John Breed m. Louisa Jones on Nov. 18, 1823. Issue:
1. Walker Breed, b. 1825, of whom later.
2. W. T. Breed, b. 1831.
3. Tom Breed, b. 1834. He came to Shiloh, La., with his brother Walker.
4. Zeptha Breed, b. 1838.
5. Frances Sarah Breed, b. ? married John Strickland in Ga. He d. prior to 1860, leaving her with three children: John, Thomas, and Susan.
6. Permelia Ann Breed, b. 1840, m. David Nutt and came to Shiloh.

WALKER BREED, born Dec. 22, 1825, married Rebecca Patrick 11/4/1850. She was the daughter of Littleberry and Ann Patrick of Henry Co., Ga., born Feb. 14, 1832. Rebecca and Walker Breed left Ga. for Louisiana prior to 1855. They had twin daughters born Nov. 22, 1851, Louiza and Ann Breed; their son John Breed was born Feb. 15, 1854, died July 1854 (Bible record.) Ann also died in childhood. Other children:
 i. William Jasper Breed, b. July 12, 1855, of whom later.
 ii. Sarah Frances Breed, m. Jake Sterling, La.
 iii. Permelia Ann Breed, m. Henry Smith, La.
 iv. Louiza, (previously mentioned) m. J.T. Spencer.

Walker Breed was a member of Shiloh Baptist Church and served in the Confederate Army in the Civil War. He died 3/27/1908. Rebecca d. 7/3/1908.

WILLIAM JASPER BREED married Palestine Youngblood, daughter of Abraham Youngblood and Caroline Skinner; she was b. 7/2/1866. William and his wife lived

on his father's farm. William Jasper Breed d. 1/20/1916.
Issue:
- (1) Lydia Breed, b. Sept. 19, 1884, m. Joe Moore.
- (2) Hallie Breed, b. Aug. 22, 1886, d. Sept. 1, 1898.
- (3) Mittie Breed, b. July 22, 1888, m. Minor Regan.
- (4) Luke Abraham Breed, b. April 10, 1892, d. Aug. 20, 1964, married Onna Weldon, daughter of Charles Weldon and Ollie Hughes, at Bernice, La., Feb. 26, 1921. He was a farmer and served in WW1. Issue:
  - a. Thelma Palestine Breed, b. Jan. 1921, m. Rufus Smith.
  - b. Luther Breed, b. Jan. 1925, m. Sudie Stokes.
  - c. Harold Breed, b. Feb. 16, 1927 in Bernice, La. He m. Arelia Barcomb. Their son William Breed was born April 3, 1954, in Montpelier, Vt.

****

Contributed by: Harold Breed
Bernice, La.

Note: For Breed (Brede) lineage see H. S. F. Vol. $\overline{X}$

INDEX

- A -

Adams, Florence, 55
  Lynn, 55
  Routh, 55
Albertson, Abraham, 141, 142
  Amous, 146
  Ann, 141, 142
  Benjamin, 142-146
  Bertha, 147
  Caroline, 146
  Chalkley, 145
  Charles, 147
  Cassandra, 142
  Frank, 147
  Hannah, 141
  Jan, 140
  Jacob, 144
  Jonathan, 144, 145
  Josiah, 142, 143
  Marmaduke, 143
  Rebecca, 141, 142
  Sarah, 144
  Susanna, 144, 145
  Thomas, 144
  Thompson, 145

Aldredge, George, 62
  Mary, 62, 64
  Sawnie, 62
Anderson, Ira, 78
Andrews, Julia, lineage of, 16
Antill, Abigail, 132
Arrington, Elizabeth, 119, 126
  Joseph, 126
  Martha, 126
  Mona, 119
  Thomas, 126
Ault, Robert, 20
  William, 20
Austin, William, 76
Avery, Carolyn, 82
  Edward, 82
  Grace, 82
  Henry, 82
  Mary, 82
  Samuel, 82
  Stephen, 82

- B -

Babers, Darling, 170, 172
Bacon, Edmund, 156
Bailey, Elinor, 54
  Ida, 54
  Isla, 152
  James, 54
  Lela, 152
  Sarah, 206
  Thomas, 54
  Troy, 54
Barne, Anne, 268
  William, 268
Barton, LeRoy, 78
Bass, Matilda, 123
Batts, Andrew, 61
  Benjamin, 59, 61, 64
  Betsy, 59
  Edward, 63
  Frederick, 59
  George, 61
  Henry, 60
  John, 59, 61
  Laura, 63
  Margaret, 62
  Mary, 59, 62, 63
  Patty, 59
  Robert, 62
  Sally, 59
  Wilkins, 61, 64
  William, 57-61
Baugh, Abraham, 231, 234-240, 242
  Amasa, 237
  Abe, 236
  Darius, 244, 248
  Elisha, 242, 245
  Elizabeth, 245
  Hollis, 246
  James, 230-233, 245
  Jane, 231
  Jesse, 244
  John, 230, 245
  Judith, 231
  Martha, 231
  Mary, 230
  Marcellus, 244
  Michael, 245
  Orpha, 246
  Priscilla, 229, 230
  Rhoda, 197, 240
  Roena, 248
  Sophronia, 245
  Sarah, 231
  Thomas, 231, 233
Beeson, Benjamin, 251, 252
  Charity, 253
  Edward, 250
  Isaac, 252
  Jane, 251
  John, 253
  Phoebe, 253
  Richard, 250, 252
Behrens, Joanne, 125
  Otto, 125
Bell, Hannah, 150
  Henry, 61
  James, 150
  Sarah, 150
Bell, Sarah, lineage of, 22
Bennett, Mark, 50
  Susan, 50
Bernard, Elizabeth, 268
  William, 268
Beverly, Ursula, 263
Billups, Ann, 155
Binns, Charles, 58
  Obedience, 206
Blackburn, Elizabeth, 190

James, 190, 237
Judith, 190
Mary, 240
Rhoda, 237, 239, 241
William, 191,192,198,241
Blackmore, Betsy, 262
Thomas, 262
Blanding, Caroline, 26
James, 26
Blaylock, Mary, 214
Bluford, Jane, 98
Boak, Harriet, 62
Boat(w)right, Alex., 210
Benjamin, 158-190, 203
214
Chesley, 187, 196
Daniel, 188
Drucilla, 188
Drury, 188
Elizabeth, 193, 197,
210, 213
Francis, 218
Jacob, 215-218
James, 184-187
Jesse, 213
John, 182, 187
Joseph, 219
Leonard, 187
Littleberry, 192
Lucy, 211
Martha, 203
Mary, 216, 219, 220,
222
Patsy, 188
Polly, 188
Rhoda, 211
Richard, 192
Samuel, 188
Susan, 209, 212
William, 188, 192, 203,
207-212, 220
Boles, John, 115

Nell, 114
Bond, Benjamin, 251
Elizabeth, 144, 251
Isaac, 251
Jane, 251
Joel, 251
John, 251
Joseph, 251
Robert, 144
William, 251
Booth, Benjamin, 266
George, 266
Hannah, 261
James, 266, 268
John, 266
Mordecai, 266
Robert, 266
Thomas, 266
William, 266
Boren, Addison, 255
Benjamin, 255
Cecil, 258
Cecil, chn. of, 258
Charles, 256
Charles, chn. of, 256
Elijah, 254, 255
Gurney, chn. of, 257
Hezekiah, 254
Jeremiah, 254
Mollie, chn. of, 256
Nancy, 255
Richard, 256
Richard, chn. of, 256
Rhoda, 255
William, 256
William, chn. of, 256
Bowles, James, 256
James, chn. of, 256
Bowmer, Susannah, 78
Bradwell, Daniel, 152
Brank, Garland, 244
Brantley, Frances, 270

Philip, 270
Brasseur, Margaret, 265
  Robert, 265
Braswell, Jane, 114
Breed, Harold, 271
  John, 270
  Luke, 271
  Walker, 271
  William, 270
Bridger, Elizabeth, 50
  John, 229
  Joseph, 48, 123, 125
  Martha, 125
  Mary, 48, 125
  Samuel, 125
Bridges, Jack, 225
Brock, John, 130
Brooke, Elizabeth, 89
  Thos. (descent of) 89, 90
Brown, Elizabeth, 242
  Jane, 156
  Mathew, 156
Buckner, Anne, 266
Buffaloe, Bryant, 176
Bullard, Wiley, 104
Burger, Sarah, 220
Burgess, Elizabeth, 171, 172
  George, 173
  John, 173
Burns, Claire, 124
Byrd, Ursula, 263

- C -

Cage, William, 262
Cain, George, 248
Call, Madeline, 258
Campbell, Mary, 76
Carver, John, 130
Chambers, Nancy, 236

Cheatham, Patience, 237
Cheatwood, John, 240
Cherry, Ann, 177
  Andrew, 177
  Allen, 178
  Augusta, 177
  Darling, 176
  Fanny, 178
  George, 177
  James, 177, 178
  Louis, 178
  Mary, 179
  Mattie, 179
  Rufus, 176
  Sarah, 177, 178
  Walter, 178
  Wiley, 176, 179
  William, 178
Chew, Ann, 143
Chezum, Samuel, 149
Chipley, Clara, 155
  Dudley, 155
  Edward, 149, 150
  Eleanor, 149
  Elizabeth, 151
  Flake, 147, 153
  George, 152
  Henry, 148
  Hunt, 155
  James, 151, 152
  Jane, 152
  John, 149, 151, 153
  Jonathan, 152
  Marshall, 152
  Mary, 155
  Rachael, 149
  Rebecca, 150
  Roy, 153
  Sarah, 152
  Simpson, 152
  Slaughter, 154
  Stephen, 153, 154

Thomas, 148
William, 149-152, 154, 155
Christian, Hattie, 221
Lenox, 221
Clarke, Anne, 267
John, 267
Clay, James, 80
Solomon, 79
Clifton, Sarah, 133
Cline, Alice, 115
Clyatt, Susan, 100
Cock, Dr. 156
Cocke, Virginia, 147
Cocks, Jesse, 60
Collier, Catherine, 262
Collins, Abington, 82
Alex., 76
Catherine, (Kate), 82
Christine, 79
Frances, 76
Harriet, 78
Henry, 82
Jane, 76
John, 76, 81, 82
Joseph, 76
Lafayette, 79
Mattie, 82
Mary, 76, 79
Nancy, 76, 79
Rosey, 79
Richard, 76-79
Rachael, 80
Sarah, 79
Thomas, 76-79, 82
William, 76-78, 80
Colman (Coleman)
Daniel, 236
Elizabeth, 236
Gulleelmeis, 236
Judith, 235
Parmenus, 236

Patience, 236
Thomas, 236
William, 236
Comfort, David, 128
Cook, Clarissa, 215
John, 256
Martha, 257
Nazareth, 215
Cooke, John, 268
Lucy, 266, 268
Mordecai, 266
Mary, 266
Coppedge, Statyra, 178
Corker, John, 265
Lucy, 265
William, 265
Cox, Elizabeth, 113
Henry, 110
Isaac, 212
John, 109
Mary, 109, 111
Richard, 109, 110
William, 109
Crafford, Carter, 125
Martha, 126
Crafton, Thomas, 68
Crosby, Sarah, 84

- D -

Dale, Elizabeth, 261
Daniel, Mary, 95
D'Autremont, Daisy, 106
Francis, 106
Davidson, Sarah, 219
Davis, Hosiah, 95
Ignatius, 84
Nancy, 84
Sophia, 95
Daws, Mary, 52
deLoach, Abba, 166

Ruffin, 173
Denning, Richard, 167
Dillworth, James, 144
  Rebecca, 144
Dodds, Rosanna, 76
Douglas, Edward, 261-263
  Elizabeth, 262
  Elmore, 262
  Ezekiel, 262
  James, 262
  John, 262
  Polly, 263
  Reuben, 262
  Sarah, 262
  Sally, 262
Doyle, Felix, 167
Drew, David, 58
Driver, Mary Sue, 64
Druett, Hannah, 141
  Morgan, 141
Dudley, Ursula, 263
Dudley - Land descent, 120
Dundas, Annie, 256
Dunn, Frances, 96
Dyer, Nancy, 78

- E -

Early, Lucy, 107
  Peter, 107
Edwards, Elizabeth, 262
  Frederick, 87
  Henry, 256
Elam, Mary, 203
Elliott, David, 17
  Mary, 17
  Roy, 17
Ellis, Joseph, 143
  Josiah, 129
Embich, John, 164
English, Henry, 130

Mary, 128
Ennis, Caty, 78, 79
  John, 78
  Mary, 78
  Rachael, 78
Evans, Mary, 95

- F -

Fannin, Elizabeth, 154
  James, 154
Farris, Sandra, 98
Faulcon, Eliz. (lineage of), 11
Fear, Virginia, 83
Feimster, Margaret, 152
Fenn, Mary, 104
Fine, Albert, 118
  Carmel, 118
  Louallen, 118
  Zachariah, 118
Fitzgerald, David, 100
  Elizabeth, 98, 104
  James, 104
Fleete, Henry, 89, 92
  William, 89
Fleming, Elizabeth, 76
  William, 225
Flint, LeRoy, 226
  Ila, 226
Fluharty, Rebecca, 149
  Stephen, 149
Foley, James, 211
  William, 210
Ford, George, 177
  Robert, 177
  William, 177
Forrest, Walter, 141
Fountain, Elizabeth, 119

Foust, Emily, 251
Frame, David, 201

- G -

Galt, Elizabeth, 154
  John, 154
  Norborne, 154
Gates, Benjamin, 208
  Eppes, 205
  Edward, 205
  Frances, 205
  Jacob, 205, 206
  James, 205, 206
  Jane, 205
  Lucy, 205
  Margaret, 205
  Martha, 205
  Rebecah, 204
  Sallie, 204
  Susannah, 206
  William, 205
Geiger, Susan, 81, 92
Gentry, Nancy, 235
George, Catherine, 263
  Henry, 263
  John, 263, 265
  Richard, 263
  Robert, 263
  Sarah, 262, 263
  Susanna, 263
Gibson, Mary, 262
Gilbert, John, 130
Glover, Ann, 107
Godwin, Elizabeth, 125
  Robert, 14
  Thomas, 125
Goff, Emmerrett, 118
Gorsuch, Ann, 268
  John, 268

Graham, Larkin, 79
  William, 30
Gray, Francis, 73
  Thomas, 69
Green, Mary, 98
  Sarah, 245
Groom, Thomas, 130
Grubb, Charity, 250, 253
  Emanuel, 254
  Frances, 254
  Henry, 250, 254
  John, 250, 253
  Joseph, 254
  Nathaniel, 254
  Peter, 254
  Phoebe, 254
  Samuel, 254
  Thomas, 250

- H -

Hack, Ann, 31
  Cave, 31
  John, 31
  Peter, 31
  Sallie, 31
Hamey, David, 68
  Edward, 68
Hammock, Mary, 103
Handy, William, 25
Harding, Thomas, 254
Hardy, Dexter, 260, 264
Harold, Rachael, 254
Harris, Wheeler, 79
Hart, John, 122, 130
  Lucy, 59
  Mildred, 122
Haskins, Aaron, 240
Hawkes, William, 71
Haworth, Stephenias, 252

Hawte, descent of Collins, 93
Heath, Richard, 254
Heggs, David, 84
  Esther, 93
  Heather, 84
  Kenneth, 83, 93
  Marye, 83
  Thomas, 83
Herring, Abigail, 151
  William, 151
Hilliard, Andrew, 99
  Elizabeth, 99
  Henry, 99
  James, 99
  Jane, 99
  Kinchen, 99
  Susan, 99
  William, 99
Hinds, Abigail, 251
  Jane, 251
Hodges, Anna, 178
  Aurora, 178
  Jubel, 178
  Laura, 178
  Nonnie, 178
  Oscar, 178
Holmes, Anna, 251
  Mary, 179
  William, 179
Holt, Earl, 124
  Henry, 58
Hooper, Charlie, 52
  Howard, 52
  James, 52
  Mary, 52
Hopkins, Elizabeth, 49
Howard, Elizabeth, 262
Humphrey, Joice, 84
Hunt, Nancy, 152
Hutchens (Hutchins)
  Agatha, 116
  Alex. 114, 115
  Anderson, 117
  Aquilla, 117
  Benjamin, 114
  Catherine, 112
  Edith, 113
  Elizabeth, 110, 114, 116
  Eliza Jane, 117
  Elkanah, 114
  Ellis, 114, 115
  Hickenson, 110
  Jane, 114
  Jesse, 114
  John, 114, 115
  Jonathan, 116
  Joseph, 115
  Lydia, 114
  Martha, 112
  Mary, 113, 116
  Nancy, 116
  Nell, 116
  Nicholas, 111, 114
  Obedience, 114
  Quintalla, 114
  Strangeman, 110, 112-117
  Susannah, 116
  Theophilus, 115
  Thomas, 114, 116
  Ulysses, 115
  William, 116, 117
  Wylie, 115
Hutchinson, Mary, 152

- I -

Irving, Levin, 29
Isakovics, Alois, 9
  Johanna, 10

Maria, 10
Rosa, 10

- J -

Jackson, Absolom, 268
  Daniel, 267
  Elizabeth, 267
  Hannah, 266, 268
  Isaac, 267
  Jonathan, 267
  Joshua, 267
  Mary, 267
  Mathias, 268
  Penelope, 17
  Priscilla, 205
  Samuel, 267, 268
  Susan, 267
  Thomas, 267
  William, 17
Jennings
  John, 57
  Martha, 57
Johnson, Daniel, 237
  Elizabeth, 237
  Frances, 101
  Martha, 236, 242
  Thomas, 101
Jolley, Elizabeth, 218
Jones, Annie, 179
  Boykin, 154
  Cave (Rev.) 32
  Inez, 179
  Josephus, 179
  Louisa, 270
  Mary, 179
  Ruth, 179
  Samuel, 179
  William, 154
Jordan, George, 68
  Joshua, 265
  Mary, 263, 265
  Robert, 265
  Samuel, 264, 265
  Thomas, 265

- K -

Kearney, Barnaby, 125
  Elizabeth, 125
Kelly, James, 198
  Martha, 198
Kemp, Edmund, 158
  Edward, 158
  Mathew, 156, 157
  Peter, 156, 157
  Richard, 158
  Robert, 156
  Thomas, 156
Kendall, Corinne, 106
  William, 106
Key, Elijah, 78
Kidd, Elizabeth, 186
  Mary, 186
Kilby, Judith, 7
  Thomas, 6
Kittrell, Esther, 218
Kline, Catherine, 164, 167
  Elizabeth, 164
  Fannie, 170, 171
  John, 163, 164
  Martha, 171
  Mary, 171
  Nicholas, 163
  Seth, 167, 171, 172
Knight Genealogy, 136
Knight, Anne, 145
  Daniel, 133
  Evan, 145
  Giles, 128, 131, 134

Jane, 134
Jonathan, 134, 145
Joseph, 128, 132
Mary, 128, 132, 135
Nancy, 255
Thomas, 130-132, 136
William, 135
Knott, William, 69
Knox, Agatha, 153

- L -

Lancaster, Benjamin, 260
  Catherine, 260
  Elinor, 260
  George, 260
  Henry, 260, 261, 266
  James, 95, 266
  John, 260
  Joseph, 260, 266
  Mallory, 261
  Philip, 260
  Robert, 266
  Sarah, 259, 261
  William, 260
Land, Carl, 120
  Cecelia, 119
  Elisha, 119
  Elizabeth, 119
  Fort, 120
  Fountain, 119
  Gertrude, 124
  Grace, 120
  Henry, 119, 124, 126
  James, 119
  John, 119
  Judith, 119
  Max, 120, 123, 126
  Maxine, 124
  Mildred, 119

  Mona, 120, 124, 126
  Nancy, 119
  Nathan, 119
  Patricia, 125
  Paul, 120
  Susan, 125
  Taylor, 125
  Thomas, 119
  William, 119, 125
Lawrason, Margarett, 108
Levridge, Rowena, 244
Liggett, Robert, 55
Lineberry, Edith, 251
  Jacob, 251
  Samuel, 251
Littleton, Anne, 262
  Edward, 262
  Nathaniel, 262
Logan, Elizabeth, 143
  George, 143
Lovelace, Ann, 268
  William, 268

- M -

Mallory, William, 260
Martin, Carolyn, 27
  James, 27
  Judith, 188
Mason, Charles, 83
  Esther, 83
  Hannah, 83
  James, 70
Mateer, Walter, 82
Mathews, Anne, 105
  Charles, 105-108
  George, 105-108
  Harriet, 105, 108
  Joel, 105, 107
  John, 105, 108

Medora, 106
Samuel, 108
Sarah, 105
Tobias, 108
Maxwell, John, 155
Middleton, Charles, 99
Irene, 99
Samuel, 99
Miller, Emma, 226
Ephraim, 225
Jacob, 225
John, 147, 224
Mary, 213, 226
Roy, 224
Willa, 225
Mitchell, Rebecca, 115
Morse, Mrs. Warren H., 260
Moseley, George, 193
Murphy, Lawrence, 97

- Mc -

McCollum, Elizabeth, 114
MacLamroc, Alan, 251
Brian, 251
James, 251
McLane, Isabella, 162
McMichael, Ada, 258
McNamara, Barbara, 84
Chester, 84
Mary, 84
Patricia, 84
Susan, 84
McNulty, Ann, 167
Charles, 166
David, 161
deLoach, 169
Elizabeth, 169
Hugh, 165
James, 161, 163-165
John, 161-163, 169
Mary, 163
Michael, 163, 165
Samuel, 165, 166
Thomas, 168
William, 165
McNulty, line of descent, 174

- N -

Nance, Martha, 255
Neale, Catherine, 24
William, 24
Noell, Poindexter, 240
Norman, Ida, 256
Norsworthy, Eliz., 48

- O -

O'Donnell, Lenore, 175
Oldham, Susannah, 85
Ozias, Emma, 224
Thomas, 224

- P -

Paker, Elizabeth, 230
Palmer, Mary, 123
Parker, Wiley, 6
Parsons, Pamela, 102
Paterson, John, 212
Julia, 212
Patrick, Littleberry, 270
Mary, 102
Rebecca, 270

Patterson, James, 244
  John, 241
  Julia, 241
Paulett, Thomas, 70
Pawson, William, 30
Pennington, Isaac, 251
  Rachael, 251
Perkins, Obedience, 110
Philips, Jonathan, 144
  Rachael, 144
Phillips, David, 49
  Leah, 49
Pinner, Ann, (lineage of), 12
Pitcher, Ann, 260
  Catherine, 260
  Henry, 259
  Isabel, 259, 264
  Lucinda, 260
  Matilda, 260
  Polly, 259
  Thomas, 259, 263, 264
  William, 259, 261, 264
Pitt, Anna, 51, 55
  Catherine, 49
  Dudley, 52
  Elizabeth, 50, 55
  Fred, 51
  Gattie, 50, 54
  Henry, 48-52
  Herman, 53
  Hester, 48, 125
  Hugh, 51
  James, 48
  Joab, 49
  John, 49
  Joseph, 48
  Lulu, 50, 55
  Margaret, 50
  Mark, 51
  Mary, 52
  Paul, 54
  Polly, 49
  Robert, 48, 50
  Stephen, 49
  Thad, 51
  Thomas, 48
  Whitney, 51
  William, 49
Pool, Nettie, 154
Porter, Penninah, 50
Poyner, Susan, 64
  William, 64
Prewitt (Pruett)
  Alexander, 122
  Jeffrey, 123
  Lucretia, 123
  Obediah, 122
Prince, Mary, 85
Proude, Mary, 251
Pryor, Thomas, 254
Pugh, George, 251
  Maxine, 251

- Q -

Quillian, Fletcher, 124

- R -

Radcliffe, Joan, 250
Radebaugh, John, 164
Radford, John, 190
Ragan, Alexander, 96, 97
  Elizabeth, 97
  Grace, 96
  Henry, 96
  Ida, 96
  James, 95
  Jane, 95
  Julia, 95

Julian, 96
Lafayette, 95
Leniaus, 96
Mary, 95, 96
Needham, 96
Robert, 95-97
Roberta, 97
Seaborn, 97
Sophia, 96
William, 96
Willard, 96
Rainey, Sarah, 61
Read, Edmund, 7
Redman, John, 254
Reynolds, Cicely, 265
Rice, Julia, 61
Richmond, Nancy, 245
Riley, Abraham, 123
　Mary Ann, 123
Roberts, Almire, 245
Robinson, Anna, 27
　Lenora, 27
　Thomas, 27
Rose, Anne, 66-74
　Christine, 75
　George, 67
　Jane, 67
　Mary, 68
　Richard, 68
　Seymour, 75
　William, 65-75
Ross, Caroline, 92
　Elizabeth, 86
　Elizabeth, chn. of, 86
　Lawrence, 85, 87
　Shapley, 85, 92
　Shapley, chn. of, 85
Routten, Mary, 219
Routon, James, 237
　Samuel, 241
Rowe, Benjamin, 169
　Eliza, 169
　Sarah, 173
Rowntree, Mary, 122
　Richardson, 122
　William, 122
Rozar, James, 95

- S -

Salway, John, 73
Sanbourne, Daniel, 265
　Elizabeth, 265
Sandel, Clarence, 84
　Nita, 84
Sandys, Ann, 268
Savidge, Elizabeth, 60
　Joel, 60
Scarf, George, 212
Scott, Deborah (descent of) 88, 91
　William, 91
Scudder, Deborah, 122
Sears, Alfred, 147
　Maybelle, 147
Seaton, Dorothy, 156
Sharpe, Isabella, 151
Sheffield, Bryan, 100
　John, 100
　Nancy, 100
　Prussia, 100, 101
　Russia, 101
　Seaborn, 100
　William, 103
Sherman, Henry, 109
Shermer, Nancy, 115
Shoemaker, George, 144
　Jacob, 144
　Susanna, 144
Simmons, Martha (lineage of), 13
Singleton, Catherine, 103

Frank, 103
Franklin, 103
George, 103
Gordon, 104
Lulu, 103
Mahala, 103
Mary, 103
Patrick, 103
Richard, 102
Rillie, 103
William, 102, 103
Skelton, John, 146
Phoebe, 146
Skipworth, Sir Grey, 158
Sloan, John, 209
Samuel, 215
Smith, Ann, 79-81, 85, 93
Anne, 6
Archibald, 251
Caleb, 6
Claiborne, 147
Clement, 255
Edward, 147
Eliza, 6
Elizabeth (lineage of) 25
Elizabeth, 147
George, 7
Henry, 84
Ida, 251
Isaac, 30
John, 6, 65, 79, 85, 255
John Custis (lineage of), 6
Mary, 81, 255
Maybelle, 147
Reuben, 251
Samuel, 255
Susan, 6
William, 84
Solomon, Deliah, 119

Soniat, Theodore, 21
Sowerby, Elizabeth, 67
Francis, 67, 69
Thomas, 73
Spence, Bluford, 98, 100
Elizabeth, 99
Hiram, 100
James, 98, 99
Joe, 98
Robert, 98
Susan, 97
William, 98, 99
Spivey, Sarah, 104
Stalcup, Frances, 248
Perry, 248
Staley, Jacob, 164
Susanna, 164
Stanley, Alice, 116
John, 113
Thomas, 113
Stanton, Richard, 72
Robert, 71
Steger, Ann, 188
Stith, Mary (lineage of), 32
Stockdale, William, 141
Stockley, Anne (lineage of), 37
Stoltz, Elvira, 52
Follene, 52
Strickland, Amous, 145
Asenath, 145
Stroud, Peggy, 262
Stuart, John, 87
Mourning, 87
Sturges, Josiah, 9
Mary, 9
Sulway, Joseph, 71
Swann, Susan, 261

- T -

Taylor, Columbus, 123
  Ettie, 256
  Francis, 123
  Gertrude, 23
  Louise, 196
  Mary, 266
  William, 123
Teackle, Anne, 30
  Elizabeth, 30
  John, 30
  Lavinia, 30
  Sarah, 30
  Thomas, 30, 31
Thias, Robert, 82
Thomas, Allison, 55
  Charles, 55
  Frank, 55
Thomson, Anna, 146
  Alexander, 146
  James, 146
Thornton, Susanna, 266
Thorpe, Sarah, 57
  Thomas, 57
Timmons, Carl, 102
  Delilah, 101
  Ethel, 101
  John, 100, 101
  Joseph, 101
  Julius, 101
  Levi, 100
  Martha, 100
  Seaborn, 101
  Thomas, 102
Tinsley, Elizabeth, 192
  Titus, John, 144
  William, 144
Tobin, Edgar, 62
Todd, Ann, 268
  Thomas, 268
Trent, Elizabeth, 109

Henry, 109
Treseder, Elizabeth, 125
Trigg, Ann, 222
Triplett, Sarah, 248
Turner, Elizabeth, 122
  Samuel, 166

- U -

Upshur family in England, 39
Upshur, Abel, 11, 21
  Anne, 9, 28, 30
  Caleb, 1-4, 11, 14
  Caroline, 28
  Catherine, 10
  Eleanor, 19
  Estelle, 21
  Elizabeth, 7, 11, 24
  Florence, 28, 29
  Harriett, 11
  Henry, 14, 29
  James, 27
  John, 1, 7, 8, 10, 18-20, 23, 41
  Leah, 5
  Mary, 9, 11, 13, 17, 32
  Margaret, 19
  Nancy, 14
  Robert, 15, 20
  Sally, 25
  Sarah, 31
  Thomas, 3, 10, 21, 22, 25, 31
  William, 3, 8, 11, 24, 27

- V -

Vane, Frances, 250
Vivian, Helen, 250

- W -

Walker, Elizabeth, 133
  Henry, 14
  Maude, 14
Wall, Mamie, 96
Wallace, Ada, 63
  John, 164
  Mary, 226
  Michael, 63
  Patricia, 226
  Priscilla, 63
  Robert, 226
Waln, Nicholas, 144
Walton, Daniel, 130
  David, 129
  Eleanor, 19
  Esther, 133
  Lydia, 139
  Martha, 225
  Sarah, 143
  Thomas, 130
  William, 130, 131
Ward, Ann, 176
Warr, John, 148
  Thomas, 148
Warren, John, 63
  Mary, 59, 63
  Thomas, 59, 63
Watkins, Benajah, 240
  Henry, 240
  Mary, 111
Watts, William, 152
Wellborn, Elijah, 122
  Mildred, 122

Wharton, Catherine, 146
Whirtler, Edith,
Willard, Joseph, 144
  Sarah, 144
Wilson, Emma, 31
  Mary, 133
  Robert, 150
  Thomas, 31
Winn, Winney, 117
Wise, George, 10
  Henry, 10
Wiser, Elizabeth, 143
  Joshua, 144
Woodhouse, Thomas, 69
Woods, Andrew, 222
  Conrad, 222
  Fannie, 226
  Grace, 224
Woolfolk, John, 86
  John, chn. of, 86
Woolston, Joshua, 145
Wormeley, Elizabeth, 158
  Henry, 158
Wright, Emma, 221
Wynns (Wynn) Daniel, 176
  Elizabeth, 176
  John, 176
  Watkin, 176

- Y -

Yerby, Elizabeth, 24
  George, 24
Young, Edward, 3
  Emma, 15
  John, 15
  Raymond, 15
  William, 79
Youngblood, Abraham, 270
  Palestine, 270